CAREER COUNSELING
Models,
Methods,
and Materials

JOHN O. CRITES, Ph.D.
Professor of Psychology
University of Maryland

McGRAW-HILL BOOK COMPANY

New York | St. Louis | San Francisco | Auckland | Bogotá
Hamburg | Johannesburg | London | Madrid | Mexico
Montreal | New Delhi | Panama | Paris
São Paulo | Singapore | Sydney | Tokyo | Toronto

Library of Congress Cataloging in Publication Data

Crites, John Orr.
   Career counseling.

   Bibliography: p.
   Includes index.
   1. Vocational guidance—Technique. 2. Vocational
guidance—Case studies. I. Title.
HF5381.C785   331.7'02   80-36815
ISBN 0-07-013781-1

CAREER COUNSELING
Models, Methods, and Materials

  3 4 5 6 7 8 9 0 D O D O 8 9 8 7 6 5

This book was set in Times Roman by The Total Book (ECU/BD).
The editor was Phillip A. Butcher;
the production supervisor was Donna Piligra.
The cover was designed by Nicolas Krenitsky.
R. R. Donnelley & Sons Company was printer and binder.

FOR LOUISE
my life, my wife

Contents

LIST OF TABLES

Foreword

It has been many years since Dr. Homer J. Smith, eminent former professor of vocational education at the University of Minnesota, used to tell students that the job or career they chose would change them and their lives more than they would change the job or career they would follow. In those days the principal efforts toward helping young people make career choices were provided in courses or segments of a course usually called "occupations" in which the student was given a mixture of information about jobs, some attempt to relate individual talents to them, culminating with each person writing a "career plan." The *homeroom* movement had caught on at this time as well. Thus many students found themselves discussing occupations or career planning in ten- to twenty-minute segments once a week under the direction of ill-prepared teachers who were of the opinion that this was an imposition on their time and professional commitments. To the extent that vocational guidance was given by those who were assigned counseling responsibilities the emphasis was largely on placement. In keeping with the times the vocational information available and the concern about careers was centered more on boys than girls.

As the guidance movement grew it was not surprising that the greatest interest and concern revolved around *counseling* and the counseling *process*. Vocational guidance went into a period of "doldrums" except for a few "voices in the wilderness." Counseling theory and process was an almost singular concern among counselor educators. For a number of different reasons *personal* counseling became the "in" thing and counselors tended to regard it as a status factor. Vocational guidance and counseling was given a very secondary role.

It was during this period that counseling theories and procedures emerged in rather significant numbers and it was a time of experimenting with many approaches for dealing with people of all ages, both individually and in groups.

The theory development was a necessary and desirable one. Counselors today can find a counseling style that has a defensible base and can function more effectively because of it. With the resurgence of interest in and emphasis on career planning as a primary concern in the life of the person, it was only natural that professionals began to consider the viability of various counseling theories or emphasis in relation to *career* counseling. The current professional literature reflects this concern.

Dr. Crites has made a significant contribution to these efforts to clarify and reconcile the various counseling theories most employed by practicing counselors as applicable to career counseling. This book does well what it has been written to do: to treat counseling theory and processes that are involved in the total process. Dr. Crites explicates the various theories in a clear, scholarly, and understandable manner. His discussion of them is "solid" but can be comprehended by even the relatively unsophisticated scholar. He has not attempted to cover in this book all aspects or topics which might be included in a course on *Career Counseling and Guidance*. The guidance aspects are not included, nor should they be.

The book is particularly well and appropriately organized to cover the counseling concepts which are involved in career planning and decision making. Thus the first chapter is a short, but enlightening introduction, with the following chapters through number six providing excellent "capsules" of the theories which have been selected for consideration. The cases which have been included as examples are particularly helpful.

Finally the last two chapters bring the reader from the theoretical to the practical, providing a "reassuring" approach for practitioners who wonder how one can deal with the many different types of clients, situations, and degrees of emotional involvement which may be present.

At this point the theories become "practical" and the practices find theoretical foundations. It is a vindication of a statement made by Stefflre in an earlier book on *Theories of Counseling* (McGraw-Hill, 1972) that there is nothing more practical than a good theory!

The book would, of course, be an excellent basic text for a course devoted exclusively to career counseling. It will also be an important text to be used where such a course is not taught exclusively. Thus it should have wide acceptance as a major part of a number of different courses: counseling procedures, career guidance courses, inservice courses and the like. The modest length of the book makes this feasible.

For too long there has been confusion on the part of the practising counselor regarding how career counseling can be carried on in a logical, consistent manner with various theoretical frames of reference. This book brings vagueness into better focus.

Walter F. Johnson
Michigan State University

Preface

Career Counseling, known by various and sundry rubrics (e.g., vocational guidance, occupational counseling, vocational counseling, etc.), has had a long and venerable but variable history. It enjoyed its heyday during the early twentieth century (1910–1940), then it suffered an eclipse during the decades of the 1950s and 1960s. Only recently has it experienced a "renaissance" in activity and applicability, not only because of the tight labor market which has made it a virtual necessity for those choosing and seeking jobs but also because people have recognized the salience—the centrality—of work in their lives. The promises of the human potential movement have fallen short of the self-fullfilment and meaningfullness that can be derived from personally and societally satisfying work experiences. As Freud has astutely observed, work *and* love (*arbeiten und lieben*) are the hallmarks of maturity. The major approaches to career counseling reviewed in this book, and the comprehensive approach synthesized from them, are conceived to assist the individual in developing and accepting an integrated picture of self and role in the world of work, to test this concept against reality, and to convert it into reality with satisfaction to self and benefit to society.[1]

How to select what might be considered the major approaches to career counseling involved judgments hardly less than controversial. The decision was mostly professional but partly personal. Although other models and methods of career counseling have been proposed, notably the sociological (e.g., Sanderson, 1954), the so-called "major" approaches chosen for discussion in this book have clearly been the most widely recognized and used. Generations of career counselors have been trained and versed in one or another of them, and all have had an impact upon how the career development of a client might be facilitated. Because of their differential contributions to the field, and because of their combined influence upon my practice of career counseling, the following five approaches were selected: Trait-and-Factor, Client-Centered, Psychodynamic, Developmental, and Behavioral. They are presented in this order largely because they appeared so historically, but also because I learned them in this sequence. One built upon another, in cumulative fashion, until the composite evolved into what is proposed as a general approach—Comprehensive Career Counseling. That they can be learned in this way has been my personal experience: the case "materials" at the end of each chapter are based upon career clients I have counseled, first from a Trait-and-Factor orientation, then Client-Centered, and so on. Comprehensive Career Counseling was extrapolated from these cases and from a synthesis of the principles and procedures of the major approaches over a period of more than twenty years.

Many mentors and exemplars have shaped and influenced my conceptualization and conduct of career counseling. Foremost among these has been Donald E. Super, whose theorizing about career choice processes and synthesizing of models and methods from different points-of-view truly qualifies him as the original comprehensive career counselor. From him I learned the Trait-and-Factor approach, embellished and enhanced by the self-concept focus of the Client-Centered, all cast meaningfully into the longitudinal context of the Developmental. From Edward J. Shoben, Jr., my therapy supervisor, I gained an abiding appreciation for, and indoctrination in, the sophistication of the psychodynamic approach, as espoused principally by the neoanalysts (Fromm, Horney, and Sullivan). But he also taught me how this

---

[1]Paraphrased from Super (1957, p. 197) to eliminate the generic masculine.

orientation could be integrated with learning theory through exposure to Dollard and Miller, Mowrer, and others, a didactic experience which was continued and augmented by over a decade of daily counseling at the University of Iowa. There, under the supervision of Leonard D. Goodstein, I developed a sense of the clinical nuances around communication and relationship, and particularly diagnosis, which only an expert can impart. It was during these years with him, and others on the University Counseling Service staff, that my career counseling came "alive" and that I acquired an intimate, habitual familiarity with the process. For the opportunity to learn from these masters, I am privileged and grateful, but I am solely responsible for interpreting their techniques.

A more personal but also professional acknowledgement brings great pleasure: this book is dedicated to my life/career partner, Dr. Louise F. Fitzgerald, who is this counselor's counselor on work and love. She has made what I call my "second career" a renaissance of interest and ideas at midlife, delightful and exciting through her intellectual competence and curiosity and her joie de vivre. Whatever satisfactions I have enjoyed in writing this book I share with her.

John O. Crites

Introduction to Career Counseling

Career counseling means different things to different people. It is a disparate field, spawned from various needs—cultural, economic, social, historical, and psychological—from disciplines that approach the analysis of career choice from often contradictory assumptions and precepts. Because of its hybrid nature, which has been a source of strength as well as weakness, career counseling has not infrequently been disdained as a field within the applied behavioral sciences, by related, supposedly more prestigious, specialities such as individual and group psychotherapy.

An understanding of the comprehensiveness and complexity of career counseling suggests that the field is much more than a "test them and tell them" operation. It is more challenging and demanding than interventions of more circumscribed focus and scope. To explicate the nature of career counseling and to compare/contrast it with other areas, this introductory chapter on the field traces its historical background and development ("Career Counseling in Perspective"), presents an overview of its purposes and processes ("Career Counseling Defined"), and anticipates its future ("Career Counseling: Challenges and Prospects"). A final section outlines the remainder of the book ("Career Counseling: Models, Methods, and Materials").

CAREER COUNSELING IN PERSPECTIVE

To look backward as well as forward on the field of career counseling is to place it in a broader context of personal and social meaning, which highlights its salience and centrality as a modus operandi for assisting individuals of all ages from all walks of life in making what is probably their most important decision—which career they will spend most of their waking hours preparing for and engaging in. As this brief historical account of career counseling attempts to bring out, it not only constitutes for the individual one of the single most effective psychological ways to attain and maintain contact with reality, i.e., through meaningful and productive work (Freud, 1962; Fromm, 1955). It also provides an economic means to effect significant social change, for example, through broadening the range of career options considered by women (Fitzgerald & Crites, 1980). What are some of the milestones, then, in the development of career counseling as a field? What are some of the major trends and resulting theoretical orientations that can be extrapolated from these milestones to define career counseling and to enumerate its challenges and prospects for the future?

Notable Events in the History of Career Counseling

Much of this material on the background and development of career counseling has been excerpted from the fiftieth-anniversary volume *Man in a World at Work,* published under the auspices of the National Vocational Guidance Association (Borow, 1964, pp. 48–53 passim). The material has been revised, however, to focus more specifically upon career counseling, rather than on the broader field of vocational guidance, which encompasses not only individual and group assistance in career decision making but also entire programs and systems of interventions (for example, high school curricula), and to update significant events since 1963. The chronology of career counseling follows:

1850–1900 Organized career counseling had no clear beginnings. The conditions from which it evolved were *economic* (for example, industrialism and the growing division of labor); *social* (for example, urbanization, child labor, immigration, and transmigration); *ideological* (for example, a restless spirit of reform and a spreading belief in the improvability of man and his status); and *scientific* (for example, the emergence of the human sciences—psychophysiology in the first half of the nineteenth century and, subsequently, the psychophysics and experimental psychology of Fechner, Helmholtz, and Wundt, and the mental testing of Cattell, Binet, and others). In the absence of any of these conditions, career counseling surely would have followed a different historical course.[1]

1890 James McKeen Cattell published an article in *Mind* in which the term "mental tests" was first used in psychological literature. Cattell, who had studied with Wundt at Leipzig, was less interested in the use of mental measurement to establish general laws of behavior than in the study of individual differences. Seeking to predict academic performance, he used his tests to measure the abilities of students first at the University of Pennsylvania, and then later at Columbia University.

1896 The first psychological clinic was established by Lightner Witmer at the University of Pennsylvania. Witmer stressed the study

---

[1]The following passages in this section are taken largely, with the substitution of "career counseling" for "vocational guidance" and some additional paraphrasing, from Borow (1964, pp. 48–62).

and treatment of learning difficulties in children. In the early 1920s, one of his students, Morris Viteles, inaugurated a vocational guidance clinic within Witmer's general clinic. Viteles' contributions included what he termed the "clinical approach" in vocational appraisal and the use of the psychographic method in job analysis to specify the psychological requirements of occupations.

1909   A banner year in the history of career counseling, 1909 marked the publication of *Choosing a Vocation* by the acknowledged "father of the field," Frank Parsons, who had died the previous year. The long-range impact and importance of Parsons' book was not felt until many years later, when it was recognized principally in the work of the Minnesota Employment Stabilization Research Institute during the 1930s. The Institute said Parsons had identified the three basic variables in the career decision-making process: (1) the individual, (2) the occupation, and (3) the relationship between them. Whatever approach to career counseling is taken must deal with these central components of choosing a vocation. This book reviews, summarizes, and synthesizes how and why the major approaches to career counseling do this.

1911   The *Vocational Guidance News-Letter* was published by the Vocation Bureau and edited by Frederick J. Allen. The first American journal devoted to vocational guidance, it was the predecessor to the *Vocational Guidance Magazine,* to *Occupations,* and when the American Personnel and Guidance Association was established in 1951, to the *Personnel and Guidance Journal.*

1912   Hugo Munsterberg published *Psychology and Industrial Efficiency* in Germany, a landmark in the application of the methods of experimental psychology to the study of vocational choice and worker performance. The American edition was published in 1913 and Munsterberg subsequently continued his studies in vocational psychology at Harvard University.

1915   The Division of Applied Psychology was established at the Carnegie Institute of Technology under Walter V. Bingham. The first academic unit of its kind, it conducted training and research on personnel selection and management, occupational performance, salesmanship, and vocational guidance.

1917 Several outstanding psychologists, including Walter V. Bingham, Walter D. Scott, E. L. Thorndike, and Robert W. Yerkes, were appointed to government positions to recommend contributions that psychology might make to the World War I effort. Emerging from these activities were testing procedures for screening military draftees with mental handicaps and for identifying intellectually superior candidates for officer training. The Army Alpha, a group test of verbal mental ability based on the prewar research of Arthur S. Otis, and the Army Beta Test, a nonverbal mental test for use with illiterates, were major products of this wartime psychological effort.

1918 James Burt Miner developed what was perhaps the first interest questionnaire at Carnegie Institute of Technology. A few years later (1921), Bruce V. Moore did his research on the technique of interest measurement with graduate engineers at the same institution, and Karl Cowdery applied a differential weighting system to interest item reponses at Stanford University. Previous research on occupational group trait differences had emphasized abilities almost exclusively. The work of Miner, Moore, Cowdery, and Max Freyd made important contributions to the research of Edward K. Strong, Jr., who published the *Strong Vocational Interest Blank* in 1927.

1925 Harry D. Kitson, a pioneer in the training of vocational counselors, first at Indiana University and for many years at Teachers College, Columbia University, published his well-known book, *The Psychology of Vocational Adjustment.* Kitson, like Parsons before him, saw career counseling as a highly specialized field for trained professionals.

1927 Elton Mayo and a team of workers from Harvard University launched a series of studies on industrial behavior at the Hawthorne (Chicago) plant of the Western Electric Company. Originally intended as an investigation of the relationship between environmental conditions of work (for example, illumination) and employee fatigue and monotony, the project ramified into an extended series of precedent-setting researches revealing the complex nature of worker performance. Roethlisberger and Dickson's classical summary of the Hawthorne studies, published in 1939 as *Management and the Worker,* traced the improvements in research design that the project had developed and made dramatically clear the importance of human relations, leadership, supervision, and worker morale as factors in worker performance and productivity.

In 1939 Clark L. Hull, then professor of psychology at the University of Wisconsin, published his pioneering work, *Aptitude Testing*. Conceiving the task of career counseling as that of predicting vocational success, Hull provided a prophetic glimpse of modern computer-based data-processing procedures in personnel work by proposing a machine that would furnish differential occupational predictions from an input of aptitude test data.

1931 The Minnesota Employment Stabilization Research Institute to study psychological factors in both employment and unemployment was established under the leadership of Donald G. Paterson of the University of Minnesota and others. Many thousands of persons were given vocational diagnoses at the Institute's Occupational Analysis Clinic and in the public employment offices of Minneapolis, St. Paul, and Duluth by means of aptitude test batteries, interviews, and occupational ability patterns. A substantial proportion of applicants were placed in jobs, despite economically depressed conditions. Among the Institute's far-reaching conclusions was the principle that improved guidance services and employment selection techniques are needed to establish a more stable labor force and to aid business recovery.

1939 The first edition of the *Dictionary of Occupational Titles* was published. Prepared by the Job Analysis and Information Section of the United States Employment Service, the dictionary titled, coded, and defined more than 18,000 American occupations. It soon became a basic reference book for vocational counselors and personnel workers in educational, industrial, social service, hospital, and military settings.

1941 In the national emergency leading up to and during participation of the United States in World War II, manpower problems became critical, and the efforts of counselors, personnel psychologists, and placement workers were greatly expanded. On the civilian front, the research, testing, and placement program of the United States Employment Service, working in conjunction with the War Manpower Commission, was broadened and intensified. In the War Department, the responsibility for developing new classification and assignment procedures for several million men under arms resulted in the preparation of tests and allied selection tools by the Personnel Research Section of the Adjutant General's Office. Similar personnel research and classification procedures were developed for the Navy by the Bureau of Naval Personnel. In the Army Air Forces, the selection and training of ground crew personnel were tasks charged to the Technical Training Command, while research on pilot selection was assigned to three psychological research units attached to air bases. Among the developments contributed by the military personnel research units were the Army General Classification Test, a variety of new psychomotor tests, refined procedures for the validation and standardization of test batteries, and the stanine method of converting raw scores to standard scores.

1942 Carl R. Rogers published his influential *Counseling and Psychotherapy*. While the book was an outgrowth of Rogers' experiences in working as a therapist with emotionally distressed clients, the nondirective (client-centered) counseling movement that it ushered in forced a searching reexamination of the assumptions and interviewing processes underlying career counseling. Among the significant developments that resulted were a revamping of the older cognitive concept of the client in career decision making to include the dynamics of affective and motivational behavior, the increased emphasis on self-acceptance and self-understanding as goals of career counseling, attention to the client's verbalized feelings as a source of information about him/her, and a new stress in research and practice upon the client-counselor interaction in interviewing. The net effect of Rogerian counseling was not to make career counseling a subspeciality within psychotherapy, but rather to broaden and modernize its conceptualizations of task and goal and to bring it into closer communication with psychology and with the related counseling arts.

1951 Donald E. Super launched the Career Pattern Study, which soon became one of the first long-range studies devoted to programmatic research on career behavior. More than any other career psychologist, Super has been instrumental in freeing career counseling from the static, single-choice-at-a-point-in-time concept of decision making, drawing attention to the potential contributions of sociology and economics to the field, and placing the study of career behavior in the context of human development. His views were set forth originally in an influential series of journal articles published during the early 1950s and subsequently synthesized and expanded into a book, *The Psychology of Careers* (1957). (See Chapter 5, "Developmental Career Counseling.")

1963   Although the motivational factors in career decision making had been implicit in the "Psychodynamic Point-of-View" in vocational psychology (Crites, 1969), they were not made explicit until presented by Bordin, Nachmann, and Segal (1963) in what they called an "articulated framework of vocational development." In this psychoanalytically oriented analysis of career choice, these theorists formulated an approach that highlighted the role of personality variables—needs, coping mechanisms, and so forth—in the process of selecting and adjusting to an occupation. Using this framework as a background, Bordin (1968) subsequently proposed a "model of vocational counseling," a chapter added to his earlier edition of *Psychological Counseling* (1955), in which he outlines how the career-counseling process can comprehend and impact the often complex interactions between personality and decision making. (See Chapter 4, "Psychodynamic Career Counseling.")

1964   This year saw the publication of the National Vocational Guidance Association's commemorative volume entitled *Man in a World at Work*, edited by Henry Borow. A compendium of several outstanding chapters, this book represented the beginning of a renaissance in career counseling, which had lagged behind the dramatic development of vocational psychology during the 1950s. This rebirth of career counseling went beyond integration with vocational development theory and research, however, by incorporating concepts and principles from theories of personality and psychotherapy, as well as occupational sociology. From the works and writings of Goldman, Holland, Roe, Samler, Super and others, there emerged a broader context for career counseling that extended its boundaries beyond those of the consulting room into the world of work, with its complexities, challenges, and uncertainties. A more pragmatic note was struck, which presaged the forthcoming research of the behaviorists.

1966   Several studies by behavioral-oriented career counselors heralded what Krumboltz (1966) called a "revolution in counseling." Adapting Skinnerian psychology to the processes and outcomes of career counseling, Krumboltz (Krumboltz & Thorensen, 1964; Ryan & Krumboltz, 1964) and his colleagues experimented with new techniques of intervening upon career decision making, including counselor modelling, goal setting, and reinforcement. This group also produced materials such as the *Job Experience Kits* (Science Research Associates, 1970), which for the first time provided the client in career counseling with vicarious explorations of the world of work through performing the duties and tasks of selected occupations. (See Chapter 6, "Behavioral Career Counseling.")

1969   Although principally a review and critique of theory and research on career choice and adjustment, Crites' (1969) text, *Vocational Psychology,* presented the first entirely *objective* taxonomy for the classification of problems in career decision making. Previous schemata relied upon interjudge agreement, which seldom exceeded 35-40 percent, whereas the new system operationally defined choice problem categories solely in terms of aptitude, interest, and choice data. (See Chapter 7, "Comprehensive Career Counseling.")

1973   Pursuing Super's (1955) concept of vocational maturity, over a period of years (1961–1971) Crites developed a measure of career choice attitudes and competencies that was published as the *Career Maturity Inventory* (CMI) in 1973 and revised in 1978. This instrument was conceived from a hierarchical model of career maturity (Crites, 1973; 1974) based upon a distinction between career choice *content* and *process* not previously articulated. The CMI provided the first longitudinally standardized measure of career-choice process variables that could be used in career counseling within a developmental framework.

1974   The sixtieth anniversary volume of the National Vocational Guidance Association, *Vocational Guidance and Human Development,* was published under the editorship of Edwin Herr. Like its predecessor, *Man in a World at Work,* it was a compendium of chapters by noted theorists and practicioners in the field. New ideas and concepts, such as group and computer-assisted approaches, were presented that augmented and broadened the theoretical and procedural foundation for career counseling.

Trends in the History of Career Counseling

Cutting across this chronology of career counseling are several major trends that culminated in different contemporary approaches to assisting clients with problems in career choice and adjustment. The predominant theme in the history of career counseling has been the Parsonian focus upon the individual, the occupation, and the relationship between them, which ultimately defines career choice (Crites, 1969, Chapter 4). This model of career decision making has constituted the cornerstone of the Trait-and-Factor approach to career counseling, with its emphasis upon test and occupational information. Juxtaposed to this orientation has been the viewpoint that career choice is largely an expression of the client's personality, whether defined as self-concept or needs. Choice problems are essentially personality problems. The Client-Centered and Psychodynamic approaches to career counseling exemplify this theoretical position.

Another major trend has been the increasing recognition of most approaches to career counseling that the choice of a career is a developmental process that unfolds over a prolonged period of time, extending from late childhood to at least early adulthood and sometimes to midlife. This precept is expressed most fully in the Developmental approach to career counseling but is also found in the Psychodynamic and newer Trait-and-Factor models (Super & Bachrach, 1957). In contrast, the Behavioral approach, being largely ahistorical in learning principles, is nondevelopmental. Krumboltz and his associates (1978) have not conceived of the choice process over time nor have they viewed behavioral interventions as influencing ongoing career maturation (Krumboltz & Baker, 1973). In this respect, the Behavioral approach represents an exception to the developmental trend in career counseling.

What Behavioral career counseling has highlighted, however, is the distinction made by Crites (1973; 1974) between career choice process and content, another major trend in the evolution and articulation of career counseling. Because of their learning orientation, Behavioral career counselors focus considerably more upon career choice process than content. In other words, they intervene principally in *how* the client makes a career choice, for example, how he or she gathers relevant occupational information, rather than shaping *which* career the client chooses. There is an interface, therefore, between the Behavioral approach and the Developmental that provides a basis for incorporating them into a more comprehensive approach to career counseling (see Chapter 7).

CAREER COUNSELING DEFINED

Implicit in these trends in the history of career counseling are various definitions of what is meant by career counseling. The variability in the terminology used over the years is confusing. The field has been referred to as: occupational counseling, vocational guidance, career counseling, vocational counseling, and career guidance. These rubrics embrace one-on-one counseling, group guidance and counseling, guidance programs, testing and information programs, computer-based systems, and paper-and-pencil booklets and inventories. It is important, therefore, not only to define the parameters of career counseling, but also to agree on nomenclature. The expression *career counseling* has been chosen for several reasons: First, the term "career" is contemporary. It has increasingly supplanted "vocational" to designate and encompass the developmental nature of decision making as a lifelong process. Second, "career" is generally more inclusive than "vocational," which has not only special connotations (such as vocational-technical education), but also historical meanings that are sometimes confused with choice as a "calling" (Tilgher, 1962). Third, "counseling" has been selected rather than "guidance" to refer specifically to an interpersonal process focused upon assisting an individual to make an appropriate career decision. Guidance often has the connotation of a comprehensive program of occupational orientation that may or may not involve a vis-à-vis relationship between counselor and client.

Implicit in this distinction between counseling and guidance is a sense of what career counseling is *not*. It is important to circumscribe the field by exclusion, but it is essential to distinguish the field from related activities that, particularly recently, have been confused with it. First, most career counselors would agree that career counseling involves a counseling relationship between the counselor and the client. More specifically, it does not consist simply of giving tests and reporting their results, as is not infrequently assumed by more therapeutically oriented counselors or psychotherapists who sometimes see career counseling as simply "test them and tell them." Second, career counseling is more than just exposure to a computer-based informational system. It involves interaction with a person (the counselor) as well as a machine (the computer), and ideally it involves active participation in the decisional process, not simply passive-receptive input of information. Third, career counseling is both more and less than personal adjustment counseling or psychotherapy. The assumption that all vocational problems are personal problems is specious and untenable. Vocational and personal problems are different, but they do interact. Thus, career counseling often embraces personal counseling but it goes beyond this to explore and explicate the client's role in the main arena of life—the world of work.

What career counseling *is* can be contrasted with and extrapolated from what it is *not*. In the pre-World War II period, when the predominant approach to career counseling was the Trait-and-Factor orientation, the National Vocational Guidance Association's (NGVA) official definition of career counseling (vocational guidance) in 1937 stated that its aim was "to assist the individual to choose, prepare for, enter upon, and progress in an occupation." As discussed above, since that time there have been at least two significant trends in the field that have necessitated a revision in the original NVGA definition. One of these has been the increasing recognition of the part played by emotional or personality variables in career choice, and the other has been the casting of the decision-making process into a developmental context. There has emerged, therefore, a more comprehensive definition of career counseling, formulated by Super (1951, p. 92), which incorporates these realities into the meaning of career counseling. It is defined as "the process of helping a person to develop and accept an integrated and adequate picture of himself (sic) and of his role in the world of work, to test this concept against reality, and to convert it into a reality, with satisfaction to himself and benefit to society." The only emendation to make this definition acceptable currently is to change the generic masculine to include women and their equitable role in the processes of career choice and adjustment. (See Chapter 8, "Comprehensive Career Counseling: Special Applications.")

CAREER COUNSELING: CHALLENGES AND PROSPECTS

Implicit in the history and definition of career counseling are stresses and strains that have questioned the applicability and viability of its models and methods. From the Trait-and-Factor tradition, there has evolved a popular (pedestrian) version of this approach to career counseling that has been caricatured as "three interviews and a cloud of dust" (Crites, 1978). Often applied mechanically in counseling centers and employment offices, the vitality and validity of this approach to career counseling, as originally formulated by the Minnesota vocational psychologists, has largely been lost. Similarly, the enthusiasm of early Client-Centered career counselors has been rebuffed by the comments of clients who came for career counseling but found themselves in personal counseling ("Well, that's all well and good, but how am I going to earn a living?"). Attempts to synthesize the two approaches in the 1950s and early 1960s resulted in an expedient eclecticism that apparently appealed to very few. Evidently, career counselors could not philosophically subscribe to cyclical use of nondirective and directive methods (Super, 1957) nor to conjoint techniques (Combs, 1947), which put the client in contact with one counselor for interviewing and with another counselor for information. As a result, career counseling in the 1960s fell into disrepute. Particularly in the last years of the decade, the *Zeitgeist* was social cause, not vocational future. One's career was eclipsed by personal concerns for others and society.

The consequence was pervasive: The staffs of counseling centers, particularly in higher education, but also in the schools and community, became almost totally engaged in counseling actitivies focused upon interpersonal relationships, drug abuse, communal living, group participation, outreach contacts, minorities, etc. There was, in effect, a nationwide abandonment of careers among counseling personnel during the late 1960s and early 1970s, until two events occurred: the emergence of the women's movement and the upheaval in the economy. Women began to realize that appropriate placement in the world of work was not only an economic wedge for equity with men but was also a sine qua non of personal esteem and self-sufficiency. The demand for competent career counseling for women increased precipitously, and the field responded with theory (Zytowski, 1969), research (Pietrofesa & Schlossberg, 1970), and career counseling principles (Fitzgerald & Crites, 1980), relevant to assisting women in establishing their equitable place in the world of work. Concurrently, there was an upsurge of interest in career counseling in high schools and in colleges and universities because of the restricted employment opportunities occasioned by economic conditions. Surveys of high school juniors and seniors and college freshmen indicated that the single, most preferred counseling service was career counseling (Prediger, Roth, & Neoth, 1973). Yet, students were not receiving it.

Paradoxically, studies (such as Gelso, Karl, & O'Connell, 1972) of counseling center staffs surveying the services they preferred to offer were at considerable variance with what large segments of their potential clientele wanted. Counselors preferred to do "therapy," whereas students wanted "career counseling." Schneider and Gelso (1972) also found in a survey of counseling training programs that preparation in personal counseling was considered stronger than in either vocational psychology or career counseling. The problem, therefore, is how to provide the counseling services clients want with those counselors prefer to offer. One solution, which underlies the raison d'etre for this book, and which represents an effort to effect a rapprochement between personal counseling and career counseling, is that career counseling not only facilitates career development (choice *and* adjustment), but it also enhances personal adjustment. The central theme of this text is that comprehensive career counseling, synthesized from the best models and methods of career counseling, also incorporates the best from theories of counseling and psychotherapy and goes considerably beyond them. This position is based upon the following five propositions:

1 *The need for career counseling is greater than the need for psychotherapy.* Comprehensive career counseling deals with both the inner and outer worlds, whereas psychotherapy treats typically only the inner world. The results from the studies cited above are conclusive: Clients want career orientation first and then personal change. Why be so presumptuous as to assume that we know better what they need when, if properly trained in psychotherapy *and* career counseling, we can offer both?

2 *Career counseling can be therapeutic.* Not only has it been established in vocational psychology that there is a moderate positive correlation between career and personal adjustment (Super, 1957; Crites, 1969), but there is also accumulated evidence that increased career adjustment is directly related to enhanced personal adjustment. Studies by Williams (1962) and Williams and Hills (1962) have demonstrated that even fairly traditional career counseling (Trait-and-Factor approach) significantly increases personal adjustment, as indexed by the discrepancy between self and ideal-self Q-sorts. Thus, there is empirical support for Super's hypothesis (1957, p. 300) that:

> . . . by relieving tensions, clarifying feelings, giving insight, helping attain success, and developing a feeling of competence in one important area of adjustment, the vocational, it is possible to release the individual's ability to cope more adequately with other aspects of living, thus bringing about improvement in his general adjustment.

3 *Career counseling should follow psychotherapy.* The Freudian dictum that no decisions concerning career or marriage should be made until the completion of psychoanalysis has been carried to the extreme in the general practice of psychotherapy. Not only are these decisions deferred during the course of psychotherapy, but they are also seldom considered afterwards. How many psychotherapists engage their clients in career counseling, either directly or indirectly by referral, after they have completed treatment? Yet if they have been successful in effecting some personality change, and if personality is related to career choice, as it appears to be (Crites, 1969, Ch. 6), then it would seem to be at least incumbent upon these psychotherapists, therapeutically if not ethically, to consider with their clients possible reorientations and new directions in their career development. There is a strong inference, as well as some research evidence (Crites, 1964), to support career counseling as a sequential adjunct to psychotherapy. Ideally, psychotherapists should be as proficient in career counseling as in psychotherapy; minimally, they should be aware of the necessary relationship between the two processes.

4 *Career counseling is more effective than psychotherapy.* Although this proposition is bound to be controversial, the evidence in support of it is not. The success rate for counseling is at least 25 percent greater than that of psychotherapy (75 percent versus 50 percent), whichever review of the literature is cited (for example, Brayfield, 1964; Garfield & Bergin, 1978). These obviously are comparisons within the treatments, not between them. That is, these percentages do not directly compare career counseling and psychotherapy, although such a comparison might be made on common criteria of success, such as self-ideal discrepancies in the studies by Williams (1962; Hills 1962). The point is that, other things being equal, there is a greater expectancy of effectiveness with career counseling than with psychotherapy.

5 *Career counseling is more difficult than psychotherapy.* Using the comprehensive approach to career counseling, which draws upon the principles and procedures of other approaches, as well as personality theory and career/developmental psychology, the career counselor must be expert not only in the basics of psychotherapy but also in the models and methods of career counseling. That is, career counseling deals with both the inner *and* the outer worlds of the individual. A psychotherapist need never know about the world of work to help a client resolve a personal or social problem, whereas a career counselor must necessarily understand the interface between these problems and the work world. In the comprehensive approach formulated in this book, the career counselor can be both psychotherapist and career counselor. Being one or the other is not sufficient to assist clients in their life/career development (Gysbers, 1975).

PLAN OF THE BOOK

To organize the extensive literature and expertise on career counseling, it is necessary to have a classification schema. A review of the theory and research on the field, augmented by actual career counseling case studies, suggests the taxonomy shown in Figure 1-1. Along the horizontal dimension are the major approaches to career counseling that have been delineated historically in the initial section of this chapter. Down the vertical axis of the schema is a categorization of the principal parameters of the various approaches to career counseling that they have in common but on which they differ. The theoretical "model"

	Trait-and-Factor	Client-Centered	Psychodynamic	Developmental	Behavioral
Diagnosis					
Process					
Outcomes					
Interview techniques					
Test interpretation					
Use of occupational information					

Figure 1-1 Taxonomy of approaches to career counseling.

is broken down into the major stages of (1) diagnosis, (2) process, and (3) outcomes. These correspond to the usual phases in the interaction between a career counselor and a client, although, as is brought out in the chapters on client-centered and behavioral career counseling, the concept of "diagnosis" is not universally accepted or defined. The techniques or "methods" of the various approaches are those which are generally identified with career counseling, although again there are some deviations in the Client-Centered and Behavioral approaches. The methods include (1) interview techniques, (2) test interpretation, and (3) use of occupational information.

One chapter is devoted to each of the major approaches to career counseling in the main part of the book (Chapters 2–6). The first section in each chapter deals with the "Model" of that particular approach, the second section is "Methods," and the third section is "Materials." Here a case study illustrative of the approach is presented. The last part of the book (Chapters 7 and 8) synthesizes the other approaches into one comprehensive approach and discusses its applications in general and to women, minorities, and handicapped/disabled clients as well as in programmatic "packages" and group settings. Again, these chapters are organized according to Figure 1-1, which provides the career counselor with a conceptual schema for formulating an approach to career counseling adapted to the needs of each client.

REFERENCES

Bordin, E. S. *Psychological counseling.* New York: Appleton-Century-Crofts, 1955.

Bordin, E. S. *Psychological counseling.* (2d ed.). New York: Appleton-Century-Crofts, 1968.

Bordin, E. S., Nachmann, B., & Segal, S. J. An articulated framework for vocational development. *Journal of Counseling Psychology,* 1963, *10,* 107–116.

Borow, H. (Ed.), *Man in a world at work.* Boston: Houghton Mifflin, 1964.

Brayfield, A. H. Research on vocational guidance: Status and prospect. In H. Borow (Ed.), *Man in a world at work.* Boston: Houghton Mifflin, 1964. Pp. 310–323.

Combs, A. Nondirective techniques and vocational counseling. *Occupations,* 1947, *25,* 261–267.

Crites, J. O. A model for the measurement of vocational maturity. *Journal of Counseling Psychology,* 1961, *8,* 255–259.

Crites, J. O. Proposals for a new criterion measure and research design. In H.

Borow (Ed.), *Man in a world at work.* Boston: Houghton Mifflin, 1964. Pp. 324–340.

Crites, J. O. *Vocational psychology.* New York: McGraw-Hill, 1969.

Crites, J. O. The maturity of vocational attitudes in adolescence. Washington, D.C.: *American Personnel and Guidance Association,* Inquiry Series, No. 2, 1971.

Crites, J. O. *Theory and research handbook for the Career Maturity Inventory.* Monterey, Calif.: CTB/McGraw-Hill, 1973; 1978.

Crites, J. O. Career development process: A model of vocational maturity. In E. L. Herr (Ed.), *Vocational guidance and human development.* Boston: Houghton Mifflin, 1974. Pp. 296–320.

Fitzgerald, L. F., & Crites, J. O. Toward a career psychology of women: What do we know? What do we need to know? *Journal of Counseling Psychology,* 1980, *27,* 44–62.

Freud, S. *Civilization and its discontents.* New York: Norton, 1962.

Fromm, E. *The sane society.* New York: Holt, Rinehart, & Winston, 1955.

Garfield, S. L., & Bergin, A. E. *Handbook of psychotherapy and behavior change* (2d ed.) New York: Wiley, 1978.

Gelso, C. J., Karl, N. J., & O'Connell, T. Perceptions of the role of a university counseling center. *Journal of College Student Personnel,* 1972, *13,* 441–447.

Gysbers, N. C. Beyond career development—life career development. *Personnel and Guidance Journal,* 1975, *53,* 647–652.

Herr, E. L. (Ed.), *Vocational guidance and human development.* Boston: Houghton Mifflin, 1974.

Krumboltz, J. D. (Ed.), *Revolution in counseling: Implications of behavioral science.* Boston: Houghton Mifflin, 1966.

Krumboltz, J. D., & Baker, R. D. Behavioral counseling for vocational decision. In H. Borow (Ed.), *Career guidance for a new age.* Boston: Houghton Mifflin, 1973. Pp. 235–283.

Krumboltz, J. D. Mitchell, A. M., & Jones, G. B. A social learning theory of career selection. In J. M. Whiteley & A. Resnikoff (Eds), *Career counseling.* Monterey, Calif.: Brooks/Cole, 1978. Pp. 100–127.

Krumboltz, J. D., & Thoresen, C. E. The effect of behavioral counseling in group and individual settings on information-seeking behavior. *Journal of Counseling Psychology,* 1964, *11,* 324–333.

National Vocational Guidance Association. Principles and practices of vocational guidance. *Occupations,* 1937, *15,* 772–778.

Pietrofesa, J. J., & Schlossberg, N. K. Counselor bias and the female occupational role. Detroit: Wayne State University, 1970. (ERIC Document, CG 006056).

Prediger, D. J., Roth, J. D., & Noeth, R. J. Nationwide study of career development: Summary of results. *ACT Research Report,* No. 61. Iowa City: American College Testing Program, 1973.

Ryan, R. A., & Krumboltz, J. D. Effect of planned reinforcement counseling on client decision-making behavior. *Journal of Counseling Psychology,* 1964, *11,* 315–323.

Schneider, L., & Gelso, C. "Vocational" vs. "personal" emphases in counseling psychology training programs. *The Counseling Psychologist,* 1972, *3* (3), 90–92.

Science Research Associates. *Job Experience Kits.* Chicago: Science Research Associates, 1970.

Super, D. E. Vocational adjustment: Implementing a self-concept. *Occupations,* 1951, *30,* 88–92.

Super, D. E. The dimensions and measurement of vocational maturity. *Teachers College Record,* 1955, *57,* 151–163.

Super, D. E. *The psychology of careers.* New York, Harper, 1957.

Super, D. E. & Bachrach, P. B. *Scientific careers and vocational development theory.* New York: Teachers College Bureau of Publications, 1957.

Tilgher, A. Work through the ages. In S. Nosow & W. H. Form (Eds), *Man, work, and society.* New York: Basic Books, 1962. Pp. 11–24.

Williams, J. E. Changes in self and other perceptions following brief educational-vocational counseling. *Journal of Counseling Psychology,* 1962, *9,* 18–30.

Williams, J. E., & Hills, D. A. More on brief educational-vocational counseling. *Journal of Counseling Psychology,* 1962, *9,* 366–368.

Zytowski, D. G. Toward a theory of career development for women. *Personnel and Guidance Journal,* 1969, *47,* 660–664.

Trait-and-Factor Career Counseling

What has become known as Trait-and-Factor career counseling has its historical antecedents in that field of psychology that has focused upon the identification and measurement of individual differences in human behavior (Anastasi, 1958; Paterson, 1930; Tyler, 1965). Although they encompass other facets of personality as well (Guilford, 1959; Mischel, 1968), the terms *trait* and *factor* refer principally to abilities (including general intelligence, special aptitudes, academic achievement, and job skills), vocational interests, and personality characteristics (Super & Crites, 1962). Together, Trait-and-Factor denote one of the major orientations in vocational psychology conceived to describe and explain career decision making. Stemming from the older "matching men and jobs" point-of-view, it is made up of three assumptions or principles (Crites, 1969, p. 336):

> **1** By virtue of his [sic] unique psychological characteristics, each worker is best fitted for a particular type of work.
> **2** Groups of workers in different occupations have different psychological characteristics.
> **3** Vocational adjustment varies directly with the extent of agreement between worker characteristics and work demands.

In Trait-and-Factor career counseling, these tenets are translated into a model and methods predicated upon assisting the client to find an optimal niche in the world of work.

MODEL

The model of this approach to career counseling was fashioned from the pragmatics of assisting men and women dislocated from their jobs during the era of the Great Depression to retrain and find new employment (Paterson & Darley, 1936). Evolving from the interdisciplinary work of the Twin Cities Occupational Analysis Clinic, early Trait-and-Factor career counseling reflected the rudiments of Parsons' (1909) tripartite emphasis upon (1) the individual, (2) the occupation, and (3) the relationship between them, but it went beyond his pioneer paradigm to incorporate the sophistication of the newly developing psychometrics and occupationology. The former produced the fabled Minnesota tests of clerical aptitude, manual dexterity, spatial perception, and so forth, and the latter yielded the fund of occupational information compiled by the U.S. Employment Service for the first edition (1939) of the *Dictionary of Occupational Titles (DOT)*. In more recent years these early foundations have been augmented by the theory and research of the Work Adjustment Project (Lofquist & Dawis, 1969) at the University of Minnesota and the Functional Occupational Classification Project in the Department of Labor (Fine & Heinz, 1958) that has culminated in the publication of the latest edition of the *DOT*.

Philosophically, Trait-and-Factor career counseling has always had a strong commitment to the uniqueness of the individual. Psychologically, this value has meant a long-time predilection for the tenets of differential psychology. As a consequence, there have been two significant implications for the model upon which this approach is based. First, it is largely *atheoretical*, other than it subscribes to the proposition that individuals differ. Addressing the real-world problems of the unemployed trying to get jobs during the 1930s and more recently difficulties of the handicapped and disabled in vocational rehabilitation, Trait-and-Factor career counseling was spawned from "dustbowl empiricism"—a singular concern with the explicitly definable and the statistically predictable. It does not posit organizing concepts or hypothetical constructs as do Client-Centered and Psychodynamic approaches. Second, it is analytical and atomistic in its orientation, as exemplified by the so-called psychograph on which are profiled the client's "traits and factors" measured by standardized tests. Moreover, Trait-and-Factor career counseling follows closely the schematic of scientific problem solving, as the following sections on its nosological concept of diagnosis, rationalistic process of counseling, and specific set of decisional outcomes illustrates.

Diagnosis

The cornerstone of Trait-and-Factor career counseling is *differential diagnosis*. Williamson (1939a, pp. 102–103) defines it as:

> a process of logical thinking or the "teasing out," from a mass of relevant and irrelevant facts, of a consistent pattern of meaning and an understanding of the [client's] assets and liabilities together with a prognosis or judgment of the significance of this pattern for future adjustments made by the [client].

To aid in diagnosing problems in career decision making, Williamson (1939b) has proposed these four categories, along with definitions of each:

1 *No choice:* When asked which occupation they intend to enter after completing their formal education or training, clients are unable to state a choice, usually responding with "I don't know what I want to do."

2 *Uncertain choice:* The client has chosen a career, and can verbalize it as an occupational title, but expresses doubt about the decision. Operationally, degree of certainty/uncertainty can be defined on a vertical rating scale as shown in Table 2-1.

3 *Unwise choice:* Defined as a disagreement between a client's abilities and interests, on the one hand, and the requirements of occupations on the other, this category encompasses all possible combinations of these variables. Usually, however, unwise choice refers to a career decision for which the client has insufficient aptitude.

4 *Discrepancy between interests and aptitudes:* Included here are three types of discrepancies: (a) interest in an occupation for which the client's aptitude is less than requisite;[1] (b) interest in an occupation below the client's ability level; and (c) interests and abilities at the same level but in different fields.

Contingent upon which problem a client is considered to have, an appropriate process of career counseling can presumably be selected. Thus, the role of diagnosis in Trait-and-Factor career counseling is much like it is in the medical model; differential courses of treatment stem from a determination of what is "wrong" with the client.

To rely upon diagnosis as a sine qua non for career counseling presumes that considerable confidence can be placed in the identification and classification of a client's choice problem(s). This has not been the case. Not only Williamson's diagnostic system but others as well have suffered from three shortcomings (Crites, 1969, Ch. 7). First, they are largely unreliable. Studies by Pepinsky (1948), Sloan and Pierce-Jones (1958), and others have established that when more than one judge is involved, agreement in classifying the problems of clients from case materials seldom exceeds 50 percent. In other words, the *best* that can be done is by chance. Second, the categories in these diagnostic systems are not independent and mutually exclusive, which accounts in part for the low interjudge agreement. A client can be classified in more than one category. One judge (or counselor) may classify a client as unrealistic because aptitude is below that required for the chosen occupation, and another judge may categorize the client as having a discrepancy between aptitude and interests. Given the diagnostic

---

[1]Note that this discrepancy is between aptitude and interest, whereas in unwise choice it is between aptitude and choice.

Table 2-1   Career Choice Certainty Scale

---

1. What is your career choice? Which occupation do you intend
    to enter full-time after you have finished your education or
    training? Be as specific as possible. Use occupational titles,
    such as electrical engineer or psychiatric nurse.

    _____

    _____

    _____

2. Rate your degree of *certainty* with your career choice on the
    scale below. Draw a mark (-) across the scale at the point that
    indicates how certain you are about the career you have cho-
    sen.

    high certainty   I have *few doubts* about my
                            chosen career. I do not expect to
                            change it. I plan to enter it and stay
                            in it.

    average certainty   I have *some doubts* about my chosen
                            career. I wonder sometimes whether I
                            have made the right choice.

    low certainty   I have many doubts about my chosen
                            career. I have a choice, but I often
                            question whether it is a good one.

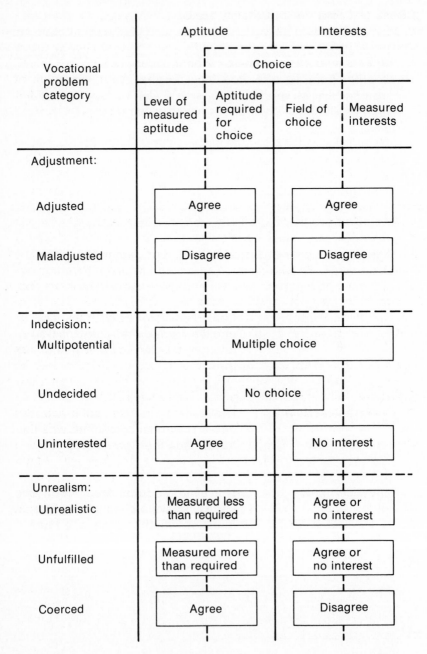

Figure 2-1 Criteria for classifying career choice problems. *(Crites, 1969, p. 300)*

system, both may be "right," but they disagree because the categories are not independent and mutually exclusive. Third, most systems for diagnosing career problems have not been exhaustive, another factor contributing to their unreliability. Because it has not been possible to classify all possible client problems into the diagnostic systems, judges have had to use the categories that were available, but they have not necessarily used the same ones, thus attenuating their percentage of agreement.

To overcome these shortcomings, Crites (1969) has devised a diagnostic system for client problems in career choice that is reliable, independent and mutually exclusive, and exhaustive, given the criteria of classification within the system for defining and categorizing a problem. These criteria are explicitly enumerated in Figure 2-1 for the problems described in Table 2-2. The underlying principle of the system is one of agreement among a client's aptitudes, interests, and choices. If a counselor has objective data on each of these variables, he or she can reliably classify the client's problem into the system, because its categories are independent, mutually exclusive, and exhaustive. The system *is* limited, however, by the variables used as criteria of classification. There are problems that clients present which must be diagnosed on bases other than those in the system. The most obvious of these is indecisiveness in career decision making. Classifying clients as undecided because they have no choice is not a sufficient basis to distinguish between simple indecision and pervasive indecisiveness (Crites, 1969, Ch. 13; also see Ch. 6). The diagnostic system identifies a client as undecided or not, but the counselor must supplement this initial classification with additional information to determine whether the client's problem is one of indecision or indecisiveness. The situation is similar with other variables that influence career choice. Their effects must be taken into account after the preliminary diagnosis based upon aptitudes and interests has been made. An illustration of how such differential diagnoses of career problems can be made is given later in the chapter (see "Materials").

Process

The process of career counseling in the Trait-and-Factor approach is what can be characterized as rationalistic. It follows closely the familiar scientific method in problem solving. Williamson (1939b, p. 214) delineates six steps in this process:

Table 2-2 Definitions of Vocational Choice Problems

Problems of Adjustment

1 The *adjusted* individual's choice is in the field of his interest and is on the appropriate aptitude level. He may have a multiple interest pattern, but his choice agrees with at least one of the patterns. In effect, he has "no problem" (Bordin, 1946), although he may come for counseling because he "lacks assurance" (Pepinsky, 1948).

2 The *maladjusted* individual's choice neither agrees with his field of interest nor with his level of aptitude. The problem here is one of complete disagreement among the variables involved in the decision-making process.

Problems of Indecision

1 The *multipotential* individual has two or more choices, each of which agrees with his field of interest and is on the appropriate aptitude level. He may have a multiple interest pattern, but his choices must be consistent with one of the patterns. His problem is that he cannot decide among these alternatives.

2 The *undecided* individual has "no choice." He may also have no interest pattern, a single or multiple pattern, and aptitude at a high, average, or low level, but regardless of his status on these variables, the fact that he cannot state which occupation he intends to enter in the future is what defines his problem.

Problems of Unrealism

1 The *unrealistic* individual's choice agrees with his field of interest, or there is no interest pattern, but it requires a level of aptitude that is higher than his tested level.

2 The *unfulfilled* individual's choice agrees with his field of interest, but it is on an aptitude level that is below his measured capability.

3 The *coerced* individual's choice is on the appropriate aptitude level, but it is not congruent with his field of interest. Although his problem may appear to be one of adjustment or indecision, it is listed

---

Table 2-2 (Continued)

---

here because a choice has been made. What makes it unrealistic is its being in the wrong interest area. Strong (1955) has found, for example, that if an individual enters an occupation for which he does not have appropriate interests ("C" on the SVIB), the chances are about 5 to 1 that he will eventually change to another occupation.

Source: Crites, 1969, pp. 298–299.

> *Analysis* collecting data from many sources about attitudes, interests, family background, knowledge, educational progress, aptitudes, etc., by means of both subjective and objective techniques.
> *Synthesis* collating and summarizing the data by means of case study techniques and test profiles to "highlight" the [client's] uniqueness or individuality.
> *Diagnosis* describing the outstanding characteristics and problems of the [client], comparing the individual's profile with educational and occupational ability profiles, and ferreting out the causes of the problems.
> *Prognosis* judging the probable consequences of problems, the probabilities for adjustments, and thereby indicating the alternative actions and adjustments for the [client's] consideration.
> *Counseling,* or *treatment* cooperatively advising with the client concerning what to do to effect a desired adjustment now or in the future.
> *Follow-up* repeating the above steps as new problems arise and further assisting the [client] to carry out a desirable program of action.

The first four steps of this process are engaged in by the counselor exclusively; only in the last two steps does the client actively participate. Most of the process, then, involves the mental activity of the counselor in gathering, processing, and interpreting data on the client.

The role of the counselor in Trait-and-Factor career counseling is clearly that of educator (Berdie, 1949), if not social engineer (Paterson & Darley, 1936). The interventive process emphasizes teaching and persuading the client, convincing the client of the inherent reasonableness of the counselor's inferences from the accumulated case data. The counselor exerts considerable influence upon the client, and in Strong and Schmidt's (1970) dimensions of counselor characteristics "expertness" would rank highest, "trustworthiness" would be second, and "attractiveness" third. This does not mean that Trait-and-Factor career counselors are unattractive, but rather that the role they typically play highlights expertness and trustworthiness. Williamson (1972, pp. 145–146) recognized the generational gap that often exists between counselor and client, particularly in the educational system, but finds no bridge for it within the context of Trait-and-Factor career counseling, other than possibly a benevolent expertness:

> While all counselors seek not to be perceived as authoritarian or even as authority figures, they are never certain how they will be perceived by the student being counseled. . . . Perhaps this is one of the reasons why so many counselors shy away from discipline, which is of course at the heart of authority, but not as [sic] authoritarianism, as is foolishly and simple-mindedly assumed by some counselors and counselor educators. It is largely an unsolved problem, it seems to me, how we will create the perception that *counselors are friendly authorities,* being older and therefore in the authority relationship of possessing professional knowledge of possible use to the student. (Emphasis added.)

In Trait-and-Factor career counseling, then, the relationship between counselor and client is largely that of teacher-to-student, expert-to-novice, older-to-younger.

Reflecting this type of counselor-client relationship, as well as the application of the scientific method in solving career choice problems, are the stages or phases typically discernible in the process of Trait-and-Factor career counseling. The first stage, which usually corresponds to the initial interview but may include additional contacts, is used to establish what earlier was known as rapport and what now is thought of more comprehensively as the relationship. The counselor listens to the client's presenting problem, gets to know the client through questions about personal background and education, and assigns tests for the client to take before the next interview. The second stage, which again may take up one or more interviews, is given to test interpretation. The client returns for a detailed synthesis of psychometric and demographic data and counseling based upon the counselor's diagnosis from the accumulated case materials. The counselor plays a highly active role, the client a more passive one, although with encouragement to react when she or he has questions or comments. Most of the time in this stage is devoted to the counselor's systematical (that is, test by test) interpretation of the client's scores on a variety of measures, such as the Differential Aptitude Tests (DAT) or the Strong-Campbell Interest

Inventory (SCII). The last stage is reserved for the dissemination of occupational information. The client is either directly informed by the counselor about occupations appropriate to his or her "traits and factors" or referred to relevant sources, such as the *DOT, Occupational Outlook Handbook,* and manuals, pamphlets, and so forth. Thus, the process of Trait-and-Factor career counseling is divided into three stages: (1) background of problem (personal data collection), (2) statement of problem (test interpretation), and (3) resolution of problem (occupational information).

Outcomes

If the diagnosis in Trait-and Factor career counseling has been accurate, and if the process has been effective, then certain outcomes are expected. The more circumscribed and immediate of these is the resolution of the client's problem. Where there was indecision, there is now decision; where there was unrealism, there is now realism. In general, the goal is for the client to arrive, through a rational process of decision making and problem solving, at a career choice which is consonant with his or her educational-vocational capabilities and which can be implemented in the world of work. The only exception to this prognosis might be the postponement or deferment of a choice for a prescribed period of time. In this case, there is still a choice, but paradoxically it is *not* to make a choice. When viewed developmentally, this happens frequently, for good reason, although it is not clear in Trait-and-Factor career counseling. It was recognized, for example, that some vocational interest patterns, such as social service, are developed later than others and, since choice should be based at least in part upon interests, a career decision might be delayed until interests have fully crystallized. Strong's (1943; 1955) data indicate that most change in interests occurs between ages fifteen and eighteen and the remainder by age twenty-one. An explicit outcome of Trait-and-Factor career counseling is a realistic choice by the time a client enters early adulthood.

A second outcome of Trait-and-Factor career counseling is that the client learns how to make decisions and solve problems, as contrasted with the decisions and solutions per se. Williamson (1965, p. 198) states this goal in terms of personal assessment and control:

> The task of the trait-factor type of counseling is to aid the individual in successive approximations of self-understanding and self-management by means of helping him to assess his assets and liabilities in relation to the requirements of progressively changing life goals and his vocational career.

Stated somewhat differently, Thompson (1954, p. 535) has pointed out that this approach should not only assist the client to make a substantive decision (career choice), but it should also help the client learn the process of how to make decisions:

> The vocational counselor's concern is not only with helping the individual to solve an immediate problem or make an immediate decision; he also recognizes that effective counseling should result in the individual's being better able to solve future problems.

Viewed this way, the scope of Trait-and-Factor career counseling expands greatly: it encompasses not only the content but also the process of career choice, a basic distinction that is discussed at greater length in Chapter 5. Neither Williamson nor Thompson articulated the counseling methods, however, to achieve this more comprehensive outcome. Consequently, as it is generally practiced, the Trait-and-Factor approach focuses more narrowly upon the client's making specific career choices as criteria of its efficacy.

The accumulated research on the Trait-and-Factor approach to career counseling is voluminous, dating from the early Minnesota studies in this country (Paterson & Darley, 1936), through those of the National Institute of Industrial Psychology in England (Hunt & Smith, 1938), to the current evaluation programs of school systems, universities, private institutions, and governmental agencies throughout the country. Reviews of these outcome studies over the years (for example, Brayfield, 1964; Crites, 1964; Myers, 1971; Tyler, 1969) have led to only one conclusion: Trait and Factor career counseling works. It may not uniformly assist all clients along all dimensions, but given its boundary conditions it results in greater decisiveness, greater certainty, and greater realism in career choice for most clients. In other words, although it may be circumscribed in its purview, relatively short-term in duration, and problem-specific in scope, there is considerable research evidence that this approach provides an experience for clients that contributes to their career decision making.

METHODS

The methods used in Trait-and-Factor career counseling reflect the rationalistic, cognitive model of this approach. Interview techniques, test interpretation procedures, uses of occupational information—taken together, they constitute a logical attack (Williamson, 1939a) upon the client's decision-making problem. They are what the thinking person would do when confronted with a choice among alternative courses of action. They are largely action-oriented, and the counselor is highly active in using these methods. Not only is most of the processing of data on the client a counselor activity, but also the lead in the interviews is typically taken by the counselor. This role should not be construed to mean, however, that the counselor is insensitive or unresponsive to the client's feelings and emotions and attitudes. Quite the contrary, as Darley (1950, p. 268) notes in discussing acceptance of the client: "The interviewer must indicate to the client that he has accepted but not passed judgment on these [the client's] feelings and attitudes."

Whether dealing with feeling or content, the Trait-and-Factor career counselor nevertheless appears to be in charge. The counselor role in this approach is probably best characterized as assertive, dominant, and participative (as contrasted with reactive and reflective), all of which earned the Trait-and-Factor counselor the appellation of "directive" during the heyday of Rogerian nondirective counseling in the 1950s. To use these methods effectively presumes that they are compatible with the counselor's personality (Forgy & Black, 1954).

Interview Techniques

Williamson (1939a) has identified five general techniques that he recommends for Trait-and-Factor career counseling:

1 *Establishing rapport* The counselor attempts to gain the confidence of the client, to appear expert, and to relate on a level that inspires the client to entrust the problem with the counselor.

2 *Cultivating self-understanding*   The client is encouraged to gain an enlightened appraisal of assets and liabilities and an insight into how they bear upon his or her problem. "The effective counselor is one who induces the [client] to want to utilize his assets in ways which will yield success and satisfaction" (Williamson, 1939a, p. 134).

3 *Advising or planning a program of action*   "The counselor must begin his advising [counseling] at the point of the student's understanding, i.e., he must begin marshalling, orally, the evidence for and against the [client's] claimed educational or vocational choice or emotional habits, practices, and attitudes. . . . Thus we see that counseling calls for resourcefulness in helping the student to think of things to be done, actions which are appropriate to the individuality of the student. It is not easy to achieve that *balance between definiteness*

and open-mindedness which produces a richness of appropriate and possible next steps for the [client] to try out" (Williamson, 1939a, pp. 135, 193).

4 *Carrying out the plan*   Once a plan of action has been agreed upon, the counselor assists the client in carrying it out by making suggestions and providing direct assistance, such as implementing a career choice.

5 *Referral*   All counselors cannot counsel all clients, a truism too often bitterly learned after the fact. Williamson (1939a, p. 143) notes that "Frequently the most appropriate advice given by a counselor is that the [client] see another counselor for assistance in understanding his problems."

More specifically, Darley (1950, p. 266) enunciates four principles of interviewing that the counselor should follow:

> **1**   Do not lecture or talk down to the client.
> **2**   Use simple words and confine the information that you give the client to a relatively few ideas.
> **3**   Make very sure that you know what it is he really wants to talk about before giving any information or answers.
> **4**   Make very sure that you sense or feel the attitudes that he holds, because these will either block the discussion or keep the main problems out of it.

A theme common to these principles, with the possible exception of the second, which is not usually associated with the Trait-and-Factor point-of-view, is implicit regard for the client. Whereas earlier explications of this approach appeared directive and paternalistic, even they evince the concern of the counselor for the client. Perhaps it is less *what* is said by the Trait-and-Factor career counselor than *how* it is said. Running through this orientation is an abiding commitment to the individuality of the client. This commitment is frequently belied by the undue attention that has been given the techniques of Trait-and-Factor career counseling. Too often this approach is followed almost mechanically, without understanding its essence, which is summed up in the question counselors should continuously ask themselves: "What is in the best interests of this client?"

Assuming that the counselor focuses on the client rather than on the techniques, what are the latter in Trait-and-Factor career counseling and how can they be used to facilitate the client's career decision making? Darley (1950, pp. 167–272) has enumerated many of the interview techniques used in this approach, which range from handling the initial contact with the client to terminating the counseling process in the last interview. These techniques are reproduced in Table 2-3. Note the casual but focused opening to the interview, which establishes rapport at the same time it leads into the subject matter of counseling. Note also the use of the open-ended question that Darley recommends throughout the communication process. It is probably the single most important modus operandi for interacting effectively with the client and eliciting content (therapeutic material) relevant to career decision making and problem solving. Using the open-ended question will also check the counselor's tendency to overtalk and cross-examine. A useful index of effective communication, predicated upon the dictum of brevity with clarity, is the *client/counselor talk ratio*. During the course of an interview, seldom should the ratio exceed 50 percent for the counselor. If it does, then the counselor is most likely overtalking, cross-examining, or breaking silences inappropriately. As a consequence, the locus of responsibility for the interview interaction may shift disproportionately to the counselor and foster dependence in the client.

Test Interpretation

This phase of Trait-and-Factor career counseling is subsumed by those interview techniques that Williamson (1939a, pp. 139–142) calls "advising or planning a program of action," and they include the following:

1 *Direct advising* In this method "the counselor frankly states his own opinion regarding the most satisfactory choice, action, or program to be made and followed out by the student." Williamson uses this method differentially with clients, depending upon their problems and personalities. He advises directly when clients are "tough-minded and insist upon a frank opinion" and when they persist in "an activity or a choice which the counselor has reason to believe will lead to serious failure and loss of morale."

2 *Persuasion* The counselor "marshals the evidence in such a reasonable and logical manner that the student is able to anticipate clearly the probable outcomes of alternative actions. The counselor seeks to persuade the student to understand the implications of the diagnosis and the outcomes of the next steps. He does not dominate the student's choosing but merely persuades him to avoid new problems."

3 *Explanation* The counselor explores the possible meanings and interpretations of the diagnosis, both test and nontest data, in an

Table 2-3 Darley's Interview Techniques

---

1 Opening the Interview If both parties in the interview are as nervous as we have indicated earlier, it is important that they both arrive quickly at a more relaxed state. A few of the ordinary rules of good manners, like greeting the client by name and asking him to sit down, come quickly to mind. Then a relatively neutral and casual statement, such as, "What do you have on your mind today?" or "What do you want to see us about?" or "What can we help you with?" may open up the interview for the client.

2 Phrasing Questions One of the best ways to cut off any conversational flow from the client is to ask a question that can be answered "Yes" or "No." For example, the question "So you want to start a small business?" is far less productive than the question "How did you happen to think of starting your own business?"; and this in turn may not be quite as effective as the simple statement "Tell me what you have in mind when you talk about starting a small business." Questions that can be answered by "Yes" or "No" or some similar terminal statement should be avoided wherever possible.

3 The Client's Experiences with Counseling Today, with the general enthusiasm about counseling, many clients coming to an advisory center will have been counseled before, either at a military separation center or at one of many possible governmental agencies. The feeling of your clients about you as a counselor will not always be a happy one, especially if he has had a bad time earlier. He will be comparing you with other counselors he has known, good or bad. He will be quoting to you his interpretations of what other counselors have told him. It will often be quite necessary to ask him what others have told him so that you will not be working at cross purposes. On the other hand, it is worth remembering that he will interpret what other people have told him primarily in terms of his own subjective feeling and attitudes and wants, not with any high degree of objectivity.

4 Overtalking the Client Many people in an interview may find it difficult to state what they mean concisely, without some fumbling for words. Do not be in such a hurry that you override or overtalk the client if he is fumbling for the phrases he wants. A very frequent error of beginning interviewers is to put words in a client's mouth, or

Table 2-3 (Continued)

---

talk faster than the client, or in some way take the conversation away from the client.

5 Accepting the Client's Attitudes and Feelings At various points in the interview the client may be trying to express the more deep-seated attitudes and feelings that control his behavior. He will get bogged down in the task simply because none of us finds it easy to put into words some of our more private attitudes, resentments, doubts, and uncertainties. He may also fear that the interviewer will not approve of what he says. The interviewer must indicate to the client that he has accepted but not passed judgment on these feelings and attitudes. Merely saying, "I see," or "I understand," or "Yes," will serve to bridge the conversational gap and keep the client talking.

6 Cross-examining Do not fire questions at the client like a machine gun. The interview is not a cross-examination. If you are filling out an interview blank and have to get names, addresses, and other items of fact, spread these items throughout the interview, don't pile them up in a series of questions at the beginning. In any event, when questions are needed, space them out and phrase them in as neutral a manner as possible.

7 Silences in the Interview Most people are embarrassed if no conversation is going on. Silences seem long and endless. If such silences were actually timed with a stop watch, they would probably be found to last not more than thirty seconds, and they do not represent necessarily a real absence of activity. The client may be groping for words or ideas; the interviewer may be studying an earlier bit of conversation that has already taken place. Do not, therefore, be frightened by the silences that sometimes fall in interviews. Do not fill them up with a lot of chattering that breaks the trend of thought or interrupts the flow of feeling. If it becomes necessary to break a silence, merely ask the client to tell you a little bit more about the point he has just finished covering. This will give him a chance to get in motion again.

8 Reflecting the Client's Feeling If the client is attempting to put a deeply emotional attitude into words, it may be a difficult and awkward process. He may have a feeling of shame or guilt attached to this attitude, or he may hesitate to appear ridiculous in the eyes of

---

Table 2-3 (Continued)

another human being. Whatever his motivations, this flow of emotion will be cut off beyond recovery if the interviewer passes moral judgment on the attitude or turns aside from the underlying feeling by asking a question that moves the interview off in another direction.

It is better to say, "You feel that people are being unfair to you," than to tell the complainer, "Everybody has trouble getting along sometimes." It is better to say, "You would like to get married now but you are not sure that you are still in love with this girl since you have not seen her in so long," than to say, "Go ahead and get married now," or, "Wait awhile until you feel better acquainted." It is better to say, "You feel that the interviewer whom you asked about jobs did not do you any good," than to say, "I am sorry, but you must go back to see the interviewer again since he is the one who must help you." Reflecting feelings and attitudes means that you hold up a mirror, so to speak, in which the client can see the meaning and significance of his deep-seated feelings.

9   Admitting Your Ignorance   If the client asks a question regarding facts and you don't have the facts, it is better to say, "I don't know," than to run off with a lot of vague generalities or in some other way try to cover up your ignorance. The client is likely to have more confidence in the interviewer who does not hesitate to admit his ignorance. It would be desirable for the counselor to get these facts later and to tell the client when to get them.

10   Distribution of Talking Time   Probably the greatest mistake of beginning interviewers is their tendency to talk the client into a coma. There are no hard or fast rules regarding the percentage of time that each of the actors in our play should talk. Within the interview itself there are certain places where the interviewer must do most of the talking. But if the interview is to have a successful effect on the client, there are certain points where he must do most of the talking in developing understanding of himself in bringing his attitudes to the surface and in formulating plans of action. Generally speaking, if the interviewer talks considerably more than one-half the time, that interview will be less productive than the one in which the client talks more than one-half the time.

Table 2-3 (Continued)

---

11   The Vocabulary of the Interviewer   We have said earlier that if the ideas and words are beyond the range of the client, he will not learn much. This means that the interviewer must make some judgment of the level of verbal ability and understanding of the person to whom he is talking. He must then choose his words accordingly, striving always to keep the words as simple as possible and to keep the ideas as clear as possible, repeating and rephrasing when necessary.

12   The Number of Ideas per Interview   It is unlikely that in the usual interview a major miracle can be wrought in the life style of another person. This means that the number of ideas and topics discussed might well be kept to a minimum in most interviews. If a man needs to be referred to four agencies in a community, he can be told all about those agencies and where they are and whom to see in forty minutes. However, the chances are that if he is told about two of the agencies in each of two twenty-minute interviews and then visits two of the agencies between the interviews, he will get more out of it than he will out of the first interview we have described. It may be suggested that a human being does not act like an automobile, all of whose needs can be met at a one-stop filling station. Just as there is a danger of giving the individual a runaround, there is an equal danger in a one-stop system that loads him up with so many ideas that he will forget most of them. Furthermore, the counselor must have time to sort out the ideas which seem relevant to the client's needs.

The same problem of the number of ideas per interview is particularly important where the ideas involved deal with emotional attitudes, resentments, failures, frustrations, and conflicts. It will do very little good if the interviewer gets the client to "tell all" that is on his mind. If by oversympathetic attention or excessive curiosity the interviewer tricks the client into saying too much about his feelings, the client will go out with very little likelihood of coming back again, since he will feel guilty and ashamed at having exposed so much to a stranger.

13   Control of the Interview   If the interview is to have the continuity and the end results that will lead to a modification of the client's behavior, the interviewer must keep control of the interview. He may have to pull the client back from conversational byways, from fruitless

Table 2-3 *(Continued)*

___

arguments, or from temporarily insoluble problems. This can be done without interrupting the free flow of the client's attitudes as mentioned in Point 8 above. Expressions like, "We were talking about ——," or, "What was it you said about ——?" or, "How does this fit into what you said earlier?" will serve to bring the conversation back to its normal course.

14 Avoid the Personal Pronoun   Most of us are inclined to use the word "I" much more than we realize. "I think you should go to see Mr. Blank," "If I were you, I would do ——," "It seems to me that," "I don't see how you can." Generally speaking, the interview will be more effective and will result in a freer conversation if the interviewer will rephrase the above questions or remarks to eliminate the use of "I" or "me" or similar references to himself. The client is not asking the interviewer for his opinion or his experiences. The client is really formulating his own opinions in a way that will permit him to criticize himself.

15 Bad News in the Interview   Not all the facts that the interviewer must give to the client are happy or favorable. It does no good in such situations to reassure the individual by saying that "everything will turn out all right," or "I am sure you won't have any trouble in doing this." If the job situation in the community is tough, nothing is gained by kidding the client about it. If the client wants to do something that cannot be done in this particular agency, no good is accomplished by agreeing to perform the miracle. If you oversell the client on the agency to which you are going to send him, he is in for a disappointment which could have been avoided by pointing out the difficulties under which that other agency works. If housing is bad, the client will eventually learn so anyhow.

16 Additional Problems   It is not the job of the interviewer to make "problem children" out of his clients. On the other hand, the interviewer must not be misled by assuming that the client's own first statement of his difficulty is either true or complete.

For example, the question may simply involve the place where a pension claim is to be filed. The answer is given and the client does not get up to leave the room. Apparently the interview is over, but the

___

Table 2-3 (Continued)

client is still there. It may well be that he has something else on his mind and it is the job of the interviewer to find out what further difficulties need to be discussed. "Was there something else you wanted to ask about?" "Do you have something else on your mind?" These may produce the desired result.

17   **The Frequent Visitor**   There is a particular group of people who love to discuss their problems. They will return periodically for a good heart-to-heart talk with the interviewer. They will give every evidence of intending to do just what the interviewer tells them to do, but for some reason they never quite get around to going to the agencies where they are referred. While it is true that the willingness of the clients to return to the interviewer is one measure of the interviewer's success, it is also true for this group of people that the interviewer is wasting his time in repeated interviews with them. They are the sympathy seekers, the complainers, the overly dependent people that clutter up the crowded time of a busy interviewer.

18   **Setting Limits on the Interview**   No matter how much an interviewer may be inclined toward lengthy sessions with each client, office routines do not permit them and successful interviewing does not demand them. It is better if the interviewer and the client realize from the beginning that the interview will last for a fixed length of time. It is the job of the interviewer to see that the interview stays approximately within that time. Other interviews may be scheduled later on if the client desires them.

19   **Plans for Action**   While it is not essential in all cases that the client rush out and do something as a result of the interview, it is generally true that he will complete the learning process about himself and about his particular world if there are certain things that he feels he has to do as a result of the interview discussion. Furthermore, much of our planning in life is based on our flexibility in modifying a course of action, or on building several plans to meet new adjustment problems. Thus it is of assistance for the interviewer and the client to work out alternative plans of action wherever possible. It is not enough for the client to decide to go to school, for instance. He should have some idea which school he is going to and what will happen if he cannot go where

Table 2-3 (*Continued*)

---

he wants to go. If he cannot get into the day school of his choice, will the alternative of night school fill the bill? The working out of alternative plans is important in the overall interviewing process.

20   Summarizing the Interview   The amount of learning that has gone on in the interview can be roughly estimated from the way in which the client summarized the interview. When the interviewer sees the time is drawing to a close, it is his job to set the stage for the summary. If possible, the client should do the summarizing. "Now suppose we see what we have accomplished in this interview," or "Tell me how you think the situation looks now." Phrases of this kind will be of assistance in calling forth a summary from the client.

21   Ending the Interview   This is not an easy task. In the general relaxation that follows the stress of interviewing, the interviewer may become expansive and start to babble about his own life and his own interests. The interview may degenerate into a most casual social conversation. This is likely to destroy much of the good work that has been done by breaking the quiet, rather objective, and apparently slow pace of the interview up until that moment. Quite often a phrase such as "Do you think we have done all we can for today?" or "Is there anything more you would like to talk about today?" will be enough to end the interview. It may help for the interviewer to stand and move toward the door. It is important in any event to learn your own technique of ending an interview when it is really over within the time limit you have set.

Source: Darley, 1950, pp. 267–299.

effort to increase the client's understanding of possible options and outcomes. Each career choice considered by the client is systematically reviewed and projected into the psychological future to estimate probable success and satisfaction in different occupations.

In Williamson's (1939a, p. 139) opinion, explanation is "by all odds the most complete and satisfactory method of counseling." He illustrates it as used in test interpretation with a client who has been considering medicine as a career choice:

> As far as I can tell from this evidence of aptitude, your chances of getting into medical school are poor; but your possibilities in business seem to be much more promising. These are the reasons for my conclusions: You do not have the pattern of interests characteristic of successful doctors, which probably indicates you would not find the practice of medicine congenial. On the other hand, you do have an excellent grasp of mathematics, good general ability, and the interests of an accountant. These facts seem to me to argue for your selection of accountancy as an occupation. Suppose you think about these facts and my suggestion, talk to your father about my suggestion, see Professor Blank who teaches accounting, and return next Tuesday at ten o'clock to tell me what conclusions you have reached. I shall not attempt to influence you because I want you to choose an occupation congenial to you. But I do urge that you weigh the evidence pro and con for your choice and for the one I suggest. Remember, that we must both look for evidence of aptitude to succeed and that a mere desire to succeed is not sufficient evidence of the required aptitude.

Thus, the counselor relies upon his or her expertise to make authoritative interpretations of the test results and to draw conclusions and recommendations from them for the client's deliberation.

In a more schematic outline, the procedure of test interpretation in Trait-and-Factor career counseling typically, although not invariably, unfolds as follows: The counselor initiates the process by introducing the test results, usually recorded on profile sheets, to the client with a comment such as "The tests you took are back, and I thought we might take a look at them today." Some counselors advocate starting with the interest inventory, which may be less threatening to the client than the more ego-invested ability tests (Super & Crites, 1962). Interest patterns are then related to scores on intelligence, special aptitude, and achievement tests that were taken, the underlying principle being to indicate which interests are congruent with capabilities and therefore realistic as bases for career choice. If personality measures have also been administered, they can be integrated with the interest and ability data toward the end of the process.

In making this presentation of test results, Trait-and-Factor counselors vary in their practice of eliciting reactions from the client. Most seem to prefer interpretation without interruption followed by discussion of all the results and their implications for career choice in one ongoing dialogue. If this method is used, synthesis and prognosis are facilitated, but the counseling relationship may be disrupted.

Once the test results have been related to feasible career options for the client, the counselor focuses the interview upon decision making. Which of the alternatives is the client going to choose? It is this decision that is the climax of Trait-and-Factor career counseling.

Occupational Information

Probably the most widely cited statement on the use of occupational information in Trait-and-Factor career counseling is that of Brayfield (1950), who has differentiated among three functions of this material.

1 *Informational*   The counselor provides a client with information about occupations in order to confirm a choice that has already been made; to resolve indecision between two equally attractive and appropriate options; or, to simply increase the client's knowledge about a choice that is otherwise realistic.

2 *Readjustive*   The counselor introduces occupational information, so that the client has a basis for reality testing an inappropriate choice, the process being something like this:

> The counselor first uses leading questions regarding the nature of the occupation or field which the [client] has chosen. In turn, the counselor provides accurate information which may enable the client to gain insight into the illusory nature of his thinking when he finds that his conception of the occupation or field does not fit the objective facts. At this point, the counselor usually is able to turn the interview to a consideration of the realistic bases upon which sound occupational choices are founded (Brayfield, 1950, p. 218).

3 *Motivational*   The counselor uses occupational information to involve the client actively in the decision-making process; to hold or maintain contact with dependent clients until they assume greater responsibility for their choice; and to maintain motivation for choice when a client's current activities seem irrelevant to long-term career goals.

Other similar strategies in presenting occupational information have been made by Christensen (1949) and Baer and Roeber (1951). The latter have expanded upon Brayfield's uses by adding the following:

1 *Exploration* The counselor uses occupational information to help the client in making an extensive study of the world of work of selected fields of occupations.

2 *Assurance* The counselor uses occupational information to assure the client that the career choice is appropriate or that an inappropriate one has been eliminated.

3 *Evaluation* The counselor uses occupational information to check the reliability and relevancy of the client's knowledge and understanding of an occupation or family of occupations.

4 *Startle* The counselor uses occupational information to determine whether a client shows signs of certainty/uncertainty after choosing a particular vocation.

Baer and Roeber (1951, p. 426) observe that: "These categories present different purposes or emphases in the use of occupational information. These categories, however, are not mutually exclusive. They overlap in the sense that one category frequently leads to or suggests another."

As in test interpretation, practice varies among Trait-and-Factor career counselors in how they present occupational information. A few are sufficiently knowledgeable about the world of work that they can verbally introduce information about occupations in the interaction with a client, possibly supplementing this information with selected pamphlets and manuals. Others bring the written materials into the interview and actually go through them with the client. This procedure often changes the nature of the relationship, with the counselor shifting roles from collaborator or facilitator to expert or teacher, the client reacting accordingly as novice or student. This disjunction in the counseling process can be counteracted considerably by the client reading the materials before the interview. Unfortunately, most counselors using this approach simply refer the client to an occupational file in the counseling agency or suggest that they go to the library for assistance. Left without the support of the counseling relationship many clients, who tend to be passive and reactive anyway, do not gather occupational information on their own and consequently this phase of career decision making is neglected. Even though a client appears to have sufficient initiative to utilize informational resources, the counselor should be actively involved in this last but critical phase of Trait-and-Factor career counseling.

MATERIALS

To illustrate the model and methods of Trait-and-Factor career counseling with actual case materials, a client representative of a cross section from a university counseling center has been chosen. An 18-year-old male freshman, Mark S., was seen for three interviews on a weekly basis during the period immediately preceding the Christmas break of his first semester. As was the practice in the center, he was seen for a short (half-hour) intake interview for disposition. He was accepted for career counseling and was assigned to a senior (full-time staff) counselor, who saw him the following week. The materials that were subsequently accumulated on the case—interview excerpts, test results, biographical and demographic data, and so forth—have been organized according to the model for Trait-and-Factor career counseling: diagnosis, process, and outcomes. The methods of interviewing, interpreting tests, and using occupational information are discussed in relation to the model, the former being the means for implementing the latter.

Diagnosis

During the initial contact with his counselor, which lasted about 40 minutes, Mark said, "I know that I need to choose a career for myself, and I have one in mind, but I'm still not set on it." The counselor, following the Trait-and-Factor procedure (Analysis) of gathering background and demographic data for Synthesis and Diagnosis, asked a series of factually oriented questions, primarily on the basis of Mark's presenting problem, to determine whether it could be taken at face value as "uncertain choice" or whether it was actually "no choice." In response, Mark explained that he had been interested in art since he was in grade school. Not only did he enjoy drawing, ceramics, and block printing, but he also had feedback, from teachers as well as parents and friends, that he was outstanding in what he did. His pictures and prints were exhibited, and he won several prizes for them. Yet he was well aware that competition in the field of art was intense, that one had to have exceptional talent to succeed. His doubts about an artistic career arose from this consideration: did he have sufficient aptitude to pursue art as a vocation? From what Mark had told him by the end of the interview, the counselor had tentatively decided upon a diagnosis of "uncertain choice" rather than "no choice": Mark had apparently chosen art but needed to reality test his decision against additional objective data.

To collect these data the counselor made arrangements with the psychometrist for Mark to take a selected battery of tests and inventories before the second interview. Aware that there are very few psychometrically adequate measures of artistic aptitude (Super & Crites, 1962), the counselor assigned only the Meier Art Judgment Test, the best of what is available, and referred Mark to a professor in the Art Department who would give them an expert evaluation of Mark's portfolio. To predict general scholastic aptitude and Mark's chances for succeeding in college irrespective of major, the counselor had the composite American College Test (ACT) score. At the 85th percentile, his score indicated that Mark's chances for getting a bachelor's degree were considerably above average. In addition to appraisal of special and general abilities, the counselor wanted an assessment of Mark's vocational interests for two reasons: (1) to confirm (or disconfirm) Mark's expressed preference for art, and (2) to identify other possible interest patterns in the event that there was no primary pattern in the artistic group or that artistic aptitude was not sufficient for success. Also, the counselor asked Mark to complete an extensive Personal Data Blank in order to elicit background information relevant to Mark's career choice. There is considerable evidence that artistic ability "runs in families" (Meier, 1942), and the counselor wanted to check this out. He did not assign a personality inventory, however, since there is equally strong negative evidence on the existence of an "artistic personality" (Roe, 1946), and there was no other immediately apparent reason for such an assessment. From the interview interaction, Mark appeared to be functioning adequately.

Process

Following the initial contact, Mark took the tests and other forms home and completed them. He then returned for the interpretation of the tests during the second interview, which was a modal sequence and time frame for Trait-and-Factor career counseling. The counselor opened the test interpretation session by telling Mark that he had received a written appraisal of Mark's portfolio from the art professor and that it was generally quite favorable. The only qualification in the report was that Mark might excel more in printmaking and lithography than in other media, an observation which Mark agreed with and which helped him focus his interest within the broader field of art. The counselor also noted that Mark's score on the Meier Art Judgment Test, which was extremely high (99th percentile as compared with college art majors,

95th percentile with artists), corroborated the art professor's opinion of his work. Likewise, there was supporting evidence from both the Strong-Campbell Interest Inventory (SCII) and Personal Data Blank (PDB) for Mark's choice of art as a career. He had only one primary pattern on the SCII occupational scales, which was in the Artistic group, and he had his highest scores on the General Occupational Theme and Basic Interest Scales in the artistic areas and activities (see Figure 2-2). To the extent that these interests, as well as artistic aptitudes, are transmitted through families (Crites, 1962), they are consonant with Mark's background, particularly in the paternal line. His father studied art, although he later became a writer; his grandfather was artistically inclined; and a first uncle was a nationally known architect. Thus, the accumulated demographic and psychometric data largely confirmed Mark's choice of art (specifically, printmaking and lithography) as a career.

Throughout the test interpretation, during which the counselor did approximately 90 percent of the talking, Mark was reactive, sometimes asking a question for clarification. When the counselor finished reviewing the test results, he asked Mark how he felt about them. He said: "Well, there doesn't seem to be anything new, but it's good to know that I have the ability to do what I want to do." The counselor responded by saying that Mark's career choice seemed to be reasonable, although he might want to reality test it further against occupational information which they could survey together at their next meeting. In the interim, Mark agreed to interview the art professor who had evaluated his portfolio about possible career options in art, such as free-lance work, teaching, owning and operating a print shop (studio), and being employed as a commercial artist. The counselor was to bring in materials relevant to each of these career paths, as well as combinations of them. During their third session they reported back to each other and attempted a prognosis based upon the information they had gathered. Two or three predictions were indicated: (1) Mark would probably have to go to graduate school eventually to be successful in the highly competitive field of art; (2) he might have to work for a few years after obtaining his Bachelor of Fine Arts to finance graduate school; and (3) he most likely would have to establish a primary source of income, through teaching or business, in order to support his artistic endeavors. The counseling terminated with Mark's comment: "I feel better. I think I can go ahead now and study art without wondering all the time whether I'm doing the right thing."

Outcomes

Follow-up on Mark occurred when he dropped in to see the counselor just before graduation. He had completed his Bachelor of Fine Arts with an overall GPA of 3.25, but he received mostly A's in his major. He had exhausted his financial resources and planned to work for at least a year before applying for graduate school. He had entered one printmaking competition, and had received an honorable mention, but felt that he needed further training before he could achieve more recognition. The counselor inferred from this feedback that the diagnosis of Mark's problem as uncertain career choice had been essentially correct. Moreover, providing test and other information about self and occupational information in reference to a career in art appeared to be an effective counseling strategy. There was direct evidence, at least, that the uncertainty had been resolved, and indirect evidence that Mark had increased his facility to make decisions. The latter was not an explicit goal of the counseling but was more a by-product manifested in Mark's planning for the future.

COMMENT

For many years, Trait-and-Factor career counseling held sway as the only approach to assisting clients engaged in the process of deciding upon their life's work. In the hands of its highly competent and enlightened originators who are still practicing, it is most likely as viable today as it was in the past (Williamson, 1972). But as practiced by too many Trait-and-Factor counselors who have not updated the model (Super & Bachrach, 1957) and methods (Williamson, 1972), this approach has gone into an incipient decline. It has devolved into what has been caricatured as "three interviews and a cloud of dust." The first interview is usually conducted to gather some background data on the client and for the counselor to assign tests. The client takes the tests, often a lengthy battery administered in "shotgun" style (Super, 1950), and then returns for the second interview, at which time the results are interpreted. Not atypically, this session amounts to the counselor teaching the client certain necessary psychometric concepts, for example, the meaning of percentile ranks or standard scores, in order to engage in a lengthy one-by-one, scale-by-scale discussion of the tests. The third interview is usually devoted to reviewing the client's career choice in light of the occupational file for possible further exploration of

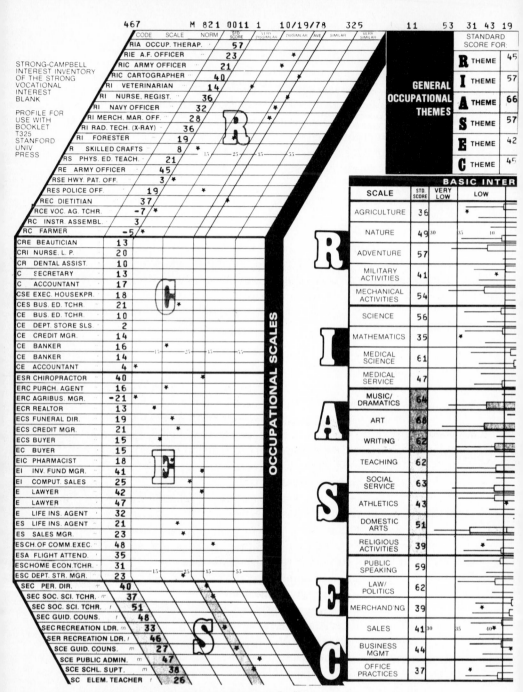

Figure 2-2 Mark's Strong-Campbell Interest Inventory Profile.

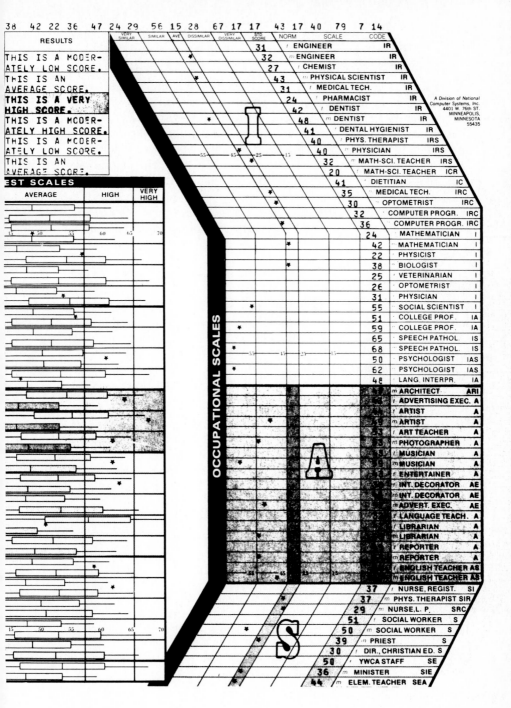

38 42 22 36 47 24 29 56 15 28 67 17 17 43 17 40 79 7 14

RESULTS
THIS IS A MODER-ATELY LOW SCORE.
THIS IS AN AVERAGE SCORE.
THIS IS A VERY HIGH SCORE.
THIS IS A MODER-ATELY HIGH SCORE.
THIS IS A MODER-ATELY LOW SCORE.
THIS IS AN AVERAGE SCORE.

EST SCALES

AVERAGE	HIGH	VERY HIGH

OCCUPATIONAL SCALES

VERY SIMILAR	SIMILAR	AVE	DISSIMILAR	VERY DISSIMILAR	STD SCORE	NORM	SCALE	CODE
						31	/ ENGINEER	IR
						32	m ENGINEER	IR
						27	/ CHEMIST	IR
						43	m PHYSICAL SCIENTIST	IR
						31	/ MEDICAL TECH.	IR
						24	/ PHARMACIST	IR
						42	/ DENTIST	IR
						48	m DENTIST	IR
						41	/ DENTAL HYGIENIST	IR
						40	/ PHYS. THERAPIST	IRS
						40	/ PHYSICIAN	IRS
						32	m MATH-SCI. TEACHER	IRS
						20	/ MATH-SCI. TEACHER	ICR
						41	DIETITIAN	IC
						35	MEDICAL TECH.	IRC
						30	OPTOMETRIST	IRC
						32	COMPUTER PROGR.	IRC
						36	COMPUTER PROGR.	IRC
						24	MATHEMATICIAN	I
						42	MATHEMATICIAN	I
						22	PHYSICIST	I
						38	BIOLOGIST	I
						25	VETERINARIAN	I
						26	OPTOMETRIST	I
						31	PHYSICIAN	I
						55	SOCIAL SCIENTIST	I
						51	COLLEGE PROF.	IA
						59	COLLEGE PROF.	IA
						65	SPEECH PATHOL.	IS
						68	SPEECH PATHOL.	IS
						50	PSYCHOLOGIST	IAS
						62	PSYCHOLOGIST	IAS
						48	m LANG. INTERPR.	IA
							m ARCHITECT	ARI
							/ ADVERTISING EXEC.	A
							/ ARTIST	A
							m ARTIST	A
							/ ART TEACHER	A
							m PHOTOGRAPHER	A
							/ MUSICIAN	A
							m MUSICIAN	A
							/ ENTERTAINER	A
							INT. DECORATOR	AE
							m INT. DECORATOR	AE
							m ADVERT. EXEC.	AE
							/ LANGUAGE TEACH.	A
							/ LIBRARIAN	A
							m LIBRARIAN	A
							/ REPORTER	A
							m REPORTER	A
							/ ENGLISH TEACHER	AS
							m ENGLISH TEACHER	AS
						37	/ NURSE, REGIST.	SI
						37	m PHYS. THERAPIST	SIR
						29	m NURSE, L. P.	SRC
						51	/ SOCIAL WORKER	S
						50	m SOCIAL WORKER	S
						39	m PRIEST	S
						30	/ DIR., CHRISTIAN ED.	S
						50	/ YWCA STAFF	SE
						36	m MINISTER	SIE
						44	m ELEM. TEACHER	SEA

A Division of National
Computer Systems, Inc.
4401 W. 76th ST.
MINNEAPOLIS,
MINNESOTA
55435

the world of work. Then the client leaves ("cloud of dust"), often without using these materials on his or her own, due to the very lack of initiative that generated the problems which brought him or her to career counseling in the first place. At best, this widespread oversimplification of Trait-and-Factor career counseling provides the client with a mass of test information, which is frequently forgotten or distorted (Froehlich & Moser, 1954). At worst, it completely ignores the psychological realities of decision making that lead to indecision and unrealism in career choice (Crites, 1969), and it fails to foster those more general competencies, for example, self-management, which are the essence of true Trait-and-Factor career counseling (Williamson, 1972).

REFERENCES

Anastasi, A. *Differential psychology.* (3d ed.) New York: Macmillan, 1958.

Baer, M. F., & Roeber, E. C. *Occupational information: Its nature and use.* Chicago: Science Research Associates, 1951.

Berdie, R. F. Counseling: An educational technique. *Educational and Psychological Measurement.* 1949, *9*, 89–94.

Brayfield, A. H. Putting occupational information across. In A. H. Brayfield (Ed.), *Readings in modern methods of counseling.* New York: Appleton-Century-Crofts, 1950. Pp. 212–220.

Brayfield, A. H. Research on vocational guidance: Status and prospect. In H. Borow (Ed.), *Man in a world at work.* Boston: Houghton Mifflin, 1964. Pp. 310–323.

Christensen, T. E. Functions of occupational information in counseling. *Occupations,* 1949, *28*, 11–14.

Crites, J. O. Parental identification in relation to vocational interest development. *Journal of Educational Psychology,* 1962, *53*, 262–270.

Crites, J. O. Proposals for a new criterion measure and research design. In H. Borow (Ed.), *Man in a world at work.* Boston: Houghton Mifflin, 1964. Pp. 324–340.

Crites, J. O. *Vocational Psychology.* New York: McGraw-Hill, 1969.

Darley, J. G. Conduct of the interview. In A. H. Brayfield (Ed.), *Readings in modern methods of counseling.* New York: Appleton-Century-Crofts, 1950. Pp. 265–272.

Fine, S. A., & Heinz, C. A. The functional occupational classification structure. *Personnel and Guidance Journal,* 1958, *37*, 180–192.

Forgy, E. W., & Black, J. D. A followup after three years of clients counseled by two methods. *Journal of Counseling Psychology,* 1954, *1*, 1–8.

Froehlich, C. P., & Moser, W. E. Do counselees remember test scores? *Journal of Counseling Psychology*, 1954, *1*, 149–152.

Guilford, J. P. *Personality*. New York: McGraw-Hill, 1959.

Hunt, E. P., & Smith, P. Vocational guidance research: Ten years' work by the Birmingham Education Committee. *Occupational Psychology*, 1936, *12*, 302–307.

Lofquist, L. H., & Dawis, R. V. *Adjustment to work*. New York: Appleton-Century-Crofts, 1969.

Meier, N. C. *Art in human affairs*. New York: McGraw-Hill, 1942.

Mischel, W. *Personality and assessment*. New York: Wiley, 1968.

Myers, R. A. Research on educational and vocational counseling. In A. E. Bergin & S. L. Garfield (Eds), *Handbook of psychotherapy and behavior change*, 1971. Pp. 863–891.

Paterson, D. G. *Physique and intellect*. New York: Century, 1930.

Paterson, D. G., & Darley, J. G. *Men, women, and jobs*. Minneapolis: University of Minnesota Press, 1936.

Pepinsky, H. B. The selection and use of diagnostic categories in clinical counseling. *Applied Psychology Monographs*, 1948, No. 15.

Roe, A. The personality of artists. *Educational and Psychological Measurement*, 1946, *6*, 401–408.

Sloan, T. J., & Pierce-Jones, J. The Bordin-Pepinsky diagnostic categories: Counselor agreement and MMPI comparisons. *Journal of Counseling Psychology*, 1958, *5*, 189–195.

Strong, E. K., Jr. *Vocational interests of men and women*. Palo Alto: Stanford University Press, 1943.

Strong, E. K., Jr. *Vocational interests 18 years after college*. Minneapolis: University of Minnesota Press, 1955.

Strong, S. R., & Schmidt, L. D. Expertness and influence in counseling. *Journal of Counseling Psychology*, 1970, *17*, 81–87.

Super, D. E. Testing and using test results in counseling. *Occupations*, 1950, *29*, 95–97.

Super, D. E., & Bachrach, P. B. *Scientific careers and vocational development theory*. New York: Teachers College Bureau of Publications, 1957.

Super, D. E., & Crites, J. O. *Appraising vocational fitness*. (2d ed.). New York: Harper & Row, 1962.

Thompson, A. S. A rationale for vocational guidance. *Personnel and Guidance Journal*, 1954, *32*, 533–535.

Tyler, L. E. *The psychology of human differences*. (3d ed.) New York: Appleton-Century-Crofts, 1965.

Tyler, L. E. *The work of the counselor*. (3d ed.) New York: Appleton-Century-Crofts, 1969.

Williamson, E. G. *How to counsel students*. New York: McGraw-Hill, 1939. (a)

Williamson, E. G. The clinical method of guidance. *Review of Educational Research*, 1939, *9*, 214–217. (b)

Williamson, E. G. Vocational counseling: Trait-factor theory. In B. Stefflre (Ed.), *Theories of counseling.* New York: McGraw-Hill, 1965. Pp. 193–214.

Williamson, E. G. Trait-and-factor theory and individual differences. In B. Stefflre & W. H. Grant (Eds), *Theories of counseling.* (2d ed.) New York: McGraw-Hill, 1972. Pp. 136–176.

Client-Centered
Career
Counseling

Superficially Client-Centered career counseling appears to be counter-point to the Trait-and-Factor approach, largely because of the opposed schools that polarized these two points of view in the early 1940s. However, Rogerian psychology and psychotherapy actually has its philosophical roots in a different rather than a necessarily antagonistic tradition. Much as the analytical (atomistic) and Gestalt systems in psychology represent different *Weltanschauung*, so do the Client-Centered and Trait-and-Factor positions. The former focuses upon the idiographic, the phenomenological, the unique ways in which the individual perceives and constructs reality, whereas the latter defines the individual nomethetically, comparatively, externally as an aggregate of traits and factors. Moreover, Client-Centered theory posits the self not only as an organizing concept, defined by those personal characteristics the individual attributes to "me," but also as the central motivating force toward actualization of one's potentialities (Rogers, 1951). Implicit in these distinctions is a theme that runs throughout the contrast between Client-Centered and Trait-and-Factor career counseling—the difference between the "inner world" of personal experience and the "outer world" of physicalistic reality.

MODEL

The conceptual framework for Client-Centered career counseling stems only indirectly and by inference from the more general system of psychotherapy proposed by Rogers (1942; 1951). In the latter, Rogers had little to say about career decision-making processes, because he was concerned primarily with the emotional-social adjustment and function-ing of the person. Some Client-Centered counselors (Arbuckle, 1961; Doleys, 1961) have contended that, if a client becomes well adjusted psychologically, she or he will be able to solve whatever career problems are encountered without specifically having to attend to them in career counseling. Referring to Doleys' contention that, from the Client-Centered position there is only one kind of counseling, not several (for example, educational, marital, career), Patterson (1964, p. 435) com-ments:

> [Doleys] presents the case for a generic counselor, pointing out that all counselors have in common a skill in developing and maintaining the counseling relationship with a total individual who is not restricted in the areas he can talk about. There has, of course, long been the belief that the

client-centered counselor does not deal differently with a client who has a vocational problem than with one who has any other kind of problem.

Patterson, however, and others of a Client-Centered bent, has recognized that, although general and vocational adjustment are related, the correlation is less than perfect (Crites, 1969), and thus a separate focus upon career choice can be justified.

During the early years of Client-Centered counseling (the 1940s), when Trait-and-Factor counselors were attempting to reconcile and synthesize its principles and procedures with established techniques, several extrapolations from the newer approach to traditional career counseling were made (Bixler & Bixler, 1945; Covner, 1947; Combs, 1947; Bown, 1947; Seeman, 1948). There ensued a heated controversy, in which the relative merits of the "directive" and "nondirective" orientations were debated loud and long, with seemingly no immediate resolution other than a contrived and tenuous eclecticism awkwardly known as "nonnondirective career counseling" (Hahn & Kendall, 1947). Not until almost two decades later was an articulate and comprehensive statement of Client-Centered career counseling formulated by Patterson (1964), although it had been presaged by Super's (1950; 1951; 1957) writings on the self concept and career development. It is primarily Patterson's conceptualization, updated to reflect more recent trends and innovations in this approach (Hart & Tomlinson, 1970; Wexler & Rice, 1974), which is drawn upon in explicating the Client-Centered position on diagnosis, process, and outcomes.

Diagnosis

Of all the concepts on which directive and nondirective counselors differed, the divergence in their viewpoints was probably greatest on diagnosis. Whereas diagnosis was the fulcrum of the Trait-and-Factor approach, Rogers (1942; 1951) has been unequivocal in his opposition to it. Here are some excerpts from his writings on diagnosis:

> When the counselor assumes the information-getting attitude which is necessary for the assembling of a good case history, the client cannot help feeling that the responsibility for the solution of his problems is being taken over by the counselor (Rogers, 1942, p. 81).

> . . . psychological diagnosis as usually understood is unnecessary for psychotherapy [counseling], and may actually be a detriment to the therapeutic process (Rogers, 1951, p. 220).

Rogers also notes the "high degree of unreliability in diagnostic formulations" (1951, p. 225) and the reluctance by those who use them to conduct research on their empirical usefulness. For these reasons, as well as for theoretical ones, Rogers eschews differential diagnosis and assumes that all clients suffer from the same problem—lack of congruence between self and experience. This state exists when "the organism denies to awareness significant sensory and visceral experiences, which consequently are not symbolized and organized into the gestalt of the self-structure" (1951, p. 510). Figure 3-1a depicts lack of congruence, in the limiting case, as nonoverlapping circles; there is no correspondence between self and experience.

Similarly, Patterson (1974, p. 166) rejects diagnosis with the observation:

> There seems to be no logical—or psychological— system of classification that is satisfying or generally acceptable, that leads to non-overlapping, discrete categories on the same level of abstraction, and that is related to differential methods of treatment.

More generally, he argues that:

> Perhaps instead of continuing to act upon the assumption that there are different kinds of emotional disorder and persisting in attempts to discover what they are, we should operate on the assumption that there is no basic essential difference and attempt to discover and understand the common etiology (Patterson, 1974, p. 167).

In Patterson's view the latter is some kind of disturbance in interpersonal relationships. In other words, he subscribes to the "unitary nature of emotional disturbance" and a "single method of treatment." Applied to career counseling, this position means that "the client-centered counselor does not deal differently with a client who has a vocational problem and one who has any other kind of problem" (Patterson, 1964, p. 435). Yet, Patterson argues that career counseling can be distinguished from other types of counseling because it focuses "upon a particular area—or problem—in an individual's life" and facilitates the "handling" of it.

The dilemma remains: if the client-centered counselor does not diagnose, how does he or she know which area of problem to focus upon? The answer to this question may lie in distinguishing between (1) disturbance in interpersonal relationships and (2) lack of information about self and work as etiological factors in a client's problem. Grummon (1972, p. 122) notes that:

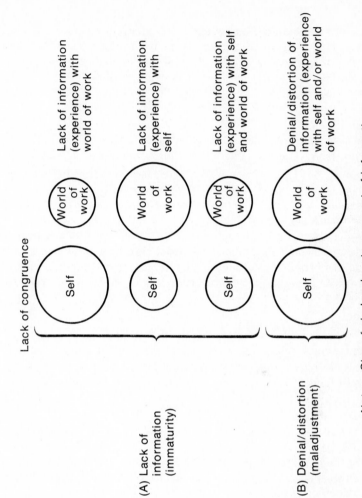

Figure 3-1 Congruence between self and world of work as a function of adjustment and information.

Note: Size of circles denotes amount of information

Lack of congruence

Lack of information (experience) with world of work

Lack of information (experience) with self

Lack of information (experience) with self and world of work

Denial/distortion of information (experience) with self and/or world of work

(A) Lack of information (immaturity)

(B) Denial/distortion (maladjustment)

World of work

Self

61

A serious weakness of client-centered theory for general counseling is that it says little about the role of information in assisting clients, or, if we confine ourselves to the terminology of the theory, the role of information in self-actualization. The theory does, of course, assume that the individual is continually interacting with his environment and is differentiating new aspects of the environment in an attempt to meet his needs.

But adequate information about self and the world of work may simply not have been available to the client, regardless of whether she or he could have accurately assimilated it. Lack of congruence as expressed in implementation of the self-concept in a compatible occupational role may, in the first instance, be a function of lack of information, as depicted in Figure 3-1b. An initial diagnostic decision, therefore, even in Client-Centered career counseling, would appear to be whether the client's problem stems from (1) a lack of information or (2) denial/distortion of information (experience). In the limiting case, of course, there can be no denial/distortion if there is no relevant information.

Process

Patterson (1964) refers generally to the process of Client-Centered career counseling but neglects to analyze it into distinct stages or phases as does Rogers (1961) for psychotherapy. Briefly defined and condensed, these are as follows:

1 *First stage* There is an unwillingness to communicate self. Communication is about externals only.
2 *Second stage* Expression begins to flow in regard to nonself topics. Problems are perceived as external to self. Experiencing is bound by the structure of the past.
3 *Third stage* Loosening of feelings with less focus upon content but no appreciable contact with deeper feelings.
4 *Fourth stage* Feelings are dealt with in greater depth and intensity. Difficulty still exists in expressing them without assistance. Rogers (1958, p. 144) says of stages three and four: "Each involves a further loosening of symbolic expression in regard to feelings, constructs, and self. These stages constitute much of psychotherapy."
5 *Fifth stage* Feelings are expressed freely as in the present. Experiencing is loosened, no longer remote, and frequently occurs with little postponement. There is an increasing quality of acceptance of self-responsibility for the problems being faced, and a concern as to how the client has contributed to them.

6 *Sixth stage* Self as an object tends to disappear. The incongruence between experience and awareness is vividly experienced as it disappears by turning into congruence. Differentiation of experiencing is sharp and basic. In this stage there are no longer external or internal problems. The client is *living*, subjectively, a phase of his or her problem.

7 *Seventh stage* The self becomes simply the subjective and reflexive awareness of experiencing. The self is less a perceived object and more something confidently and tangibly felt in process. Internal communication is clear, with feelings and symbols well matched, and meanings are integrated. There is the experiencing of effective choice of new ways of being.

Relating these stages in psychotherapy to career counseling, it can be inferred that clients enter career counseling at a stage of "experiencing" roughly equivalent to that at which personal clients leave psychotherapy. This is the sixth stage in experiencing, during which a higher level of congruence is achieved by the client, so that she or he "owns" feelings and problems rather than externalizing them. A fuller definition of the sixth stage follows:

> The client is clearly examining the significance of his/her feelings or self-concept and is able to arrive at conclusions about them, or to use the results of this self-assessment as the point of departure for further self-exploration. His formulations about himself provide the links between any elaborations of events or expressions of feeling. In stage 6 the client is able to use the results of self-examination in specific areas to arrive at a deeper and more comprehensive self-understanding (Gendlin & Tomlinson, 1961).

Although some clients in career counseling are clearly not at this stage of experiencing, most seem able to relate to self and the world with a fairly high level of congruence (Gaudet & Kulick, 1954; Goodstein, Crites, Heilbrun, & Rempel, 1961). Table 3-1 presents a scale for rating experiencing developed by Gendlin and Tomlinson (1961) that can be used by the career counselor listening to taped interviews to determine generally which stage the client has reached.

That career counseling can intervene with the client at the sixth stage and take him or her beyond to the highest stage of experiencing, thereby enhancing personal as well as career development, has been demonstrated in a study by Williams (1962). He obtained Q-adjustment scores on vocational-educational clients and compared them with

Table 3-1   Experiencing Scale

Stage One   The chief characteristic of this stage is that the content or manner of expression is impersonal. In some cases the content is intrinsically impersonal, being a very abstract, general, superficial, or journalistic account of events or ideas with no personal referent established. In other cases, despite the personal nature of the content, the speaker's involvement is impersonal, so that he reveals nothing important about himself, and his remarks could as well be about a stranger or an object.

Stage Two   The association between the speaker and the content is explicit. Either the speaker is the central character in the narrative or his interest is clear. The speaker's involvement, however, does not go beyond the specific situation or content. All comments, associations, reactions, and remarks serve to get the story or idea across but do not refer to or define the speaker's feelings.

Stage Three   The content is a narrative or a description of the speaker in external or behavioral terms with added comments on his feelings or private experiences. These remarks are limited to the events or situation described, giving the narrative a personal touch without describing the speaker more generally. Self-descriptions restricted to a specific situation or role are also at stage three.

Stage Four   The content is a clear presentation of the speaker's feelings, giving his personal, internal perspective or feelings about himself. Feelings or the experience of events, rather than the events themselves, are the subject of the discourse. By attending to and presenting this experiencing, the speaker communicates what it is like to be him. These interior views are presented, listed, or described, but are not interrelated or used as the basis for systematic self-examination or formulation.

Stage Five   The content is a purposeful exploration of the speaker's feelings and experiencing. There are two necessary components. First, the speaker must pose or define a problem or proposition about himself explicitly in terms of feelings. The problem or proposition may involve the origin, sequence, or implications of feelings or relate feelings to other private processes. Second, he must explore or work with the problem in a personal way. The exploration or elabora-

---

Table 3-1 (Continued)

tion must be clearly related to the initial proposition and must contain inner references so that it functions to expand the speaker's awareness of his experiencing. *Both* components, the problem and the elaboration, must be present.

Stage Six The content is a synthesis of readily accessible, newly recognized, or more fully realized feelings and experiences to produce personally meaningful structures or to resolve issues. The speaker's immediate feelings are integral to his conclusions about his inner workings. He communicates a new or enriched self-experiencing and the experiential impact of the changes in his attitudes or feelings about himself. The subject matter concerns the speaker's present and emergent experience. His manner may reflect changes or insights at the moment of their occurrence. These are verbally elaborated in detail. Apart from the specific content, the speaker conveys a sense of active, immediate involvement in an experientially anchored issue with evidence of its resolution or acceptance.

Stage Seven The content reveals the speaker's expanding awareness of his immediately present feelings and internal processes. He demonstrates clearly that he can move from one inner reference to another, altering and modifying his conceptions of himself, his feelings, his private reactions to his thoughts or actions in terms of their immediately felt nuances as they occur in the present experiential moment, so that each new level of self-awareness functions as a spring board for further exploration.

Source: Kiesler, 1973, pp. 443–444.

personal clients from Dymond's (1954) research on Client-Centered psychotherapy, the precounseling mean of the former being 50.53 and the postcounseling mean of the latter being 49.30. From these findings, Williams (1962, p. 26) concluded that "the adjustment level of personal clients *following* counseling is approximately that of [vocational-educational] clients *before* counseling." Since the vocational-educational clients' postcounseling mean was 58.76, indicating a still higher level of adjustment, it would appear that career counseling largely encompasses the seventh (and highest stage) in Rogers' (1961) schema of counseling process:

> The client does not need a narrative as a point of departure. He (sic) can travel freely among feelings and understands them quickly. The client has no difficulty in tying together what he is saying and presenting a clear picture of himself—what meaning his thoughts, actions, and feelings have for him. He moves easily from one inward reference to another and is able to integrate them into his experiential frame of reference (Gendlin & Tomlinson, 1961).

Outcomes

Implicit in this conceptualization of process are the assumed outcomes of Client-Centered career counseling. Grummon (1972, p. 110) observes that:

> It is difficult to distinguish clearly between process and outcomes. When we study outcomes directly, we examine the differences between two sets of observations made at the beginning and end of the interview series. Many process studies make successive observations over a series of counseling interviews and, in a sense, are miniature outcome measures which establish a trend line for the case.

In other words, the outcomes of Client-Centered career counseling can be defined in terms of the gains achieved during the process of client-counselor interactions. Patterson (1974) concurs with Grummon that the immediate goal of counseling (or psychotherapy) from the Client-Centered point of view is client growth in the process but considers the ultimate goal to be self-actualization, defined by Rogers (1959, p. 218) as greater congruence, greater openness to experience, and less defensiveness on the part of the client.

In Client-Centered career counseling, however, the "successful resolution of many educational and vocational problems (as well as other presenting problems) does not require a reorganization of self" (Grummon, 1972, p. 119). Rather, the goal is to facilitate the clarification and implementation of the self-concept in a compatible occupational role, at whatever point the client is on the continuum of career development. Patterson (1964, p. 442) cites Super's (1957, p. 197) revision of the NVGA definition of "vocational guidance" as delineating the desired outcomes of Client-Centered career counseling:

> [It] is the process of helping a person to develop and accept an integrated picture of himself and of his role in the world of work, to test this concept against reality, and to convert it into reality, with satisfaction to himself and benefit to society.

These outcomes of Client-Centered career counseling can be viewed within the more general theoretical framework outlined in Figure 3-1, where the relationship of self to the world of work is depicted. To the extent that an implementation of self in a compatible occupational role is achieved through counseling, that is, the degree of congruence attained (Figure 3-1), the counseling has been effective in terms of the desired outcomes of Client-Centered career counseling.

How these outcomes can be measured is not as clear as the definition of them. In the study by Williams (1962) mentioned earlier, a modified version of the Butler-Haigh Q-sort (Rogers & Dymond, 1954) was used to assess congruence between self and ideal self. The drawback to this procedure, however, is that the content of the items in the Q-sort is nonvocational. Consequently, the implementation or translation process that Super (1951) states is the essence of career choice is not directly measured. He and his associates (Super, Starishevsky, & Matlin, 1963) have experimented with a technique, based upon a modification of Kelly's (1955) Role Construct Repertory Test, which is designed specifically to fill the need for a measure of career self-concept and its relationship to occupational roles. In brief, the procedure is to elicit from an individual what Super calls "psychtalk," or self-descriptive statements (possibly culled from an autobiography), and translate them into "occtalk" by means of an occtalk-to-psychtalk dictionary, much like an English-to-French dictionary might be used. Occtalk is composed of the individual's career options, for example, psychologist, lawyer, accountant, engineer, and so forth. The dictionary consists of equivalencies, such as physician = intelligent + healthy +

narrow-minded (Super, et al., 1963, p. 36). Initial research with this instrument has been promising. The procedure is cumbersome and time-consuming, but it has the distinct advantage over other modes of assessing self-concept, for example, adjective checklists, in that it is idiographic. The language in it is generated from the individual, not devised by the test constructor. Until it has been refined further, the career counselor might elicit comparable psychtalk and occtalk from the client during the interview and discuss the translation of one into the other with the client, not only as a counseling technique but also as a measure of outcomes as the counseling progresses.

METHODS

The methods by which the outcomes of Client-Centered career counseling are attained presume certain basic attitudes on the part of the counselor. Much as Rogers (1957) emphasized such conative dispositions as necessary for successful client-centered psychotherapy, so Patterson (1964, p. 442) has observed that the Client-Centered approach to career counseling is "essentially an attitude rather than a technique." In psychotherapy, there are three attitudes that characterize the ideally functioning client-centered counselor (Rogers, 1957; 1961):

   1 *Congruence*   being genuine and open; not playing a role or presenting a facade; the counselor "is aware of and accepts his own feelings, with a willingness to be and express these feelings and attitudes, in words or behavior" (Patterson, 1973, p. 396).
   2 *Understanding*   perceiving the client's phenomenal field; sensing the client's inner world "as if" it is the counselor's; not diagnostic or evaluative; empathic.
   3 *Acceptance*   "unconditional positive regard"; the counselor accepts the client "as an individual, as he is, with his conflicts and inconsistencies, his good and bad points" (Patterson, 1973, p. 396).

   Communicating these counselor attitudes to a client experiencing at least a minimal degree of incongruence as a source of motivation for treatment results in a relationship in which change, i.e., increased client congruence, can occur. These counselor attitudes are communicated in Client-Centered career counseling via distinctive techniques of interviewing, test interpretation, and use of occupational information.

Interview Techniques

Once stereotyped as "uh-huh" counseling in its early days of development because of Rogers' (1942) emphasis upon nondirective interview techniques, the Client-Centered approach has evolved into a much more sophisticated repertoire of counselor interview behavior in recent years. In tracing this evolution, Hart and Tomlinson (1970, p. 4) have delineated three periods during which different interview techniques predominated:

1 *Nondirective period* (1940–1950) Counselor used verbal responses with a minimal degree of "lead" (Robinson, 1950), such as simple acceptance, clarification, and restatement, to achieve client insight.

2 *Reflective period* (1950–1957) Counselor concentrated almost exclusively upon reflection of feelings, which was substituted for clarification from the preceding period, the goal being to "mirror the client's phenomenological world to him" (Hart & Tomlinson, 1970, p. 8).

3 *Experiential period* (1957–present) Counselor engages in a wide range of interview behaviors to express basic attitudes and, in contrast to previous roles, relates relevant personal experiences to the client, in order to facilitate the latter's experiencing. Thus, in contemporary client-centered psychotherapy the counselor is much more active than ever before, as indexed, for example, by client/counselor talk ratios. (Presumably the same would be true of Client-Centered career counseling, although neither Patterson nor others have made this application as yet.)

Assuming that the above presumption is justified, the Client-Centered career counselor would make responses during the interview with a higher degree of "lead," such as approval, open-ended questions, and tentative interpretations. The purpose would be to enrich client experiencing as it relates to implementing the self-concept in an occupational role. In research extending over a long period of time, Snyder (1945; 1963) has developed an interview classification system for Client-Centered counseling that defines these response categories and provides a frame of reference for the counselor to determine which of them is used most frequently and how appropriately. The initial version of the system (Snyder, 1945) is given in Table 3-2, where each of the different response categories is defined. In 1963, these categories were

Table 3-2   Counselor Response Categories

DEFINITIONS OF COUNSELOR CATEGORIES

A. Lead-taking categories (those which seem to determine the direction of the interview; which indicate what the client should be talking about).

XCS *Structuring*   Remarks that define the counseling situation. Remarks indicating the purposes the interview may be expected to accomplish, or the responsibilities of both individuals, i.e., telling "what we can do here." Also includes remarks setting the time and limits of the interview; would include "You can have just an hour," but wouldn't include "I see you've come to the end of the hour."

XFT *Forcing client to choose and develop topic*   Includes all efforts of the counselor to reject responsibility for the direction of the interview. For example: "What shall we talk about today?" or "Well, how do you feel about it?"

XDC *Directive questions; specific types of questions*   Asking outright question which requires the giving of a factual answer. It does not include interrogative statements which are merely intended to redefine, clarify, or redescribe a feeling. It would include "What do you think of that?" "How old are you? " "Do they resent the fact that you are not aggressively going out after jobs?" It would not include "And you aren't too happy about it?" or "It's rather unpleasant for you, is that right?" particularly when such questions follow somewhat similar statements.

XND *Nondirective leads and questions*   Statements that encourage the client to state the problem further. This excludes leads that would greatly limit the client in what he could bring out about the problem or his feelings about it. It would include "Tell me more about it," or "Would you like to tell me how you feel about it?" or "How are you today?" (asked in a general sense). In general this type of lead is one that encourages a statement without limiting the nature of the response except in a very general way, as in "Tell me more about it."

Table 3-2 (Continued)

B. **Nondirective response-to-feeling categories** (those which seem to attempt to restate a feeling that the client has expressed, but not to interpret or to offer advice, criticism, or suggestions).

XSA *Simple acceptance* "Yes," "Mm-hmmm," "I see," "That's right," (if not answer question) or similar responses. Must not imply approval or criticism.

XRC *Restatement of content or problem* A simple repeating of what the client has said without any effort to organize, clarify, or interpret it, or any effort to show that the counselor is appreciating the feeling of the client's statement by understanding it. The wording need not be identical with that of the client.

XCF *Clarification or recognition of feeling* A statement by the counselor that puts the client's feeling or affective tone in somewhat clearer or more recognizable form. "It makes you feel very much annoyed." "You love your mother but you resent her telling you what to do," "I think sometimes you wish you'd never been born."

C. **Semidirective response-to-feeling category** (those responses that are interpretive in character).

XIT *Interpretation* Responses in which the counselor points out patterns and relationships in the material presented. This category is always used when causation is implied or indicated. "You do this because . . . ." If the counselor attempts even vaguely to say "why" the client does or feels something, it is considered interpretation. "Perhaps you are revealing feelings of inferiority." "When people feel frustrated they often act the way you do." "There's your problem."

D. **Directive Counseling Categories** (those categories of responses that imply a relationship in which the counselor attempts to change the immediate ideas of the client or to influence his attitude toward them).

XAE *Approval and encouragement* "That's fine." "You've

Table 3-2 (Continued)

---

covered a lot of ground today." "You bet!" Any statement which lends emotional support or approval to alleviate the client's insecurity.

XIX *Giving information or explanation*   Answers to any questions about the nature of psychology or any other informational material; anything which is recognized as a generally established fact; any personal information about the counselor.

XCA *Proposing client activity*   Any statement that implies that the client should take any sort of action.

XPS *Persuasion*   Attempts to convince the client that he should accept the counselor's point of view. "Don't you think it would be better that way now?"

XDE *Disapproval and criticism*   "You need to get hold of yourself."

E.   **Minor categories** (those responses that do not seem to be related to the principal problem of the client).

XEC *Ending of the contact*   Any responses dealing with the bringing to a close of the contact, or with the setting of a time for future contact.

XES *Ending of the series*   Responses relating to the bringing to a close of the series of interviews, or to the beginning of the client's feeling that he does not need further contact.

XFD *Friendly discussion*   Material unrelated to the client's problem, and serving only the purpose of establishing good rapport between client and counselor.

XUN *Unclassifiable*   Any response which cannot be classified in one of the above categories.

Source: Snyder, 1945.

reorganized and classified somewhat differently, without associated definitions. The later categories were:

Lead-taking responses	Relationship response
structuring	relationship
nondirective lead	Supportive responses
directive lead	reassurance
question	offer of help
Reflective or reeducative responses	approval
restatement	Redirecting responses
clarification	calling attention
interpretation	challenging
attenuation	withholding support
advice	persuasion
information	disapproval

Underlying the use of these response categories are the counselor attitudes mentioned previously. They have been given explicit definitions by several client-centered theorists, the most notable of whom are Truax and Carkhuff (1967). The scales they constructed for rating accurate empathy (understanding), nonpossessive warmth (acceptance), and genuineness (congruence) are reproduced in Table 3-3, with the definitions of stages on each scale. These definitions differ from those originally given by Rogers in the following ways:

> Accurate empathy involves more than just the ability of the therapist to sense the client or patient's "private world" as if it were his own. It also involves more than just his ability to know what the patient means. Accurate empathy involves both the therapist's sensitivity to current feelings and his verbal facility to communicate this understanding in a language attuned to the client's current feelings (Truax & Carkhuff, 1967, p. 46).

> Nonpossessive warmth . . . involves valuing the patient as a person, separate from any evaluation of his behavior or thoughts. Thus, a therapist can evaluate the patient's behavior or thoughts but still rate high on warmth if it is quite clear that his valuing of the individual is uncontaminated and unconditional (pp. 59–60). [This is the same distinction that Ellis (1961) makes between what he calls "being" and behavior.]

> A high level of self-congruence does not mean that the therapist must overtly express his feelings but only that he does not deny them. Thus, the therapist may be actively reflecting, interpreting, analyzing, or in other ways functioning as a therapist; but this functioning must be self-

Table 3-3   Scales for Empathy, Nonpossessive Warmth, and Genuineness

---

A TENTATIVE SCALE FOR THE MEASUREMENT OF ACCURATE EMPATHY

Stage 1   Therapist seems completely unaware of even the most conspicuous of the client's feelings; his responses are not appropriate to the mood and content of the client's statements. There is no determinable quality or empathy, and hence no accuracy whatsoever. The therapist may be bored and disinterested or actively offering advice, but he is not communicating an awareness of the client's current feelings.

Stage 2   Therapist shows an almost negligible degree of accuracy in his responses, and that toward only the client's most obvious feelings. Any emotions which are not clearly defined he tends to ignore altogether. He may be correctly sensitive to obvious feelings and yet misunderstand much of what the client is really trying to say. By his response he may block off or may misdirect the patient. Stage 2 is distinguishable from Stage 3 in that the therapist ignores feelings rather than displaying an inability to understand them.

Stage 3   Therapist often responds accurately to client's more exposed feelings. He also displays concern for the deeper, more hidden feelings, which he seems to sense must be present, though he does not understand their nature or sense their meaning to the patient.

Stage 4   Therapist usually responds accurately to the client's more obvious feelings and occasionally recognizes some that are less apparent. In the process of this tentative probing, however, he may misinterpret some present feelings and anticipate some which are not current. Sensitivity and awareness do exist in the therapist, but he is not entirely "with" the patient in the *current* situation or experience. The desire and effort to understand are both present, but his accuracy is low. This stage is distinguishable from Stage 3 in that the therapist does occasionally recognize less apparent feelings. He also may seem to have a theory about the patient and may even know how or why the patient feels a particular way, but he is definitely not "with" the patient. In short, the therapist may be diagnostically accurate, but not empathically accurate in his sensitivity to the patient's current feelings.

Table 3-3 (Continued)

Stage 5 Therapist accurately responds to all of the client's more readily discernible feelings. He also shows awareness of many less evident feelings and experiences, but he tends to be somewhat inaccurate in his understanding of these. However, when he does not understand completely, this lack of complete understanding is communicated without an anticipatory or jarring note. His misunderstandings are not disruptive by their tentative nature. Sometimes in Stage 5 the therapist simply communicates his awareness of the problem of understanding another person's inner world. This stage is the midpoint of the continuum of accurate empathy.

Stage 6 Therapist recognizes most of the client's present feelings, including those which are not readily apparent. Although he understands their content, he sometimes tends to misjudge the intensity of these veiled feelings, so that his responses are not always accurately suited to the exact mood of the client. The therapist does deal directly with feelings the patient is currently experiencing although he may misjudge the intensity of those less apparent. Although sensing the feelings, he often is unable to communicate meaning to them. In contrast to Stage 7, the therapist's statements contain an almost static quality in the sense that he handles those feelings that the patient offers but does not bring new elements to life. He is "with" the client but doesn't encourage exploration. His manner of communicating his understanding is such that he makes of it a finished thing.

Stage 7 Therapist responds accurately to most of the client's present feelings and shows awareness of the precise intensity of most of the underlying emotions. However, his responses move only slightly beyond the client's own awareness, so that feelings may be present which neither the client nor therapist recognizes. The therapist initiates moves toward more emotionally laden material, and may communicate simply that he and the patient are moving towards more emotionally significant material. Stage 7 is distinguishable from Stage 6 in that often the therapist's response is a kind of precise pointing of the finger toward emotionally significant material.

Stage 8 Therapist accurately interprets all the client's present, acknowledged feelings. He also uncovers the most deeply shrouded of the client's feelings, voicing meanings in the client's experience of

Table 3-3 (*Continued*)

---

which the client is scarcely aware. Since the therapist must necessarily utilize a method of trial and error in the new uncharted areas, there are minor flaws in the accuracy of his understanding, but these inaccuracies are held tentatively. With sensitivity and accuracy he moves into feelings and experiences that the client has only hinted at. The therapist offers specific explanations or additions to the patient's understanding so that underlying emotions are both pointed out and specifically talked about. The content that comes to life may be new but it is not alien.

Although the therapist in Stage 8 makes mistakes, these mistakes are not jarring, because they are covered by the tentative character of the response. Also, the therapist is sensitive to his mistakes and quickly changes his response in midstream, indicating that he has recognized what is being talked about and what the patient is seeking in his own explorations. The therapist reflects a togetherness with the patient in tentative trial and error exploration. His voice tone reflects the seriousness and depth of his empathic grasp.

Stage 9   The therapist in this stage unerringly responds to the client's full range of feelings in their exact intensity. Without hesitation, he recognizes each emotional nuance and communicates an understanding of every deepest feeling. He is completely attuned to the client's shifting emotional content; he senses each of the client's feelings and reflects them in his words and *voice*. With sensitive accuracy, he expands the client's hints into a full-scale (though tentative) elaboration of feeling or experience. He shows precision both in understanding and in communication of this understanding, and expresses and experiences them without hesitancy.

A TENTATIVE SCALE FOR THE MEASUREMENT OF NONPOSSESSIVE WARMTH

Stage 1   The therapist is actively offering advice or giving clear negative regard. He may be telling the patient what would be "best for him" or in other ways actively approving or disapproving of his behavior. The therapist's actions make himself the locus of evaluation; he sees himself as *responsible for* the patient.

Table 3-3 (Continued)

Stage 2 The therapist responds mechanically to the client, indicating little positive regard and hence little nonpossessive warmth. He may ignore the patient or his feelings or display a lack of concern or interest. The therapist ignores the client at times when a nonpossessively warm response would be expected; he shows a complete passivity that communicates almost unconditional lack of regard.

Stage 3 The therapist indicates a positive caring for the patient or client, but it is a *semipossessive* caring in the sense that he communicates to the client that his behavior matters to him. That is, the therapist communicates such things as "It is not all right if you act immorally," "I want you to get along at work," or "It's important to me that you get along with the ward staff." The therapist sees himself as *responsible for* the client.

Stage 4 The therapist clearly communicates a very deep interest and concern for the welfare of the patient, showing a nonevaluative and unconditional warmth in almost all areas of his functioning. Although there remains some conditionality in the more personal and private areas, the patient is given freedom to be himself and to be liked as himself. There is little evaluation of thoughts and behaviors. In deeply personal areas, however, the therapist may be conditional and communicate the idea that the client may act in any way he wishes, *except* that it is important to the therapist that he be more mature or not regress in therapy or accept and like the therapist. In all other areas, however, nonpossessive warmth is communicated. The therapist sees himself as *responsible to* the client.

Stage 5 The therapist communicates warmth without restriction. There is a deep respect for the patient's worth as a person and his rights as a free individual. At this level the patient is free to be himself even if this means that he is regressing, being defensive, or even disliking or rejecting the therapist himself. At this stage the therapist cares deeply for the patient as a person, but it does not matter to him how the patient chooses to behave. He genuinely cares for and deeply prizes the patient for his human potential, apart from evaluation of his behavior or his thoughts. He is willing to share equally the patient's joys and aspirations or depressions and failures. The only channeling by the

---

Table 3-3 *(Continued)*

---

therapist may be the demand that the patient communicate personally relevant material.

A TENTATIVE SCALE FOR THE MEASUREMENT OF THERAPIST GENUINENESS OR SELF-CONGRUENCE

Stage 1   The therapist is clearly defensive in the interaction, and there is explicit evidence of a very considerable discrepancy between what he says and what he experiences. There may be striking contradictions in the therapist's statements; the content of his verbalization may contradict the voice qualities or nonverbal cues (i.e., the upset therapist stating in a strained voice that he is "not bothered at all" by the patient's anger).

Stage 2   The therapist responds appropriately but in a professional rather than a personal manner, giving the impression that his responses are made because they sound good from a distance but do not express what he really feels or means. There is a somewhat contrived or rehearsed quality or air of professionalism present.

Stage 3   The therapist is implicitly either defensive or professional, although there is no explicit evidence. (Two patients are present in the sample given.)

Stage 4   There is neither implicit nor explicit evidences of defensiveness or the presence of a facade. The therapist shows nonself-incongruence.

Stage 5   The therapist is freely and deeply himself in the relatiohip. He is open to experiences and feelings of all types—both pleasant and hurtful—without traces of defensiveness or retreat into professionalism. Although there may be contradictory feelings, these are accepted or recognized. The therapist is clearly being himself in all of his responses, whether they are personally meaningful or trite. At Stage 5 the therapist need not express personal feelings, but whether he is giving advice, reflecting, interpreting, or sharing experiences, it is clear that he is being very much himself, so that his verbalizations match his inner experiences.

Source: Truax and Carkhuff, 1967.

congruent, so that he is being himself in the moment, rather than presenting a professional facade (pp. 68–69).

These attitudes are as applicable in Client-Centered career counseling, even during informational aspects of the process, as they are in psychotherapy, since they provide the conditions for the acceptance of personal responsibility for career decision making and for the reduction of anxiety associated with career choice.

Test Interpretation

One of the central issues with which Client-Centered career counselors have had to contend has been how to reconcile the use of tests with the tenets of the Rogerian approach. Rogers' (1946, p. 140) position was that:

> psychometric tests which are initiated by the counselor are a hindrance to the counseling process whose purpose is to release growth forces. They tend to increase defensiveness on the part of the client, to lessen his acceptance of self, to decrease his sense of responsibility, to create an attitude of dependence upon the expert.

He modified this critical stance on tests to allow that:

> tests are not necessarily completely excluded from the counseling process, however. The client may, in exploring his situation, reach the point where, facing his situation squarely and realistically, he wishes to compare his aptitudes or abilities with those of others for a specific purpose. . . . Consequently, when the request for appraisal comes as a real desire of the client, then tests may enter into the situation. It should be recognized, however, that this is not likely to occur frequently in practice.

This last observation most likely came out of Rogers' background in personal adjustment counseling, where the focus of both the client and the counselor is upon the inner world of phenomenal experience rather than on the outer world of work and related activities.

To resolve what appears to be a basic incompatibility between nonevaluative counselor attitudes (acceptance, congruence, and understanding) on the one hand, and the evaluative information derived from tests on the other hand, Client-Centered career counselors have proposed that tests be used primarily for the client's clarification of self rather than for the counselor's objective understanding (for example, analysis and diagnosis as in Trait-and-Factor career counseling) of the client. Patterson (1964, p. 449) argues that "The essential basis for the use of tests in [Client-Centered] career counseling is that they provide information which the client needs and wants, information concerning questions raised by the client in counseling." Similarly, Grummon (1972, p. 126) concludes that "Tests can be useful in [Client-Centered career counseling], provided that the information they supply is integrated into the self-concept." His rationale for using tests in the Client-Centered approach fits into the larger context of Super's (1951) self-concept theory of vocational choice as an implementation of the self in a compatible occupational role. To make this translation the individual, according to Super, must be able to answer the question "What kind of person am I?" Not only life experiences but also information from standardized tests can give the individual a basis for identifying and describing characteristics relevant to career choice.

To achieve this "client-centeredness" in using tests, several innovative procedures have been proposed. First, tests are introduced as needed and requested by the client, "precision" testing as opposed to "saturation" testing (Super, 1950). In other words, the client can take tests whenever appropriate throughout the course of career counseling, rather than as a battery before counseling starts. Second, the client participates in the test selection process (Bordin & Bixler, 1946). The counselor describes the kind of information the client can gain from the various tests available, and the client decides which behaviors she or he wants to assess. Then the counselor usually designates the most appropriate measures with respect to their psychometric characteristics (applicability, norms, reliability, validity). Finally, when the tests have been taken and scored, the counselor reports the results to the client in as objective, nonjudgmental a way as possible and responds to the latter's reactions within a client-centered atmosphere. An excerpt from an actual counseling interview illustrating how this is done is given in Table 3-4. Bixler and Bixler (1945, p. 192) summarize this approach as follows: (1) give the client simple statistical predictions based upon the test data; (2) allow the client to evaluate the prediction as it applies to himself or herself; (3) remain neutral towards test data and the client's reaction; (4) facilitate the client's self-evaluation and subsequent decisions by the use of therapeutic procedures; and, (5) avoid persuasive methods—test data should provide motivation, not the counselor. Compare and contrast this approach to test interpretation with that of Trait-and-Factor career counseling in Table 3-5.

Table 3-4 Test Interpretation in Client-Centered Career Counseling

---

C: Two or three students out of one hundred with scores like yours succeed in pre-med.

S: I knew they'd turn out like that. (disappointed)

C: Even though you expected this, it's pretty hard to take.

S: Yes, sir, but I got off to a bad start this year. It's the same story. My advisor discouraged me, so did Mr. R. in Dean X's office, and now the test discourages me. I want to try another quarter next fall with a fresh start. I think starting new with a good rest, I can do it. If I fail, then I'll know I can't be a doctor, but I'm not satisfied with that yet.

C: You feel everything discourages you, but you haven't given yourself a fair trial. You think next fall will tell the story.

S: Yes, I do, even though they didn't agree with me, and the tests are on their side.

Source: Bixler and Bixler, 1946.

Occupational Information

The principles underlying the use of occupational information in Client-Centered career counseling are much the same as those governing test interpretation. Patterson (1964, pp. 453–455) enumerates four of them:

1 *"Occupational information is introduced into the counseling process when there is a recognized need for it on the part of the client . . ."* The principle underlying this procedure is that the counselor accepts the client as she or he is. Thus, if a client seems to ask for occupational information prematurely, the counselor provides it; conversely, the counselor does not volunteer occupational information until the client is ready for it.

2 *"Occupational information is not used to influence or manipulate the client . . ."* The counselor may suggest possible career options the client has not considered by introducing relevant occupational information, but, from the Client-Centered point of view, she or he should not try to persuade the client to consider certain occupations in preference to others, the principle being not to use occupational information in an evaluative way.

Table 3-5 Test Interpretation Procedures in Trait-and-Factor and Client-Centered Career Counseling

Trait-and-Factor	Client-Centered
1 Begins with presentation of the test profile. The meaning and implications of the test scores are provided in considerable detail by means of verbal elaborations by the counselor.	**1** The counselor begins by encouraging the student to consider the evidence he already has as to student's aptitudes and interests, success with and liking for various high-school subjects, his hobbies, his work experiences, etc.
2 No effort is made by the counselor to elicit responses from the subject, although subject's comments and questions are not discouraged. Questions are answered; client comments are recognized by attentive listening, reflecting responses.	**2** Where client's evaluation of abilities or interests seems at variance with test results, he/she is asked to consider the matter further. Test results are then compared with estimates made on nontest evidence, with discussion of discrepancies and agreement between the two kinds of indications. A completed profile is not presented to the student, but test results are presented one at a time in the form of a scratch-paper profile, in order to avoid giving over-attention to the test data once a particular test result is introduced.

3 *"The most objective way to provide occupational information and a way which maximizes client initiative and responsibility is to encourage the client to obtain the information from original sources, that is, publications, employers, and persons engaged in occupations . . ."* Here the principle is to foster independence in the client through his or her assumption of personal responsibility, rather than the counselor gathering and digesting the information for the client.

4 *"The client's attitudes and feelings about occupations and jobs must be allowed expression and be dealt with therapeutically."* The counselor attends to not only the objective aspects of occupational information but also the subjective meanings of the information for the client. That an occupation, for example, which a client had decided upon has prerequisites she or he had not realized may have considerable personal significance which the counselor needs to work through with the client using the interview techniques of Client-Centered career counseling.

Grummon (1972, p. 122) emphasizes further that, in the process of presenting occupational information, the career counselor should not lose sight of the Rogerian dictum, stemming from phenomenological theory, that "reality for the individual is his perception of that reality." Rusalem (1954, pp. 85–86) reiterates this observation when he says that "the presentation of occupational information must assume that for the client it becomes a process of selective perception."

Likewise, Samler (1964, p. 426) states that "The process of occupational exploration is psychological in the sense that the client's perceptions are taken into account." He points out that the selective perception mentioned by Rusalem may be a very useful source of material for discussion of the client's needs and values. Why is it, for example, that a client singles out a particular aspect of an occupation, such as the opportunity for travel, upon which to focus in considering it as a career option? What subjective value does it have, and how does it relate to the decision-making process? These are all questions which are relevant to Client-Centered career counseling and which often stand in marked contrast to traditional presentation of occupational information, which is typically didactic and cognitively oriented. To summarize, this approach recognizes that the client's perceptions of the world of work are idiosyncratic and that the counselor's role is to assist the client in exploring and clarifying them, not to evaluate them.

MATERIALS

This case study in Client-Centered career counseling is a 25-year-old male veteran, Brad Johnson, who was returning to civilian life after the Korean War. He was seen in the Counseling Psychology section of a large Veterans Administration Hospital for ten weekly one-hour interviews after treatment for injuries sustained in combat. He had been a tenant farmer before his service and, although his combat injuries had not left him disabled, he felt vaguely different about himself and wanted to reconsider farming as a career. He had completed an undergraduate degree in agriculture before he was drafted, accumulating an overall GPA of 3.49, but he was entitled to further education or training under the G.I. Bill.

Diagnosis

When Brad first came for counseling, he seemed depressed and distracted. He had stepped on a land mine in Korea and was lucky to be alive, especially with no permanent disabilities. But his physical system had undergone a severe insult, and the surgery to remove the shrapnel had been a nightmare of pain and sleepless nights. It was not unusual, therefore, that he was depressed, but the counselor sensed that it was more pervasive than a reaction to his hospitalization. It bordered upon what Kierkegaard has called "sickness unto death," that feeling of despair and desolation that accompanies an existential crisis in one's life. For Brad, this crisis appeared to be a questioning of his identity, an inability to say what kind of person he was, and especially an inability to translate this diffused self-concept into a meaningful occupational role.

The counselor's initial diagnosis was the implicit and general one of Brad's lack of congruence between the way he saw himself and the way he viewed the world. Whether this discrepancy stemmed from distortion and denial or from lack of information about self and work posed the next diagnostic decision for the counselor. During the early interviews, Brad was largely noncommunicative and reactive. He passively put the locus of responsibility for the interaction upon the counselor, making it difficult for him to gain an impression of Brad's felt difficulty, to enter his phenomenal field and know reality from his perspective. By the third interview, however, the client-centered conditions of acceptance, empathy, and genuineness that the counselor was attempting to create in the relationship were sufficiently potent that Brad felt less threatened. He started to talk more and to express feelings he had previously kept to himself. He revealed that he had majored in agriculture only because, as the eldest son, there was a strong parental expectation that he would take over the family farm after his father was too old to work it. He had acquiesced to this expectation, which was largely unspoken but assumed, because he had extreme difficulty in communicating with his parents, much as he did with the counselor in the early interviews. He had learned to deny his feelings, and the counselor concluded that this mechanism accounted for at least a part of Brad's lack of congruence. But there was another part which seemed to come from his apparent naïveté about the world, and the counselor thought this lack of sophistication or information, possibly stemming from growing up in the country, might also be a contributing factor.

He discussed this possibility with Brad in the fourth interview and suggested that he take an interest inventory to compare his likes and dislikes with those of others employed in a variety of occupations. The counselor explained that the interest inventory he had in mind, the Strong Vocational Interest Blank (SVIB), offered a convenient way to explore the self in relation to the world of work. The inventory takes a large sampling of self-percepts (400 items on personal preferences for occupations, avocations, school subjects, people, and so forth) and translates them into career options by expressing them as scores on the SVIB occupational scales. Brad thought that taking the SVIB might be helpful, since he was experiencing anxiety about who he was and what he might do. He voiced some concern, however, that the inventory would show that he had no interests similar to those of the occupational groups. The counselor responded that, if this should be, then they could work together on *why* his interests were unpatterned. This, in fact, was the case, as Brad's SVIB profile in Figure 3-2 indicates. He has no A's and B+'s, although his occupational level (OL) score is quite high, a pattern that Crites (1960) found was related to lesser ego strength or poor adjustment status. It is characteristic of clients who manifest personal maladjustment in an undifferentiated high level of vocational aspiration. With his inability to clarify his self-concept and his naïveté about the workaday world, Brad appeared to fit this syndrome— personal incongruence expressed in career indecision and diffusion.

Process

Client-Centered career counseling seemed singularly appropriate for Brad, whose lack of congruence reflected both his inner and outer worlds of experience. From the ongoing interaction over the ten

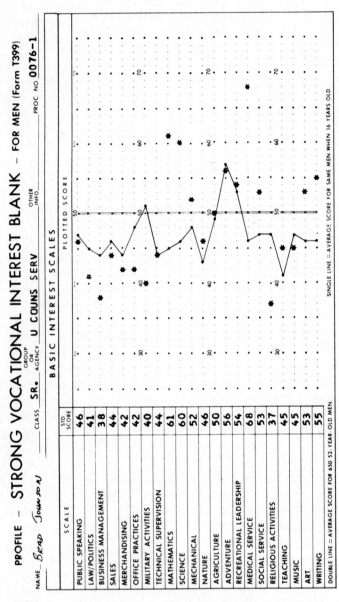

Figure 3-2 Brad Johnson's Strong Vocational Interest Blank Profile.

OCCUPATIONAL SCALES

OCCUPATION	STD SCORE	C	B−	B	B+	A
I						
DENTIST	44					
OSTEOPATH	36					
VETERINARIAN	32					
PHYSICIAN	50					
PSYCHIATRIST	38					
PSYCHOLOGIST	32					
BIOLOGIST	39					
II ARCHITECT	32					
MATHEMATICIAN	24					
PHYSICIST	33					
CHEMIST	44					
ENGINEER	32					
III PRODUCTION	30					
ARMY OFFICER	19					
AIR FORCE OFFICER	33					
IV CARPENTER	25					
FOREST SERVICE MAN	11					
FARMER	30					
MATH-SCIENCE TEACHER	33					
PRINTER	27					
POLICEMAN	23					
V PERSONNEL DIRECTOR	18					
PUBLIC ADMINISTRATOR	21					
REHABILITATION COUNS.	20					
YMCA STAFF MEMBER	24					
SOCIAL WORKER	18					
SOCIAL SCIENCE TEACHER	14					
SCHOOL SUPERINTENDENT	16					
MINISTER	15					

OCCUPATION	STD SCORE	C	B−	B	B+	A
VI LIBRARIAN	29					
ARTIST	33					
MUSICIAN PERFORMER	43					
MUSIC TEACHER	24					
VII C.P.A. OWNER	22					
VIII SENIOR C.P.A.	14					
ACCOUNTANT	16					
OFFICEWORKER	18					
PURCHASING AGENT	23					
BANKER	17					
PHARMACIST	29					
FUNERAL DIRECTOR	27					
IX SALES MANAGER	13					
REAL ESTATE SALESMAN	22					
LIFE INS. SALESMAN	19					
X ADVERTISING MAN	27					
LAWYER	29					
AUTHOR-JOURNALIST	32					
XI PRESIDENT-MFG. CO	19					

SUPP OCCUPATIONAL SCALES

OCCUPATION	STD SCORE	C	B−	B	B+	A
CREDIT MANAGER	25					
CHAMBER OF COM. EXEC.	29					
PHYSICAL THERAPIST	48					
COMPUTER PROGRAMMER	26					
BUSINESS ED TEACHER	11					
COMMUNITY REC. ADMIN	27					

NON-OCCUPATIONAL SCALES

59	42	57	58	52	36	58	34
AACH	AR	DIV	MFII	MO	OIE	OL	SL

ADMINISTRATIVE INDICES

399	7	9	11	55	34
TR	UNP	FC	LP	IP	DP

87

interviews, beginning with the one-sided, halting, reactive communication of the first stage, proceeding through the increasingly open expression of the middle stage, and terminating with a greater acceptance of self in the final stage, Brad moved significantly along the underlying continuum of experiencing. The counselor estimated from tape recordings of the first three interviews that Brad was at approximately the fourth stage in Rogers' (1961) process conception of psychotherapy. He was struggling to express his feelings, but they were largely blocked by his previous familial experiences and inhibitions. By the fourth, fifth, and sixth stages, however, responding to the counselor's predominantly reflective style, Brad had progressed to Rogers' fifth stage, in which "feelings are expressed freely," "experiencing is loosened, no longer remote, and frequently occurs with little postponement," and "there is an increasing quality of acceptance for the problems being faced." During the last four interviews, Brad had achieved the sixth stage in Rogers' schema, which was characterized by his greater congruence and particularly his "owning" his problems. The counselor had a distinct sense of a nascent integration in Brad's self-concept, a merging of the inner and outer worlds; but, although it had begun, it was still incomplete. Brad was approaching, but had not reached, the seventh and final stage along Rogers' continuum.

The counselor's techniques throughout Brad's career counseling were a blend of reflection and restatement. For example, here is an excerpt from the latter part of the third interview, during which Brad started to talk about communication within his family circle:

Brad: They never talked about much of anything, except the weather and the crops. We all just assumed that I would stay on the farm.

Counselor: It was hard to talk with them about what *you* wanted to do, what your feelings were.

Similarly, in discussing the SVIB, the counselor was matter-of-fact and descriptive rather than evaluative and predictive. He made such statements as "Your interests do not seem to be similar to those of people in any of these occupations" and "Your Occupational Level score is quite high." Brad responded by asking what the low-interest scores and the high OL score meant, and the counselor commented that they reflected the way he was seeing himself at the time. He aspired to higher-level occupations but was uncertain about which direction to head. In the eighth interview, Brad asked how he could learn more about occupations he might consider, and the counselor referred him to the occupational alcove in the hospital library. Brad used it extensively and started to develop some interest in farm-related careers, such as county agricultural agent, feed plant manager, and farm equipment salesperson. In the last interview, Brad decided he wanted to gain some first-hand knowledge of these occupations by talking with people in these fields and to return for some follow-up interviews with the counselor at a later date.

Outcomes

The trend line of movement in the career counseling with Brad was generally positive. In the beginning, the gains were admittedly slight, but the fact that he maintained contact during this time was in itself a sign of progress. Then in the often critical middle stage of the process he appeared to break through some of his previous inhibitions and feel freer to accept himself and to begin coping with the world about him. At the end, he had not actually made a career choice, but whereas before he had been closed to engaging in the decision-making process, he was now open to being involved in it. There was a dawning of personal responsibility that indicated greater confidence and integration in his functioning. He was more effective and regnant in his life. He was reaching out, rather than pulling back, and his intention to learn more about farm-related occupations and then schedule some follow-up interviews was noteworthy.

When he returned two months later for two more interviews, he wanted to take the SVIB again and to reality test his tentative choice of pursuing a career in farm equipment sales with a large manufacturer such as Allis-Chalmers or International Harvester. He felt he could fulfill his high-level vocational aspirations with one of these firms and still draw upon his agricultural and farm background as well. He saw his choice as a compromise (integration?) between staying on the farm and leaving it entirely. His second SVIB tended to confirm Brad's insights: He now had a primary interest pattern in the Business Contact group and a secondary in Technical, which included Farmer. A year later, he reported that he was working as a sales representative with International Harvester, was well satisfied with his work, and had recently received a promotion to district manager.

COMMENT

The model and methods of Client-Centered career counseling represent not only an application of Rogerian principles to decision making, but they also synthesize this approach with core concepts from Trait-and-Factor and developmental theory. Patterson (1964, p. 441) incorporates a refined "matching men and jobs" concept of career choice when he states that it "may still be broadly conceived as the matching of the individual and a career, but in a manner much more complex than was originally thought," and he draws heavily upon Super's (1957) self-theory of career development to introduce this dimension into the otherwise ahistorical, "right now" focus of client-centered psychotherapy. It is questionable, however, whether even this comprehensive a synthesis, which might also include the contemporary Client-Centered emphasis upon greater counselor activity, meets some of the criticisms that have been leveled at Client-Centered career counseling.

Theoretically, Grummon (1972, p. 123) has expressed concern over the almost exclusive phenomenological orientation of the Client-Centered approach, which ignores the effect of stimulus variables upon the acquisition and processing of information about self and the world of work. He observes that: "The theory's failure to elaborate how the environment influences perception and behavior is for the writer [Grummon] a significant omission which has special relevance for many counseling situations." Pragmatically, the principal pitfall also concerns the potential disjunction and disruption that the introduction of information into the interview process by the counselor often creates. It is still not clear from Patterson's formulation how the counselor informs the client about occupations without shifting from a Client-Centered role to a didactic one and thereby compromising the very attitudes which supposedly promote self clarification and actualization. His suggestion that the counselor *read* occupational information aloud to the client does not appear to be the panacea.

REFERENCES

Arbuckle, D. S. *Counseling: An introduction.* Boston: Allyn & Bacon, 1961.

Bixler, R. H., & Bixler, V. H. Clinical counseling in vocational guidance. *Journal of Clinical Psychology,* 1945, *1,* 186–190.

Bixler, R. H., & Bixler, V. H. Test interpretation in vocational counseling. *Educational and Psychological Measurement,* 1946, *6,* 145–156.

Bown, O. H. The client-centered approach to educational and vocational guidance. *The Personnel Counselor,* 1947, *2,* 1–5.

Combs, A. Nondirective techniques and vocational counseling. *Occupations,* 1947, *25,* 261–267.

Covner, B. J. Nondirective interviewing techniques in vocational counseling. *Journal of Counsulting Psychology,* 1947, *11,* 70–73.

Crites, J. O. Ego-strength in relation to vocational interest development. *Journal of Counseling Psychology,* 1960, *7,* 137–143.

Doleys, E. J. Are there "kinds" of counselors? *Counseling News and Views,* 1961, *13,* 5–9.

Dymond, R. F. Adjustment changes over therapy from self-sorts. In C. R. Rogers & R. F. Dymond (Eds), *Psychotherapy and personality change.* Chicago: University of Chicago Press, 1954. Pp. 76–84.

Ellis, A. *Reason and emotion in psychotherapy.* New York: Lyle Stuart, 1962.

Gandet F. J., & Kulick, W. Who comes to a vocational guidance center? *Personnel and Guidance Journal,* 1954, *33,* 211–215.

Gendlin, E. T., & Tomlinson, T. M. Psychotherapy process rating scale: Experiencing (EXP) Scale. Unpublished manuscript. Madison, Wisc.: Wisconsin Psychiatric Institute, 1961.

Goodstein, L. D., Crites, J. O., Heilbrun, A. B., Jr., & Rempel, P. P. The use of the California Psychological Inventory in a university counseling service. *Journal of Counseling Psychology,* 1961, *8,* 147–153.

Grummon, D. L. Client-centered theory. In B. Stefflre & W. H. Grant (Eds), *Theories of counseling.* (2d ed.) New York: McGraw-Hill, 1972. Pp. 73–135.

Hahn, M. E., & Kendall, W. E. Some comments in defense of non-nondirective counseling. *Journal of Counseling Psychology,* 1947, *11,* 74–81.

Hart, J. T., & Tomlinson, T. M. (Eds), *New directions in client-centered therapy.* Boston: Houghton Mifflin, 1970.

Kelly, G. A. *The psychology of personal constructs.* New York: Norton, 1955.

Patterson, C. H. Counseling: Self-clarification and the helping relationship. In H. Borow (Ed.), *Man in a world at work.* Boston: Houghton Mifflin, 1964. Pp. 434–459.

Patterson, C. H. *Theories of counseling and psychotherapy.* (2d ed.) New York: Harper & Row, 1973.

Patterson, C. H. *Relationship counseling and psychotherapy.* New York: Harper & Row, 1974.

Robinson, F. P. *Principles and procedures in student counseling.* New York: Harper, 1950.

Rogers, C. R. *Counseling and psychotherapy.* Boston: Houghton Mifflin, 1942.

Rogers, C. R. Psychometric tests and client-centered counseling. *Educational and Psychological Measurement,* 1946, *6,* 139–144.

Rogers, C. R. *Client-centered therapy.* Boston: Houghton Mifflin, 1951.

Rogers, C. R. The necessary and sufficient conditions of therapeutic personality change. *Journal of Consulting Psychology,* 1957, *21,* 95–103.

Rogers, C. R. A process conception of psychotherapy. *American Psychologist,* 1958, *13,* 142–149.

Rogers, C. R. A theory of therapy, personality, and interpersonal relationships, as developed in the client-centered framework. In S. Koch (Ed.), *Psychology: A study of a science.* Study I. *Conceptual and systematic.* Vol. 3. *Formulations of the person and the social context.* New York: McGraw-Hill, 1959. Pp. 184–256.

Rogers, C. R. *On becoming a person.* Boston: Houghton Mifflin, 1961.

Rogers, C. R., & Dymond, R. F. (Eds), *Psychotherapy and personality change.* Chicago: University of Chicago Press, 1954.

Rusalem, H. New insights on the role of occupational information in counseling. *Journal of Counseling Psychology,* 1954, *1,* 84–88.

Samler, J. Occupational exploration in counseling: A proposed reorientation. In H. Borow (Ed.), *Man in a world at work.* Boston: Houghton Mifflin, 1964. Pp. 411–433.

Seeman, J. A study of client self-selection of tests in vocational counseling. *Educational and Psychological Measurement,* 1948, *8,* 327–346.

Snyder, W. U. An investigation of the nature of nondirective psychotherapy. *Journal of General Psychology,* 1945, *33,* 193–223.

Snyder, W. U. *Dependency in psychotherapy: A casebook.* New York: Macmillan, 1963.

Super, D. E. Testing and using test results in counseling. *Occupations,* 1950, *29,* 95–97.

Super, D. E. Vocational adjustment: Implementing a self-concept. *Occupations,* 1951, *30,* 88–92.

Super, D. E. *The psychology of careers.* New York: Harper, 1957.

Super, D. E., Starishevsky, R., Matlin, N., & Jordaan, J. P. *Career development: Self-concept theory.* Princeton, N.J.: College Entrance Examination Board, 1963.

Traux, C. B., & Carkhuff, R. R. *Toward effective counseling and psychotherapy: Training and practice.* Chicago: Aldine, 1967.

Wexler, D. A., & Rice, L. N. (Eds), *Innovations in client-centered therapy.* New York: Wiley, 1974.

Williams, J. E. Changes in self and other perceptions following brief educational-vocational counseling. *Journal of Counseling Psychology,* 1962, *9,* 18–30.

Psychodynamic
Career
Counseling

The Psychodynamic approach to career counseling has its roots in the psychoanalytic tradition but goes beyond it by incorporating concepts and techniques from both Trait-and-Factor and Client-Centered career counseling. It utilizes test information for the client as well as the counselor, and it introjects these data into the career decision-making process in unique ways. It builds upon the foundation of "matching men and jobs"; however, it elaborates upon the foundation to draw on complex notions of how choices are made (process). Some of its interview and test interpretation techniques are avowedly "client-centered," yet again they extend that approach, at least as formulated during the "nondirective" and "reflective" periods (see Chapter 3), to include methods from other orientations. In fact, in their discussion of "experiential" Client-Centered counseling, Hart and Tomlinson (1970, p. 17) acknowledge that it resembles psychoanalytically oriented psychotherapy.

In short, the Psychodynamic approach is the most comprehensive one we have as yet considered. It embraces central aspects of Trait-and-Factor and Client-Centered career counseling and adds to them an articulate and complex focus upon the client's internal motivational states and external coping mechanisms.

MODEL

The model that is comprehensive enough to comprehend these divergent viewpoints—to be "pan-theoretical" (Bordin, 1968)—must necessarily be both general and specific. It must be more general than a "cookbook" of counseling techniques (for example, Trait-and-Factor) and more specific than general assumptions about personality functioning (Client-Centered). In an effort to accomplish such a rapprochement, Bordin (1968), who has been the principal theorist in defining Psychodynamic career counseling, although supplemented by other formulations (for example, King & Bennington, 1972), has proposed a synthesis that integrates several concepts and precepts into a coherent psychodynamic approach. He starts with what he calls the "centralist principle":

> . . . it is that in an individual we expect to find systems of motives which are relevant to a wide range of his behavior, along with other systems, either independent of the more comprehensive ones or loosely related to them, which are relevant only to a narrow segment of behavior (Bordin, 1968, p. 137).

These systems take form developmentally and are differentially influenced by parental pressures (for example, withdrawal of love) at successive stages in the psychosocial process. Bordin (1968, p. 138) cites Freud's emphasis upon the purpose of this parental pressure and the defense mechanisms the individual acquires as going beyond the generalities of Rogerian theory, thus making the Psychodynamic point of view more veridical with "the subtlety and complexity of human behavioral phenomena." To these core concepts he adds the Rankian notion of integration and differentiation (Allen, 1942) and Erikson's (1963) life-span formulation of the stages (or "crises") in the development of the healthy personality.

Throughout his conceptualization of Psychodynamic career counseling, Bordin (1968) applies the principles of this orientation to the career decision-making process (Bordin, Nachmann, & Segal, 1963). He articulates the essence of his theoretical (and counseling) commitment, which is twofold: Career choice involves the client's needs, and it is a developmental process. He asserts that:

> Our pivotal assumption is that insofar as he has freedom of choice an individual tends to gravitate toward those occupations whose activities permit him to express his preferred ways of seeking gratification and of protecting himself from anxiety . . . Psychoanalytic theory suggests that a developmental approach to vocation should examine the full sweep of influences shaping personality from birth, even from conception (Bordin, 1968, p. 427).

To "prevent crippling psychological conflicts" in the course of personality-vocational development, the psychodynamically oriented career counselor intervenes at the "traditional points in the life cycle," utilizing the following concepts of diagnosis, process, and outcomes.

Diagnosis

On the issue of whether or not to diagnose, Bordin (1968, p. 296) is unequivocal: "We are convinced that counselors should not undertake counseling responsibility without at least a rudimentary knowledge of diagnosis and diagnostic techniques." But his view of diagnosis is not the traditional, nosological one of Trait-and-Factor career counseling. In fact, Bordin (1946) was the first to seriously question such nondynamic taxonomies of client problems and proposed instead more psychologically based constructs. He delineated five problem categories:

1 *Dependence* Some individuals experience difficulties in assuming personal responsibility for the solution of their problems and with mastering the developmental tasks of life. They rely heavily upon others to run their lives for them and become inordinately dependent upon others for the mediation of their needs.

2 *Lack of information* Individuals from impoverished economic or educational circumstances may often not have relevant information for career decision making, simply because they have not been exposed to appropriate sources. They may appear dependent, but actually they are ill-informed.

3 *Self-conflict* Bordin (1946, p. 178) defines this category as "a conflict between the response functions associated with two or more self-concepts or between a self-concept and some other stimulus function." An example would be a woman who has conflicting role expectancies concerning career and marriage.

4 *Choice anxiety* States of anxiety are created around making a career choice, if the individual wants to do one thing but a "significant other" (parent, spouse) wants him or her to do something else or if the individual experiences internal conflict between positive and negative valences associated with occupations.

5 *No problem* This is an "anchor" category in Bordin's system, although he cites cases of lack of assurance as falling within it, such as a client who has made a realistic career choice but comes for counseling to "check it out."

More recently, in analyzing the sources of motivational conflict experienced by clients seeking career counseling, Bordin and Kopplin (1973, pp. 156–159 passim) have proposed a new diagnostic system consisting of seven major categories, with some subdivided into more specific problems. The more general problems are defined as follows:

1 *Synthetic difficulties* A limiting case of minimum pathology and conflict in which the major problem is to be found in the difficulty of synthesizing or achieving cognitive clarity. The client is able to work productively in counseling.

2 *Identity problems* These are assumed to be associated with the formation of a viable self and self-percept (not necessarily fully conscious).

3 *Gratification conflicts* This classification takes its inspiration from the point of view that examines occupations in terms of the opportunities each offers for finding particular forms of psychosocial gratification in the work activities.

4 *Change orientation* The client is dissatisfied with himself and struggles via vocational choice to change himself.

5 *Overt pathology* Even though the contact was initiated around

vocational choice, it becomes evident that the disturbance makes it impossible for the student to do any kind of work on this question.

6 *Unclassifiable* Except that it is a problem involving motivational conflict.

7 *Unclassifiable* Except that it is a problem involving no motivational conflict.

To assess the reliability of this system, two judges classified the career motivational conflicts of eighty-two former clients. On the first forty-seven cases, they reconciled disagreements through consultation, but still attained only 51 percent exact agreement, with partial agreement in a remaining 28 percent. From these results, Bordin and Kopplin (1973, p. 159) concluded that:

> In general, we must concede that, though tolerable, our level of agreement was not satisfying. However, we do not find it discouraging because we take into account the sparseness of the case notes in so many instances that forced us into the guessing situation that the reliability figures document. A further factor in unreliability is that the counselors were not oriented to the issues raised by our categories.

Even granting that the reliability of this new system might be increased to a satisfactory level, however, of what use is it to the career counselor? It is wholly *post hoc*: The diagnosis is made from reading the notes and summaries of cases that have already been closed out. Such a procedure may have some value for research purposes, but it does not provide the career counselor with the requisite data for diagnosis *before* a course of career counseling is formulated. As Bordin (1946, p. 172) stipulated many years ago: "The most vital characteristic of a set of diagnostic classifications is that they form the basis for the choice of treatment."

Crites (in press) has formulated a psychodynamically oriented diagnostic system which can be used before or during career counseling and which can be directly linked to choice of treatment strategies and techniques (see "Methods" below). It is based upon a synthesis of Horney's (1945; 1950) theory of personality/psychotherapy and the Edwards Personal Preference Scales (EPPS). The latter measures the needs shown around the perimeter of the circumplex in Figure 4-1, brief definitions of which are given in Table 4-1. They have been ordered according to the sign and magnitude of their intercorrelations. Because the EPPS is ipsative (Radcliffe, 1963), about half the scales are negatively correlated with the other half. In the circumplex, all the

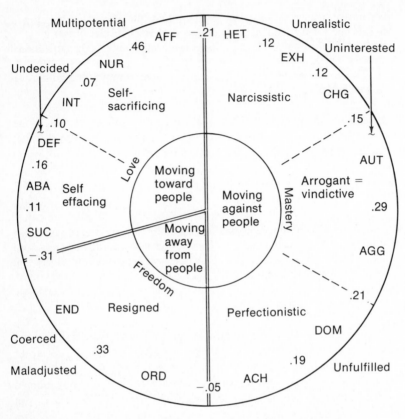

Figure 4-1 Edwards Personal Preference Schedule (EEPS) Circumplex.

scales to the right of the vertical axis are positively correlated with each other, but they are negatively related to those on the left of the vertical axis. Within the latter, Endurance and Order are negatively correlated with the others and hence constitute a subgroup on the left side of the circumplex. The scales are then ordered by the principle that they be more highly correlated with adjacent than nonadjacent scales—and in every instance they are (Edwards, 1954, p. 20). Following these rules, the three distinct sectors of scales shown in Figure 4-1 can be identified.

Theoretically, these sectors bear a remarkable correspondence to Horney's (1945; 1950) interpersonal orientations (moving against, toward, and away from people) and to her psychical types (narcissistic; arrogant-vindictive, and so forth). Although the EPPS was developed

Table 4-1 Definitions of Needs Measured by the Edwards Personal Preference Schedule (EPPS)

Variables	Manifest needs associated with variables[a]
Achievement	To successfully accomplish tasks of social and personal significance
Deference	To conform to convention and follow the leadership of others
Order	To stress organization and neatness in one's activities
Exhibition	To attract attention to oneself by dress or behavior
Autonomy	To act independently of others and of conventions
Affiliation	To engage in many activities with friends
Intraception	To think in terms of the motives underlying behavior
Succorance	To receive encouragement, sympathy, and affection from others
Dominance	To assume leadership roles in relationships with others
Abasement	To feel guilty and at fault when things go wrong; generally timid and inferior
Nurturance	To provide help, sympathy, and affection to others
Change	To seek new experiences and avoid routine
Endurance	To work hard and keep at a task until it is completed
Heterosexuality	To engage in social and sexual experiences involving the opposite sex
Aggression	To attack, criticize, or make fun of others

[a]Modified from descriptions in Edwards' manual.

from Murray's (1938) needs, the definitions of these variables in Table 4-1 combine when cast into the circumplex to describe Horney's orientations and types (with the exception of "self-sacrificing," which I have added). In turn, the types can be related to the career choice problems on the outside of the circumplex, which were originally proposed by Crites (1969) and discussed as part of the Trait-and-Factor approach (see Chapter 2). Here, however, they are linked to the personality dynamics of the client to suggest possible diagnoses of the motivational conflicts that may be producing problems in the career decisional process. Using this conceptual framework, which as yet has not been researched but has been used clinically for many years, the counselor can administer the EPPS to the client and relate the high and low scores to problem classifications based upon aptitude, interest, and choice data. From a synthesis of this psychometric information with Horney's personality constructs, a dynamic diagnosis can be made while the career counseling is in progress.

Process

Bordin (1968) breaks the process of career counseling down into three stages, which are a microcosm of the overall process of career development. In the first stage, *exploration and contract setting,* the critical task of the Psychodynamic career counselor is to avoid a superficial rationalistic examination of the client's choice problem as well as a seductive attempt to engage the client in nonvocationally oriented psychotherapy. Rather, as the name of this approach implies, the focus should be upon the psychodynamics of career decision making, the interface between the personal and the vocational in the client's life. The counselor strives to articulate the relationship between these two—to extrapolate the implications, for example, of a fearful, defensive identification of a failing engineering student, who wants to change majors, with an overdemanding and stern father. This process is what the writer calls *rehearsing,* the first of three "r's" in Psychodynamic career counseling. The other two "R's" are *refocusing* and *reconstructing.*

In the first stage the client retells his or her "story," which has been recounted innumerable times to others in the extraclinical world but without resolution. Now, the counselor hears the client out but within the context of a developing therapeutic relationship based upon what Shoben (1956) terms warm concern, nonretaliatory permissiveness, and honesty of communication, rather than gratuitous advice. These aspects of the relationship largely correspond to those of empathy, unconditional positive regard, and genuineness in Client-Centered career counseling (see Chapter 3).

The second stage is that of *critical decision,* not necessarily of career but between the alternatives of counseling limited to choice or broadened to encompass personality change. Bordin (1968, p. 440) observes:

A more than superficial examination of an individual in the throes of vocational choice usually uncovers a struggle for growth and change. The occupations he considers will reflect both his views of himself as he is and as he would like to be. As the client becomes increasingly aware of this struggle, he also begins to see the counseling process not only as a means for effecting a decision but also, if he desires it, as a part of a process of personality change. He then begins to struggle with the question of whether he should retain his more limited original objective or seek broader goals in counseling.

In other words, the Psychodynamic career counselor offers to the client the option of becoming engaged more extensively in the process of dealing with the interrelationship of personal and career development. If the client chooses to work on this goal, it is what the writer calls *refocusing*—a changing of orientation in the client from a narrow viewing of career choice as an externally imposed task to an "owning" of it as an integral part of his or her personality. The counselor facilitates this acceptance of self-in-relation-to-decision through a cooperative interaction with the client, in which each actively participates essentially equally.

The last stage in the process of Psychodynamic career counseling is *working for change* (Bordin, 1968). It is presumed that the client will opt for at least some change in personality, even if it is circumscribed to vocational identity. The thrust of this final stage is toward increased awareness and understanding of self. The process of *reconstructing* or redefining the kind of person a client is moves ahead principally along the relationship dimension of career counseling, although it is facilitated by communication (see "Methods" below). Utilizing Sullivan's emphasis upon what is going on in the relationship "right now," the Psychodynamic career counselor responds largely in terms of the feelings the client elicits in her or him. In response to a client's inability to assume personal responsibility for making a choice ("I just can't seem to decide on what I want to do—what do you think?"), the counselor may feel impatience and frustration, bordering on rejection, and might say: "I want to help you choose, but I feel you are putting the responsibility mostly on me. I feel like we are not working on this together—that it's not fifty-fifty. What do you think?" The counselor may add, to extrapolate to the client's life in general: "I wonder, too, whether others have the same feelings as I do when you ask them to tell you what to do, and I wonder how this affects your relationships with them." In this way, the counseling relationship is used as a prototype for other relationships and what is learned through counseling can be adapted to the client's interactions outside the consulting room (Magaret, 1950).

Outcomes

Although not explicitly stated (Bordin, 1968), the expected outcomes of Psychodynamic career counseling are apparent from an analysis of the stages in the process. One objective is to assist the client in career decision making. The problems that clients may present run the gamut of those enumerated previously in the discussion of "Diagnosis," for example, synthetic difficulties, gratification, conflicts, and so forth. If the counseling is successful, presumably, these problems will be resolved. Horney (1950) makes a useful distinction here between problem *solution* and problem *resolution*. The former reduces the anxiety associated with being undecided or unrealistic in career decision making, but only temporarily. After being given test and occupational information, an undecided client may declare a choice in order to feel less anxious about not having a goal. But she or he may select an occupation that is not consistent with aptitudes or interests. It is the motivating properties of the anxiety that prompt the decision rather than a consideration of its appropriateness. In contrast, problem resolution eliminates the conditions thwarting realistic career decision making. Thus, an unrealistic client who aspires to an occupational level beyond his or her intellectual capabilities may come to accept a downward adjustment of career aspiration and thereby not only reduce choice anxiety but also effect a long-term resolution of the choice problem.

To achieve lasting problem resolution in career decision making, it is necessary to achieve some positive change in the client's personality. This can be accomplished in two principal ways. Even though the client may choose a more narrowly defined type of career counseling, salubrious effects upon personal development can be realized. For example, a juxtaposition of a pervasive indecisiveness in decision making with submission to an authoritarian father may motivate a dependent client to assume greater personal responsibility without the counselor directly dealing with the latter. If the client is willing to undertake personal counseling, relatively free from career emphasis, the avowed outcome is some kind of personality change, albeit only symptomatic anxiety reduction. Both career decision and personality change, achieved through whatever modes, are the desired end states of the client following successful psychodynamic career counseling. Bordin

(1968, p. 444) sums up the rationale for this approach by commenting that there is a:

> close link between personality and career development which provides a basis for eliminating the spurious dichotomy between vocational and personal counseling without reducing one to the other. It permits us to relate a person's difficulties with his vocational choices to the vicissitudes of his personality development and, through helping with these choices, to influence the fullness of that development.

METHODS

The methods of Psychodynamic career counseling, as explicated primarily by Bordin (1968), are an amalgam of techniques derived not only from psychoanalytic practices, but also from the Trait-and-Factor and Client-Centered approaches. More than a mere eclectic gathering together of disparate counseling procedures, however, they are a true synthesis of theories and methods, leavened by Bordin's many years of experience as an active counselor. As the ensuing descriptions of Psychodynamic interview techniques, test interpretation processes, and uses of occupational information bring out, they provide sophisticated and refined methods for assisting clients in their career decision making.

Interview Techniques

Drawing upon the work of Colby (1951), a psychoanalytically disposed psychotherapist, Bordin (1968, pp. 179–180) enumerates three interpretative counselor response categories that can be used to conduct an interview. The first of these, *clarifications,* is intended to focus the client's thinking and verbalization upon material relevant to the presenting problem. It also serves to open up new areas of discourse and summarize others. Typically, clarifications take the grammatical form of "questions, mild imperatives or simplified restatements." Because of their form and content, their highest incidence is usually during the beginning stage of counseling. In exploring and rehearsing with the client the parameters of his or her problem, they can be used with another type of counselor response that Colby terms *interpositions.* These include advisory suggestions and some explanations as well as open-ended questions. They draw the client out and, at the same time, establish a "working relationship." At the beginning of career counseling, clarifications and interpositions accomplish two objectives, particularly in the form of open-ended questions. First, because these questions cannot usually be answered "yes" or "no," the locus of responsibility for communication is placed upon the client—this is essential especially for those who tend to be "passive dependent." Second, the questions are less threatening to the client than declarative statements, which often are interpreted as critical or unqualified. Thus, communication and relationship are furthered more during the early interviews by the counselor's saying: "Are you having a hard time telling me about how your father always decided things for you?" than by "You really resent your father for always making decisions for you." The latter may be true, but the client may have difficulty "owning" such feeling toward the father at this stage and reject the counselor's interpretation out-of-hand.

A second type of counselor response is *comparison,* in which two or more topics are juxtaposed to present in sharper relief the similarities or differences among dynamic phenomena. This technique is central to explicating the interrelationship of personal and career development. To illustrate, a counselor might respond to an indecisive client's unconscious rebellion against imposed parental career aspirations by saying: "On the one hand, your parents want you to be something you don't want to be, yet, on the other hand, you cannot decide what you want to be. Do you see any connection between the two?" What may appear obvious to the counselor (or an outside observor) may never have occurred to the client until stated in this way. Similarly, the client's past behavior may be compared to present behavior to indicate both progress in career counseling and to identify new directions in its course. For example, the counselor might point out: "When we first started talking about how you made decisions, you told me you seldom if ever gathered information before you made up your mind about what you were going to do. As a result, many of your decisions didn't work out. But now, before you decide, you take time to get the information you need. That's very good." And then, the counselor might add: "Next, we might talk about what you do *after* you have made a decision. What do you do then?" Comparisons such as these can be used throughout career counseling, but they are most characteristic of the middle stage.

The third technique, which is more pointedly therapeutic in purpose than the other two, is the *interpretation of wish-defense* systems, as exemplified in a case study cited by Cautela (1959). A client who was well suited for medicine by virtue of both abilities and interests, and who was doing well in his premed courses, expressed a desire in career counseling to change his major to architecture, for which he had no apparent talent. In subsequent interviews, he reported that shortly before his decision to consider architecture his mother was almost completely paralyzed due to a cerebral hemorrhage and that his father had intimated that the son was partially responsible because his mother had waited on him continually. On the psychodynamic hypothesis that "buildings symbolically represent the female figure," the counselor interpreted the client's contemplated shift to architecture as a way of "*re*building his mother" and hence reducing his guilt over having originally precipitated her paralysis.

Pursuing the implications of this wish-defense interpretation over a span of twenty interviews (which Psychodynamic career counseling not infrequently runs), the client finally decided that architecture was an unrealistic, reactive choice and that he would pursue his studies in pre-med. In interpreting the wish-defense system, the counselor attempts to bring into the client's awareness the linkage between internal motivational states and the career decision-making process.

Test Interpretation

Bordin has made major contributions to testing in Psychodynamic career counseling. In collaboration with a colleague (Bordin & Bixler, 1946) and in the spirit of the Client-Centered approach, he proposed that the client be an active participant in selecting the tests she or he would take. A description of different types of tests (for example, aptitude, interest, personality) is given to the client, who then determines which kind of self-appraisal information might be most useful in resolving the choice problem. But the counselor actually selects the specific tests (for example, the Strong-Campbell Interest Inventory) to be administered, since she or he knows their psychometric characteristics. Here is an excerpt from Bordin and Bixler (p. 365) illustrating how the counselor might orient a client to an interest inventory:

> Many times these tests can help a person along in this process of puzzling things out by giving them new slants on how they felt about themselves. In one test you would indicate how you feel about yourself in terms of occupational or occupationally-related activities (SVIB). From this you might get a new slant on how you see yourself in terms of occupations.

In other words, the counselor informs the client about the possible benefits of various tests but does not go into a discussion of their technical (psychometric) characteristics. A study by Seeman (1948) indicates that this test selection procedure results in greater client participation and involvement in the career counseling process.

Once the client has taken the tests, Bordin (1968, pp. 296–298) delineates four ways in which they may be used. One is to provide diagnostic information for the counselor. As mentioned previously, diagnosis is central to the Psychodynamic approach, and it is based upon both test results and interview data. Another use is to aid the client in developing more realistic expectations about counseling. Bordin (p. 297) comments that:

> Awareness that the information he gets from tests has not removed his indecision may prepare the defensive client for interpretations, leading to enlightenment concerning his true motives: that he is attempting to use this issue of information as a defense against having to examine himself as a possible source of difficulty.

A third purpose is to make appraisal data available to the client. A central focus of Psychodynamic career counseling is to provide the client with an opportunity for reality testing aspirations and preferences against reliable and relevant test information. Fourth, tests can stimulate the client to greater self-exploration, if used descriptively. This means interpreting scores with reference to the test norms, rather than validity data, so that the client can gain a clearer concept of self. For example, he or she may discover an above average capacity for status but a below average capacity in tolerance. In communicating test results to the client for reality testing and self-exploration, Bordin subscribes to the procedure developed by Bixler and Bixler (1946), in which scores are reported in as nonevaluative a way as possible. The counselor simply gives the client a statistical prediction, such as, "The chances are about 3 ½ to 1 that if you go into this occupation you will stay in it for 20 years or more," and then discusses the client's reaction to this factual statement.

Bordin (1968) has suggested that this method of test interpretation is enhanced by the counselor's verbally relating the client's scores rather than presenting them visually on profile sheets or psychographs. Several advantages accrue from this approach:

1 The counselor can maintain a consistent role as a "collaborator" with the client, rather than shifting to one of "expert" or teacher who explains the psychometric meaning of test scores;

2 The test results can be introduced into the client-counselor interaction as needed, rather than all at once as is routinely done in Trait-and-Factor career counseling;

3 The client has a greater likelihood of remembering the implications of the testing, because they have been expressed and integrated into his or her vernacular and thinking about career choice.

There is compelling research evidence that clients either forget or distort test information disseminated by the traditional method (Froeh-lich & Moser, 1954; Kamm & Wrenn, 1950), a problem that can be largely circumvented by the counselor's verbal presentation of test results as part of the ongoing dialogue with the client. This process is structured initially by the counselor explaining before testing that she or he will *not* present score profiles but rather will discuss their import in counseling as the occasion arises. Most clients agree to this method. Then as the client *needs* test information for career decision making, the counselor responds with it during the interview. For example:

Client: Since I saw you last week, I've been thinking more and more about accounting. What do you think?

Counselor: Well, the interest inventory you took indicates that your interests are very similar to those of accountants. If you went into that occupation, the chances are about 3 to 1 that you would stay in it for a long time—20 years or more—and that you would probably be satisfied with it.

Client: Sounds like a good possibility. Any others I should consider?

Detailed explanations of scores (stanines, percentiles, and so forth) are avoided in this type of presentation; the test results are integrated into the ongoing career decisional and counseling process; and the relationship remains a collaborative, interactive one.

Occupational Information

The type of information about occupations that is integral to Psychody-namic career counseling might best be described as based upon "need analysis" of job duties and tasks. A series of such studies has been conducted under Bordin's general sponsorship at the University of Michigan on accountants and creative writers (Segal, 1961); on dentists, lawyers, and social workers (Nachmann, 1960); on clinical psychologists and physicists (Galinsky, 1962); and on engineers (Beall & Bordin, 1964). In addition, Bordin, Nachmann, and Segal (1963) have delineat-ed several dimensions of psychosexual development along which occupational groups can be characterized in terms of need-gratifying activities and instrumental modes of adjustment to work. Knowledge of

how and why members of specific occupations engage psychodynamically in their jobs as they do can be used to assist clients in choosing
careers in which they may have the greatest probability of satisfying
their needs. Thus, although this is clearly the Trait-and-Factor paradigm
of "matching men and jobs," the variables are personality dynamics
(needs) and gratifying work conditions (satisfiers), rather than the static
characteristics of the individual and occupation.

MATERIALS

To illustrate the psychodynamic approach to career counseling, a case
that exemplifies the intimate relationship between personality dynamics
and career decision making has been selected. This client was a
20-year-old male college student named Randy Grant, a math major in
the middle of his junior year. At the time he applied for counseling,
Randy had a GPA of 3.91, with freshman entrance test scores (ACT
battery) all above the 95th percentile, yet he told the receptionist that he
wanted "academic advising." She noted on his application, however,
that he seemed to be very depressed as well as distracted.

Diagnosis

The first interview was painful for both client and counselor. Randy was
obviously confused and uncomfortable, fidgeting in his chair and talking
in monosyllables. The counselor was trying in vain to find out why
Randy was there and was feeling more and more frustrated with the
convoluted communication. Finally, the counselor decided to move
from the communication dimension to that of relationship, in an effort
to establish some contact. He first reached out and touched Randy
lightly on the shoulder and then said, "Maybe I can tell you a little bit
about myself so you can get to know me better." Randy relaxed visibly
at this gesture and listened intently as the counselor talked about
himself. It was not until half-way through the second interview,
however, that Randy was able to say why he had come for counseling
and, even then, although he was evidently upset personally, he couched
his problem completely in educational and vocational terms. He said
that he was majoring in mathematics, was enjoying it, and was doing
well, although he was self-critical that he had "only" a 3.91 rather than a
4.00 GPA.

By the third interview, the emerging dynamic diagnosis the
counselor was formulating was that Randy had introjected rigid parental
expectations of achievement that demanded almost exclusive interper-

sonal isolation to fulfill. Layered on top of this achievement orientation was intense anxiety associated with any decision making, and particularly with a decision as major as that of career. Randy came from a fundamentalistic religious family, in which his father's authority was complete and unquestioned. His father had either made decisions for Randy or was highly critical of decisions his son made. Either way, Randy felt totally inadequate in decision making and paralyzed by anxiety in career choice. On the Edwards Personal Preference Schedule, which the counselor used to check Randy's diagnostic impressions from the interviews, his highest scores were in Deference, Abasement, and Succorance, with above-average scores in Endurance and Order. His lowest scores were on the "Moving against others" scales.

The counselor interpreted this profile as confirming his interview hypotheses and more fully explicating them. Randy's scores placed him primarily in the "Self-Effecting" sector of the circumplex, with a secondary pattern in the "Resigned" sector. The counselor interpreted these orientations as conflicting ones, with "Moving away from people" being a solution to the problems involved in "Moving toward people" (Horney, 1945; 1950). He saw "Moving against people" as being completely repressed, even when it would be appropriate. Confounded with these interpersonal tendencies was Randy's career indecision ("Undecided" bordering upon "Coerced"): torn by conflicting interpersonal tendencies he became immobilized in deciding what he wanted to do.

Process

Randy's presenting problem, despite his obvious personal involvement, was defined by him as educational and vocational. At the time he entered career counseling, he was hardly emotionally ready to deal with career choice, much less the strong aversive feelings he experienced about it. Consequently, the counselor took Randy on his own psychological level, first making a personal overture to establish some kind of basic contact with him, upon which a counseling relationship might be built. In the beginning, then, exploration of Randy's problems was deliberately circumscribed and contract setting was left implicit, the counselor's expectation being that goals would become more articulate as the relationship strengthened. This was largely what happened, although the counselor realized by the fourth or fifth interview (critical decision stage) that Randy could not work directly upon his personality problems. An indirect approach seemed called for, in which personal and vocational dynamics were juxtaposed. The counselor's technique was to yoke the two with responses such as this: "You came to see me about choosing a career, but you have a hard time talking to me about it. Why is that, Randy?" Randy could respond in this context without feeling threatened by the probability of punishment by a significant other, especially a man.

In the last stage of Randy's career counseling (working for change), he started to actively assume responsibility for his life and career. What had earlier appeared as schizoid tendencies—his depression (or anhedonia) and his interpersonal aversiveness—were definitely ameliorated. His countenance brightened, and he seemed more alert and less distracted during the later interviews. Although he still talked very little, he obviously valued the relationship with the counselor, and never missed an appointment throughout the ten-interview series of his counseling. It was this relationship that was clearly the therapeutic agent for Randy. As he became more and more involved in the relationship, he moved away from what Mowrer (1950) has termed a *defensive* identification with his father, as a means of reactively protecting himself, to a *developmental* identification with the counselor, which provided him with a *modus operandi* for proactively coping with life. Much of this change was nonverbal but nonetheless apparent. Some of it was communicated verbally, when Randy reported a greater engagement with life, a fuller contact with life on a daily basis. And as Freud (1962) astutely observed in *Civilization and Its Discontents,* but unfortunately obscured in a footnote, Randy's principal points of contact with reality were his schoolwork and his career plans. For the first time in college, he was gaining intrinsic satisfaction from his studies, rather than achieving for achievement's sake, and he had applied for a fellowship for graduate training in mathematics.

Outcomes

Career counseling usually involves making a career choice as an outcome, but with Randy it was acting upon a choice that had been made implicitly. Not only was he successful in mathematics; he also seemed to be well-suited to it. He was afraid to "own" his covert decision, however, because of his previous punishment for making decisions. It was not until he experienced a genuine closeness with the counselor that his defensiveness mitigated sufficiently for him to openly act upon what he wanted to do *and* to enjoy it. The experience of joy in his studies, against the background of years of unhappiness, was particularly profound for Randy. He found a new freedom and revelled in it. He had always lived alone on campus, in one of the dorms, but in his senior year he moved off-campus and rented a large, older house with some newly made friends. The summer after he graduated his father wanted (ordered!) him to come home and work on the farm, but after discussing it with the counselor, Randy decided to resist his father's authority and found a highway construction job to earn enough money to start graduate school in the fall. Four years later, he received his Ph.D. with high honors from a major university and took a job as a mathematician with the space program. On that inchoate, almost primordial level of the relationship, Randy had gleaned a subjective synthesis of feeling and meaning that integrated him personally with reality and vocationally with a life's work.

COMMENT

As has been true of psychoanalytic theory in general, the model of Psychodynamic career counseling suffers from the limitation that it disproportionately emphasizes internal factors as the most salient ones in career choice and minimizes external ones (Ginzberg, Ginsburg, Axelrad, & Herma, 1951). The assumption is that "insofar as the client has freedom of choice," career choice is a function of individual psychodynamics, but scant attention is given to the conditions and variables that impose constraints upon the decision-making process (Crites, 1969, Ch. 3).

Moreover, from a behavioristic point of view, the overconcern of the Psychodynamic career counselor with motivational (nonobservable) constructs introduces unnecessary complexity into the conceptualization of career determination. This overconcern rests upon the tenuous assumption that overt decision-making behaviors are somehow mediated by internal needs. This criticism might be less telling were it not that Bordin has not as yet devised an a priori diagnostic system which is linked to differentially effective career counseling methods. He is acutely aware, however, of the need for such a conceptualization when he and Kopplin (1973, p. 160) observe "it would be useful to make more explicit the differential treatment implications of this classification of motivational conflicts related to vocational development." They then propose some general considerations that the psychodynamic career counselor should make in treating clients with different problems. However, these recommendations (for example, "the counselor must explore the family constellation and client's experience of it so as to understand how identity formation is influencing his learning" [Bordin & Kopplin, 1973, p. 169]) are hardly specific enough to guide interview behavior. Their value lies not on this tactical level, but on the strategic one of fashioning career counseling to the psychodynamics of each client, a flexibility and perspicacity in approach that is too often missing from the pedestrian practice of Trait-and-Factor and Client-Centered career counseling.

REFERENCES

Allen, F. H. *Psychotherapy with children.* New York: Norton, 1942.

Beall, L., & Bordin, E. S. The development and personality of engineers. *Personnel and Guidance Journal,* 1964, *43,* 23–32.

Bordin, E. S. Diagnosis in counseling and psychotherapy. *Educational and Psychological Measurement,* 1946, *6,* 169–184.

Bordin, E. S. *Psychological counseling.* (2d ed.) New York: Appleton-Century-Crofts, 1968.

Bordin, E. S., & Bixler, R. H. Test selection: A process of counseling. *Educational and Psychological Measurement,* 1946, *6,* 361–373.

Bordin, E. S., & Kopplin, D. A. Motivational conflict and vocational development. *Journal of Counseling Psychology,* 1973, *20,* 154–161.

Bordin, E. S., Nachmann, B., & Segal, S. J. An articulated framework for vocational development. *Journal of Counseling Psychology,* 1963, *10,* 107–116.

Cautela, J. R. The factor of psychological need in occupational choice. *Personnel and Guidance Journal,* 1959, *38,* 46–48.

Colby, K. M. *A primer for psychotherapists.* New York: Ronald, 1951.

Edwards, W. The theory of decision making. *Psychological Bulletin,* 1954, *51,* 380–417.

Erikson, E. H. *Childhood and society.* New York: Norton, 1963.

Freud, S. *Civilization and its discontents.* New York: Norton, 1962.

Froehlich, C. P., & Moser, W. E. Do counselees remember test scores? *Journal of Counseling Psychology,* 1954, *1,* 149–152.

Galinsky, M. D. Personality development and vocational choice of clinical psychologists and physicians. *Journal of Counseling Psychology,* 1962, *9,* 299–305.

Ginzberg, E., Ginsburg, S. W., Axelrad, S., and Herma, J. L. *Occupational choice.* New York: Columbia University Press, 1951.

Hart, J. T., & Tomlinson, T. M. (Eds), *New directions in client-centered therapy.* Boston: Houghton Mifflin, 1970.

Horney, K. *Our inner conflicts.* New York: Norton, 1945.

Horney, K. *Neurosis and human growth.* New York: Norton, 1950.

Kamm, R. B., & Wrenn, C. G. Client acceptance of self-information in counseling. *Educational and Psychological Measurement,* 1950, *10,* 32–42.

King, P. T., & Bennington, K. F. Psychoanalysis and counseling. In B. Stefflre & W. H. Grant (Eds), *Theories of counseling.* New York: McGraw-Hill, 1972. Pp. 177–242.

Magaret, A. Generalization in successful psychotherapy. *Journal of Consulting Psychology,* 1950, *14,* 64–70.

Mowrer, O. H. *Learning theory and personality dynamics.* New York: Ronald, 1950.

Murray, H. A. *Explorations in personality.* New York: Oxford University Press, 1938.

Nachmann, B. Childhood experience and vocational choice in law, dentistry, and social work. *Journal of Counseling Psychology,* 1960, *7,* 243–250.

Radcliffe, J. A. Some properties of ipsative score matrices and their relevance for some current interest tests. *Australian Journal of Psychology,* 1963, *15,* 1–11.

Segal, S. J. A psychoanalytic analysis of personality factors in vocational choice. *Journal of Counseling Psychology,* 1961, *8,* 202–210.

Shoben, E. J., Jr. Work, love, and maturity. *Personnel and Guidance Journal,* 1956, *34,* 326–332.

Developmental Career Counseling

Neither the Trait-and-Factor nor the Client-Centered approaches to career counseling make mention of the development of the client across the life span as a factor that impinges upon the career choice process. Although the Psychodynamic orientation includes development as a phenomenon related to decision making, it does not articulate the interface between them. Only in Developmental career counseling have the parallels between the individual's overall career maturation and the decisional problems the client talks about in career counseling been drawn.

Developmental career counseling stands in juxtaposition to general career development as microcosm to macrocosm, and as such follows many of the same principles. It is an ongoing process that, although saccadic at times, moves ahead to specifiable outcomes. It can be broken down into discernible stages that unfold in a systematic sequence. It has the now-familiar two dimensions of all career counseling, communication and relationship, but these take on a special significance when viewed within a developmental context. It also intertwines with other facets of development, such as the personal and social, so that intervention in the client's career development can have effects upon cognate developmental processes. Thus, the Developmental approach introduces the time dimension into career counseling and the possibility of all the changes in behavior, whether vocational, personal, or social, which can occur along the time dimension.

MODEL

A confluence of several streams of conceptualization in career counseling has contributed the theoretical foundation upon which the developmental approach to assisting clients engaged in decision making has been built. Foremost among the architects of this frame of reference, and the recognized progenitor of it, is Donald E. Super, who has formulated the precepts and principles of Developmental career counseling since the early 1940s. At that time, when the Trait-and-Factor orientation was predominant, he adapted Buehler's (1933) life-stage schema to the analysis of career behavior in his book, *The Dynamics of Vocational Adjustment* (1942). He did not neglect the demonstrated value of the "actuarial method," as he referred to it later (1954), which he considered to be the "cornerstone of vocational guidance." Indeed his monumental volume, *Appraising Vocational Fitness* (1949), represents the traditional approach at its best, but throughout his treatment of vocational appraisal by means of psychological tests there is interwoven his longstanding commitment to developmental psychology and his nascent self-concept theory. This is evidenced particularly in his summary of the "Nature of Interests," where he proposes that: "Interests are the product of interaction between inherited neural and endocrine factors, on the one hand, and opportunity and social evaluation on the other" (p. 420). He then elaborates upon the role of the self in the formation of interests and projects this process over the developmental continuum by describing the crystallization of interest patterns during adolescence.

His synthesis of these diverse, and often manifestly contradictory, substantive areas evolved through a series of landmark papers (1951; 1954; 1955; 1957a; 1960), a book on the *Psychology of Careers* (1957b), and a Career Pattern Study monograph (Super & Overstreet, 1960). Out of this synthesis there has emerged an orientation, best character- ized as Developmental career counseling, that is unique primarily because of its emphasis upon the total span of career development from childhood through late adulthood. Super (1957) says that orientation to the career choice process should start early and continue until after retirement from the world of work. He sees career development as a continuum "coterminal" with ongoing Developmental career counsel- ing. He likens the relationship between counselor and client in career counseling to the relationships people have with doctors and lawyers: they have continuity over long periods of time. This broad perespective, looking both backward and ahead, is central to Development career counseling:

> The counselor needs to ask himself what has been the patterning of the client's previous educational and vocational career, what its extrapolation or projection into the future suggests may be in store for him, what have been the subsequent careers of others whose early careers resembled that of this client, how this client's personal and social resources may be expected to make his career pattern deviate from the norm, and what he and the client can do together to bring other resources to bear in order to improve his prospects (Super, 1967, p. 320).

Implicit in these considerations is a model of Developmental career counseling based upon distinctive concepts of diagnosis, process, and outcomes.

Diagnosis

Super (1957a) uses the term *appraisal* instead of diagnosis, but he considers them to be essentially synonymous. It is apparent from his discussion of appraisal, however, that this concept is not only broader in scope than diagnosis, but that it also has a more positive connotation and portent. He delineates three kinds of appraisal that focus upon the client's potentialities as well as problems (compare with Witryol & Boly, 1954):

1 *Problem appraisal* The client's experienced difficulty and expectations of career counseling are assessed, much as in the psychodynamic approach, presumably using some classification system such as Bordin's (1946), although Super does not discuss the diagnostic constructs he would use.

2 *Personal appraisal* A psychological picture of the client is obtained from a variety of demographic, psychometric, and social data, the analogue being the clinical case study (Darley, 1940). Both vocational assets and liabilities are assessed and expressed in normative terms (for example, "The client is above average in fine-finger dexterity but below average in clerical speed and accuracy.").

3 *Prognostic appraisal* Based largely upon the personal appraisal, predictions of the client's probable success and satisfaction—the two principal components of career adjustment (Crites, 1969)—are made. More specifically, appraisal data can be collected and organized according to the format shown in Table 5-1, which has been adapted from Super's formulation.

This outline (Table 5-1) can be used for both cross-sectional and developmental appraisals, although Super (1942; 1954) clearly opts for the latter if the appropriate data are available. What he terms the "thematic-expolative" method of appraisal, as contrasted with a more narrowly conceived actuarial model, strives to provide an impression of the client's behavior within a developmental context.

> The assumption underlying this approach is that one way to understand what an individual will do in the future is to understand what she or he did in the past. It postulates that one way to understand what she or he did in the past is to analyze the sequence of events and the development of characteristics in order to ascertain the recurring themes and underlying trends (Super, 1954, p. 13).

From data on the patterning of the client's educational and vocational experiences, from knowledge of the subsequent careers of others like the client at the same life stage, and from assessment of the client's personal resources and competence to use them (Super, 1957b, p. 320), the counselor derives what Pepinsky and Pepinsky (1954) have

Table 5-1 Outline for a Career Appraisal

This outline is applicable to either a counseling or a personnel situation. It might also be used for research purposes. It is designed to summarize background, interview, and test data on an individual in a systematic fashion. Changes in the outline may be necessary, however, to adapt it to special problems or situations.

Title ("Vocational Appraisal of _____ ")

Personal Appraisal (description of the individual in terms of his or her status on psychological, sociological, and physical dimensions).

Present Status and Functioning (1) How does the individual stand on the various pertinent dimensions? What are his or her general and special aptitudes? Interests? Personality characteristics? Attitudes? Educational background and achievement? Socioeconomic status? (2) How is the individual adjusting to the various aspects or areas of his or her physical and psychological environment, including self? What is his or her "self-concept"? Daily pattern of living (sleeping, eating, personal hygiene, study, work, and recreational habits)? What are the nature and quality of his or her relationships with peers? Family? Teachers? Superiors and subordinates? General authorities (administrative officers, police)? What is his or her general level of adjustment? Personality integration? What are his or her predominant adjustment mechanisms?

Developmental History (1) Has the individual had any significant physical illnesses that either affected his or her psychosocial development or left the individual with special disabilities and handicaps? (2) What is the family background of the individual? Intact or broken home? Number and order of siblings? Parents living? Parental attitudes (acceptance, concentrations, avoidance)? Parental identification? What were the individual's relationships to peers (accepted as equal, leader, follower, isolated, and so forth)? (3) Early interests and abilities (hobbies, sports, organizations, and so forth)? (4) Early vocational choices and plans (preferred occupations, age of first choice, motives for choices, indecision)? (5) School achievement and adjustment (grades, attitudes toward school, best- and least-liked subjects, favorite teachers, and so forth)?

Table 5-1 (Continued)

Problem Appraisal (identification of the individual's problem; assessment of strengths as well as weaknesses, for example, motivation to change self or assume responsibility for problem solution, adaptability and flexibility, equanimity and sense of humor, constructive and integrative behavior).

Vocational Problem (1) Classify according to one of the currently available diagnostic systems. (2) Assess the individual's vocational thinking (how involved is she or he in the decision-making process? How does she or he perceive occupations—as ends in themselves or as means to other ends? Does she or he think in "either-or" terms about occupations? How does she or he reason through the problem of vocational choice? Is his or her thinking logical or does it have "psychological" fallacies in it, for example, parataxic distortions? (3) Evaluate whether the individual's vocational problem arises because of immaturity or maladjustment. Does she or he simply not know how to choose an occupation, or is she or he conflicted to the extent that she or he cannot make the appropriate response?

Factors Related to Vocational Problem (1) What part is played by the individual's family in his or her choice problem? (2) What is the relationship of his or her personality to his or her choice problem? (3) What other factors, such as financial resources, military obligations, marriage plans, academic achievement, and so forth, are relevant?

Prognostic Appraisal (predictions about the individual's future behavior in counseling or on the job).

Vocational Counseling (1) Motivation: How well will the individual respond to counseling? Will she or he work on the problem, or will she or he want the counselor to solve it for him/her? Why did she or he apply for counseling? What are his or her expectations? (2) Interview behavior: How will the client respond verbally? Will she or he talk readily or not? How will she or he relate to the counselor? Will she or he be dependent, aggressive, aloof, and so forth? (3) Counseling goals and plans: What can be achieved with this individual? Should the counselor simply give him or her test and occupational information, or should she or he try to think through the vocational problem with the individual? Should the counselor focus only upon the specific choice

---

Table 5-1 (Continued)

problem of the individual, or should she or he help him or her learn how to solve other vocational problems that she or he may encounter in the future? Can the counseling be primarily vocational in nature, or should personal adjustment counseling precede a consideration of the individual's vocational problem? How can the counseling best be implemented? What techniques should be used?

Vocational Adjustment (1) Success: Which occupations are within the limits of the individual's capabilities? (2) Satisfaction: In which occupation is the client most likely to find satisfaction? What problems might his or her personality create for him/her on the job with respect to doing the work itself, getting along with others, and adjusting to the physical conditions of the work, and in realizing his or her aspirations and goals (material rewards, recognition, prestige, etc.)? (3) Contingencies: what factors which are known might either facilitate or adversely affect the individual's future vocational adjustment if they should occur? For example: military service, marriage, change of job duties, transfer to another region of the country, slow or fast promotion, incompatible social life and obligations, etc.

Summary (a "thumb-nail" sketch of the individual that pulls together the various parts of the vocational appraisal).

called a "hypothetical client," which serves as a basis for making predictions about future career development. That is, from this personal appraisal, and with cognizance of the problem appraisal, extrapolations are made as to the client's future career behavior and the effect which interventive career counseling may have upon it.

Throughout this process of accumulating data and making appraisals, the client is an active participant in extrapolating themes concerning his or her career choice and development. Super (1957b, p. 307) states that "the best appraisals are made collectively" and that the counselor's "sharing the results of his appraisal with the client" constitutes a safeguard against faulty inferences (Super, 1957a, p. 158): "The client's reactions to the data and to the counselor's tentative interpretations (often put in the form of a question beginning with 'Could that mean . . .') provide a healthy corrective for the counselor's own possible biases" (Super, 1949, pp. 536–540). By including the client in the appraisal process, Super largely resolves the dilemma, posed by the opposition of Client-Centered theory to the counselor's assuming an evaluative attitude, of whether to diagnose or not. No longer is the counselor solely responsible for the appraisal process. Endorsing and elaborating upon a similar viewpoint proposed by Tyler (1953, p. 103), Super (1957a, p. 156) observes that: "It will be instead a course of action for which the client is completely willing to take the consequences, *leading to a goal which is based on a cooperative realistic appraisal of the factors involved*" (italics are Super's addendum to Tyler). Thus, in Developmental career counseling, as formulated primarily by Super but widely received and refined by others, appraisal (or diagnosis) plays a central role in "getting to know" the client, both hypothetically from life history data and personally from his or her active engagement in the appraisal process.

Process

The course of Developmental career counseling follows closely the broader spectrum of career development. What takes place in the contacts between client and counselor depends upon the point the client has reached on the continuum of career development. The counselor must first determine the career life stage of the client and assess his or her degree of career maturity (Super, 1955). If the client is relatively immature in career behavior, as compared with his or her age or peers (Super & Overstreet, 1960), then Developmental career counseling concentrates upon orientation and exploration, which precede decision making and reality testing in the macrocosm of career development. With the career-immature client, Super and Overstreet (1960, p. 157) observe that:

> It is not so much counseling concerning choice, as counseling to develop readiness for choice, to develop planfulness. It involves helping [the client] to understand the personal, social, and other factors which have a bearing on the making of educational and vocational decisions, and how they may operate in his own vocational development.

In contrast, if the client is more career-mature, that is, has a more fully developed awareness of the need to choose a career, then the counselor proceeds differently.

Working with a client who is vocationally mature is essentially the familiar process of vocational counseling. It involves helping him to assemble, review, and assimilate relevant information about himself and about his situation, which will enable him to draw immediately called-for conclusions as to the implications of these choices for future decisions (Super & Overstreet, 1960, p. 150).

In sum, the overall process of career development progresses from orientation and readiness for career choice to decision making and reality testing, and the Developmental career counselor initiates counseling at that point in the process which the client has reached.

To determine objectively which stage of career development the client is in, Crites (1973; 1978) has constructed the Career Maturity Inventory (CMI), as part of a longitudinal study of career maturity over the past fifteen years. The CMI consists of two parts, each assessing different facets of career maturity: the Attitude Scale and the Competence Test. The former surveys the client's attitudes toward career choice process, the "dispositional response tendencies" that are intimately involved in making a decision. These include: (1) Involvement, (2) Independence, (3) Orientation, (4) Decisiveness, and (5) Compromise. The Competence Test measures the more cognitive aspects of career choice process. They are: (1) Self-Appraisal, (2) Occupational Information, (3) Goal Selection, (4) Planning, and (5) Problem-solving.

Together, the Attitude Scale and the Competence Test encompass the major components in the process of making a career choice. Each item in them was standardized by relating it to either chronological age or school grade (6 through 12). In other words, because all items are time-related, they measure a developmental variable—career maturity.

Other research on the CMI in relation to a host of factors, including indices of both career choice realism and personal/social adjustment, substantiates its validity as an inventory of career maturity. Along with extensive grade/life stage norms, then, it can be used to identify the client's stage of career development and to supplement developmental diagnosis of choice problem by pinpointing those dimensions of career maturity on which the client is relatively behind his or her peers.

Consider the CMI Career Maturity Profile in Figure 5-1 for an undecided ("no career choice") 19-year-old male college freshman who applied for career counseling about midway through his second semester. Comparing him with others of the same chronological age and educational development, he is below average in his rate of career

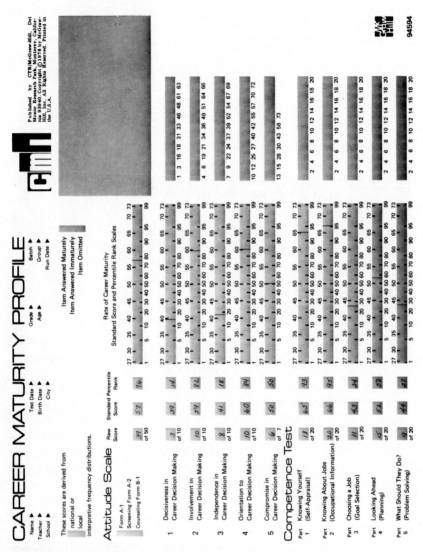

Figure 5-1 Career Maturity Inventory Profile of an undecided client. *(From Career Maturity Inventory devised by John O. Crites. Reprinted by permission of the publisher, CTB/McGraw-Hill, Del Monte Research Park, Monterey, CA 93940. Copyright © 1978 by McGraw-Hill, Inc. All rights reserved. Printed in U.S.A.)*

maturity on the Goal Selection and Problem-solving subtests of the Competence Test and the Independence and Decisiveness subscales of the Attitude Scale, although his total scores on both are about at the norm. Overall, he would appear to be in the Exploratory stage but unable to crystallize a career choice because of certain immature competencies and attitudes. More specifically, his low Goal Selection and Problem-solving scores in relation to his high Self-Appraisal and Occupational Information scores suggest that his decisional problem is *not* one of having adequate information about self and the world of work but of how to relate these to each other.

Because attitudes tend to mediate competencies, his immature Goal Selection and Problem-solving are probably exacerbated by his low Independence and Decisiveness scores. Even if all his competencies were mature, he might still be unable to make a career choice because of his dependence and indecisiveness. The implication for career counseling is twofold: First, information giving in the tradition of the Trait-and-Factor approach would *not* be appropriate. The client is already above average on the informational dimensions of career maturity (S-A and OI). Second, experiences to facilitate the maturation of both those competencies and attitudes that are below average *would be* appropriate. Focusing on one or the other might still leave him undecided about his career choice.

Outcomes

The immediate and more circumscribed objective of Developmental career counseling is to facilitate the client's career development, whether this means fostering increased awareness of the world of work or mastering the career developmental tasks of choosing and implementing a career goal. The maturation of the client toward these outcomes of career development can be charted on a CMI Profile, as shown in Figure 5-1. The CMI can be given both before and after career counseling and scores can be plotted on the profile sheet to determine what gains were made. On the average, without career counseling or other interventions (for example, occupational orientation courses, computer-assisted programs), there is a developmental gain of approximately 2 raw score points on the CMI from one year to another. Consequently, if this much increase is achieved from career counseling, it can be considered highly significant; it is equivalent to about a year's growth in "normal" career development. Actually, there is a considerable amount of accumulated research that indicates the gains from even informal treatments (talking with others about jobs) are greater than the average (2 raw score points). Evidently, the CMI is highly sensitive as an outcome measure to the effects of Developmental career counseling and related experiences (Crites, 1978). It can also be used as part of the treatment process to model optimal career decision making for the client (see "Test Interpretation" below).

The broader, more inclusive goal of Developmental career counseling has been proposed by Super (1955, p. 217) as follows:

> One underlying hypothesis has been that, by relieving tensions, clarifying feelings, giving insight, helping attain success, and developing a feeling of competence in one important area of adjustment, it is possible to release the individual's ability to cope more adequately with other aspects of living, thus bringing about improvements in his general adjustment. A second hypothesis underlying the approach used is that this is best done by building on the individual's assets, by working with his strengths rather than his weaknesses.

The first hypothesis is predicated upon the well-established relationship between general and vocational adjustment, which is moderate positive ($r = .40$) in magnitude. If vocational adjustment can be improved as a function of Developmental career counseling, then general adjustment may also be enhanced. The second hypothesis builds upon the emphasis that developmental psychology places upon growth potentialities in the personality. Rather than necessarily attempting to correct a client's weaknesses, Developmental career counseling capitalizes upon strengths, upon removing the obstacles to and encouraging the fulfillment of potentialities. It augments and facilitates those processes in the client that are conducive to greater career maturity.

That these hypotheses are viable ones is evidenced not only by the demonstrated empirical relationship (moderate positive) between general and career adjustment (Super, 1957; Crites, 1969), but also by the studies of Williams (1962; and Hills, 1962). Here it was found that self-ideal congruence, as an index of personal adjustment status, significantly increases as a by-product of career counseling *without* direct treatment of the client's personality functioning. In short, career counseling can further both career and personal development. There are at least two reasons why this relationship obtains: One is that most of the individual's waking hours are spent either in preparing for or engaging in work. Work is central to life; consequently, how we adjust to work constitutes a major component in overall or general adjustment. If career counseling enhances the client's vocational adjustment, it will most likely have a positive effect upon his or her general adjustment.

The second reason this relationship exists is that career counseling is an interpersonal process. The client is involved in a meaningful relationship with the counselor where the ability to get along with another is both modeled and learned. As much research has demonstrated (Crites, 1969), this is a critical factor in career adjustment. Workers who cannot get along with others on the job are more likely to be failures. Thus, career counseling impacts an interpersonal dimension that also cuts across career and general adjustment.

METHODS

Much as the model of Developmental career counseling reflects an integration of different conceptual and substantive emphases, so, too, the methods of this approach are a synthesis of diverse counseling procedures. They have been drawn by Super and others primarily from the Trait-and-Factor and Client-Centered orientations, although the influence of developmental principles is also apparent. That the synthesis is more than a superficial eclecticism follows from Super's (1951) interweaving of career counseling conceived as information giving and as personal therapy. His basic premise is that people are both rational *and* emotional and that, therefore, "the best vocational counseling is a combination of the two, somewhere between the theoretical extremes" (Super, 1951, p. 91). He then describes such a middle road in terms of the kinds of questions the counselor may assist the client in answering:

> What sort of person do I *think* I am?
> How do I feel about myself as I think I am?
> What sort of person would I *like* to be?
> What are my values and needs?
> What are my aptitudes and interests?
> What can I do to reconcile my self-ideal with my real self?
> What outlets are there for me with my needs, values, interests, and aptitudes?
> How can I make use of these outlets?

Consonant with the foci of these questions, upon both the objective and subjective facets of the client's personality and environment, are the modus operandi of Developmental career counseling: its interview techniques, test interpretation procedures, and uses of occupational information.

Interview Techniques

Because Super sees career counseling as dealing with both the rational and emotional aspects of self-exploration, decision making, and reality testing, he contends that, if the techniques of interviewing are appropriate and consistent, they should occur in approximately the following cycle (Super 1957, p. 308):

  1 Nondirective problem exploration and self-concept portrayal
  2 Directive topic setting, for further exploration
  3 Nondirective reflection and clarification of feeling for self-acceptance and insight
  4 Directive exploration of factual data from tests, occupational pamphlets, extracurricular experiences, grades, etc., for reality testing
  5 Nondirective exploration and working through of attitudes and feelings aroused by reality testing
  6 Nondirective consideration of possible lines of action, for help in decision making

Kilby (1949) has outlined a similar sequence of the cyclical use of directive and nondirective interviewing techniques in career counseling. The essence of this cyclical approach is to respond directively to content statements by the client and nondirectively to expressions of feeling. Thus, the counselor ranges back and forth among such response categories as restatement, reflection, clarification, summary, interpretation, and confrontation (Robinson, 1950).

Super does not link these counselor interview techniques directly to the process of Developmental career counseling. Extrapolating from the Psychodynamic approach and relating its counselor response categories to the major stages in career development, however, the two can be synthesized as follows: During the opening phase of Developmental career counseling, when the focus is upon exploration of the range of career options open to the client, clarifications and interpositions (see Chapter 4) can be used by the counselor to increase the client's awareness of a broader range of career options that she or he has considered previously. A possible response might be: "Have you thought about any other occupations like singing but which would combine your artistic interests with your verbal abilities?"

To assist the client in narrowing down the career options available to him or her, which typically occurs during the middle stage of Developmental career counseling, and which parallels the crystallization stage in career development (Ginzberg et al., 1951), the counselor can respond with juxtapositions, thereby highlighting the desirable/undesirable aspects of different occupations. To illustrate: "On the one hand, sales work means good income but, on the other hand, you have to travel a lot. How can you resolve this?"

Finally, in the last stage of the career counseling process within the Developmental framework, when the client has specified career goals and is planning how to achieve them, the counselor can rely more and more upon declarative statements (for example, "That sounds like a good idea to me. Get your application in for a direct student loan as soon as possible.") to facilitate implementation of career choice. Thus, interview techniques appropriate to the corresponding stages in the macrocosm of the client's career development and the microcosm of Developmental career counseling can be used differentially by the counselor.

Two other interview techniques available to the counselor in Developmental career counseling are the career autobiography and the decisional diary. To gain some understanding of how the client has made decisions in the past, a career autobiography can be useful not only as a review for the client, but also as a catalyst for discussion during the interview. The autobiography recounts such major choices as high school curriculum (college preparatory, business, industrial arts, and so forth) as well as college selection, post-high-school training, part-time work experience, and other life decisions. It illuminates who the "significant others" who most influenced the client's decision making were—parents, relatives, friends, teachers, counselors?

Answers to these and similar questions indicate to the counselor the extent to which the client has assumed personal responsibility for choice and its consequences, has utilized informational resources in decision making, has coped with bad decisions and obstacles to plans, and myriad other aspects of the career choice process. The decisional diary supplements the career autobiography with a current account of how the client is making daily decisions. These should include not only thinking about one's career but any life decision confronted by the client—what to do, what to wear, what to buy, and so forth.

Together, these interview aids stimulate discussion topics relevant to career choice, and they constitute part of the career counseling. There is a reactive effect, an increased awareness and sensitization, upon the client simply by engaging her or him in the activities of writing a career autobiography and keeping a decisional diary. The client can then better articulate and participate in the process of career decision making.

Test Interpretation

The philosophy and pragmatics of using tests in Developmental career counseling which Super has evolved, as is true of his entire approach, synthesizes the best of other orientations into a coherent method for disseminating psychometrics to the client, so that they will be maximally useful. The rationale for his use of tests stems from the distinction between *saturation* and *precision* testing, the former referring to a battery of tests administered to the client usually after a short, preliminary interview (as in Trait-and-Factor career counseling) and the latter designating individual test administration throughout the course of career counseling. With reference to precision testing, Super (1950, p. 96) describes it as:

> testing which is done as part of the counseling process, to get needed facts as these facts are needed and as the individual is ready to use them. It is *testing-in-counseling.*

As such, the client is intimately involved in selecting, taking, and interpreting the tests, and, as a consequence, the likelihood increases that "the test results will be accepted and used intelligently by the client." Adding to this procedure the verbal (rather than visual) presentation of the test results to the client (see Chapter 4) facilitates even more the incorporation of this information into the client's thought processes about career choice.

Particularly is this the case, if the counselor orients the client with respect to the precision use of tests in career counseling. Structuring how the process will unfold, both verbally and nonverbally, gives the client an explicit expectation of what is going to happen and counteracts the stereotype of saturation testing which many clients bring to the initial interview (Super & Crites, 1962, pp. 613–620). The "test them and tell them" tradition, especially in the secondary schools, is so strong that it is critical for the Developmental career counselor to fully inform and discuss with the client the precision use of tests. If the counselor plans to introduce the test results verbally into the counseling interaction, she or he should explain to the client that, possibly in contrast to expectations, profiles and psychographs will not be used. Should the client object to this procedure, then it can become an issue in the counseling for discussion and negotiation. To prepare for precision, verbal interpretation of test scores, the counselor must review them before each interview, so that she or he is current on what they are and what their significance is. The thrust of using tests in Developmental career counseling, then, is to maximize their value in decision making by (1) administering them in a discriminating way and (2) involving the client in every phase of the process.

The prototypic test interpretation process in Developmental career counseling can be illustrated with the Career Maturity Inventory. Because considerations of career choice process usually precede considerations of content, the CMI is typically administered early in career counseling. During the first couple of interviews, the Developmental career counselor may take a decision-making history from the client, possibly keyed to the career autobiography. Then the counselor would suggest the administration of the CMI as a means of gaining a further understanding of the client's career choice attitudes and competencies. If the counselor decides to interpret the CMI verbally rather than visually (that is, presenting the Career Maturity profile sheet), then this approach should be discussed with the client. The counselor might say: "After you have taken the Career Maturity Inventory, I'll discuss the results with you as we talk about your career choice and plans." If the counselor interprets the CMI from the profile sheet, the Career Maturity Guide can be used as a supplementary aid for the client. This is a workbook keyed to the CMI "Response Record" on the profile sheet. It suggests to the client resources and experiences that are designed to increase career maturity. The Guide can also be completed by the client alone, since it is a self-administering, programmed booklet (Crites, 1978).

Occupational Information

To inform the client about the structure of the world of work, occupational trends and forecasts, job duties and tasks, and employment opportunities, traditional types of occupational information can be presented by brochures, pamphlets, or volumes like the *Occupational Outlook Handbook*. The most appropriate information for Developmental career counseling, however, is the description of career patterns in different occupational pursuits. There have been some studies of career patterns, notably those of Davidson and Anderson (1937) and

Miller and Form (1951), but they are out-of-date now and dealt only with occupational level, not field. Super (1954, pp. 17–18) observes that there are at least six kinds of descriptive data on career patterns that are needed for Developmental career counseling:

   1 What are the typical entry, intermediate, and regular adult occupations of persons from different socioeconomic levels?
   2 To what extent do "regular adult occupations" exist, and what is the relationship between parental socioeconomic level and having a regular adult occupation?
   3 What are the lines and rates of movement from entry toward regular adult occupation?
   4 What factors are related to the direction and rate of movement from one job or occupation to another?
   5 What is the relationship between occupational field and factors such as accessibility of the occupation or industry, and the possession of various aptitudes, values, and personality characteristics?
   6 What is the relationship of differences between actual and parental occupational levels to possible causal factors such as accessibility of the occupation or industry, and the possession of aptitudes, interests, values, personality characteristics?

Unfortunately, both private publishers and governmental agencies, as well as professional organizations, continue to proliferate occupational information that is largely irrelevant for Developmental career counseling. In lieu of career pattern data, the career counselor must rely upon his or her knowledge of career psychology, leavened with astute observation and personal experience.

MATERIALS

Ideally, a case study of the Developmental approach to career counseling would span several years. Unfortunately, it is rare for a counselor to maintain extended contact with former clients, and subjects in long-term, ongoing research projects are not usually exposed to counseling. Thus, some compromise on a developmental case is necessary. The individual chosen to exemplify Developmental career counseling, a 20-year-old college junior female, was first seen by another counselor in high school (10th-12th grades), who provided observations on her earlier career behavior. The client's name was Susan Gotham, and she completed the time span from high school to the present by periodically writing about what she was doing and how she felt about her life.

Diagnosis

When Susan was first seen at her college counseling center, she said she was struggling with the choice of a major. It was at the beginning of her junior year, and she had let the decision go to the eleventh hour. Her advisor was pressing her to declare her area of concentration, and she had become increasingly anxious about making a decision, yet concomitantly less able to do so. She experienced intense conflict, dating back to high-school years, around pursuing a career or becoming a homemaker. Case notes from her high school counselor, as well as standardized ability and interest scores, indicated that she had superior scholastic aptitude and primary interests in the professions, yet she was expected by her parents to be a housewife without any career commitment, although they supported her going to college to get "a liberal education" and to "find a husband." Similarly, most of her closest girlfriends in high school had either married upon graduation or intended to do so as soon as possible. Susan responded subjectively to these interpersonal influences, but she was objectively disquieted by her outstanding academic achievement, which placed her at the top of her class, and how she might fulfill her intellectual capabilities and potentialities without working. The counselor interpreted her dilemma as not uncommon for bright, young women who are caught in the developmental "contra-trends" of being career mature in the decision-making process, but unrealistic in career choice because of the overdetermining potency of the socialization process, which often exerts inordinate pressure upon them to get married or enter highly sex-stereotyped occupations (Crites, 1975).

His developmental diagnosis of Susan's choice problem, based upon her former counselor's summary and his interview interactions with her, was that she could not resolve the home/career dilemma. He supplemented these impressions with the Career Maturity Inventory, which Susan took after the second interview, following a discussion of her decision-making attitudes and competencies, and the California Psychological Inventory, which she had completed between the intake and initial interviews upon his request to gain a fuller understanding of her personality characteristics and functioning. The results from these inventories confirmed and extended the counselor's diagnosis. On the

CMI, Susan's scores were mostly above average, with the exception of the Goal Selection subtest of the Competence battery. On the Attitude Scale, she was at the 95th percentile. The items that she endorsed in the keyed "immature direction," however, revealed two response tendencies. One reflected her decisional conflict, not being able to choose between home and career, and the other her inclination to rely upon extraneous events, that is, chance occurrences and trial-and-error, to resolve the choice problem for her. These aspects of her career maturity interfaced with her personality development as assessed by the CPI. The overall elevation of her profile, keyed by the high Ie (Intellectual efficiency) score, substantiated the counselor's interview evaluation of her as a generally well-adjusted person who was functioning well intellectually. Her predominant mode of adjustment was one of social ascendance and dominance, the core of which was a desire to accommodate and please others, to make the socially desirable response. Herein lay a large part of her choice problem: She experienced extreme difficulty in saying what *she* wanted and running the risk of alienating or incurring the disfavor (or criticism) of others. She wanted a career, but others wanted her to have a home. The consequence: conflict and indecision.

Process

Both the developmental and therapeutic implications of the diagnosis for Susan's career counseling were complex. Along the dimension of career choice process, as assessed by the CMI, she was relatively mature, but on the dimension of career choice content, she was immature because she had not chosen a college major when confronted by this career developmental task. From her personality characteristics, as measured by the CPI, the counselor concluded that these contra-trends in Susan's career development were a function of her personality development. Her approach to life was to live within a largely nondiscriminating audience and communality based upon strong denial mechanisms that almost precluded her making the negative decisions essential to the "choice act." Her indecision stemmed from her inability to say "no" to either options or others. In short, like a child who likes everything and everybody, Susan was personally immature. To assist her in differentiating this generalized "yeasaying" response tendency, on the hypothesis that intervention in her personal development would facilitate her career development with respect to choice content, the counselor used essentially two techniques. First, he asked Susan to keep a daily "decisional diary," which they reviewed at the beginning of each interview, focusing upon whatever negative decisions she had made and how she felt about them. This procedure heightened her awareness of the decision-making process (that is, the reactivity of keeping the diary) and emphasized the necessity of excluding options to arrive at a decision.

Second, the counselor engaged Susan in a series of role-playing sessions, during which he asked her to do something she did not want to do. For example, she had a part-time job teaching blind and deaf children certain rudimentary personal and social skills three times a week. The counselor took the role of her supervisor and asked her whether she would take the children, on her own time, for a picnic in the park. He explained that the staff member who usually did this was sick. In the past, Susan's inclination would have been to immediately acquiesce to the supervisor's request and then later have vague but unconscious feelings of resentment. In the role-playing, which the counselor video-taped, she tried out several alternative ways of coping with the situation, some of which involved saying "yes," but only after she had fully expressed what she wanted. After the role-playing, the counselor played the video-tape back with Susan and explored with her how she felt at different times during the interaction. He supplemented this approach with the administration of ipsative-type inventories of Susan's interests and values, including the Kuder Occupational Interest Survey (Form DD) and the Allport-Vernon-Lindzey Study of Values. These "forced choice" instruments not only gave Susan experience in choosing between given options, but also the scores indicated the intra-individual similarity/strength of her interests and values.

Outcomes

Susan's career counseling extended over eleven interviews, with periodic follow-up correspondence during the next two years. The developmental trend line, both vocational and personal, was generally positive—toward greater maturity. Her decisional diary, for example, evinced increasing negative decision-making facility. By the terminal interview, she was not only able to tell others what she wanted but also able to say "no" when she felt it appropriate, without the fear of lost affection or approval. By this last interview she had decided upon a college major and future career, which she could combine with homemaking but which she could pursue as a bona fide career: recreational therapy. This occupation combined her two strongest academic interests, physical education and psychology, and it provided an outlet for her people-oriented personality characteristics. Academically, she was more than capable enough to take a double major in physical education and psychology and to complete her master's degree in recreational therapy. She found out that job opportunities in this field were plentiful and eventually entered it after completing her graduate work with straight A's. She had no difficulty in finding a position to her liking and wrote that she was enjoying her work. She also reported that she felt her interpersonal relationships were more cooperative and equitable and that she was no longer assuming more than her share in them. Thus, we see in her career counseling a confluence of career and personal development that culminated in a career choice she could convert "into a reality, with satisfaction to [herself] and benefit to society" (Super, 1957b, p. 197).

COMMENT

The hallmark of Development career counseling is its synthesis of several theoretical and procedural strands, particularly the Trait-and-Factor and Client-Centered. But it goes beyond these and casts them into the context of the client's ongoing career development, which Super (1957b) aptly characterizes as "coterminal" with career counseling. Some may contend, however, that even as comprehensive an approach as this suffers from conceptual lacunae which make it less than optimally effective. Psychodynamically oriented career counselors might question the basically descriptive or normative, rather than explanatory, nature of developmental concepts and principles, whereas certain behavioristically inclined career counselors might contend that the historical focus of Developmental career counseling is unnecessary, since career behavior is largely conditioned by its consequences, not its antecedents. Perhaps these are less shortcomings of commission than they are of omission. Only recently have measures of career maturity (Super, 1974) been constructed and related to other aspects of personality functioning (Crites, 1973). Likewise, conceptualization of learning models of career development has just begun (Crites, 1971), but research designed to test them has been initiated (Oliver, 1973). All of which leads to the conclusion that, although Developmental career counseling may still be incomplete in certain respects, it is the most comprehensive and coherent system of assisting clients with career problems which has as yet been formulated, and it may be refined even further by articulating its relationship to learning phenomena and processes.

REFERENCES

Buehler, C. *Der menschliche Lebensauf als psychologisches Problem.* Leipzig: Hirzel, 1933.

Crites, J. O. The maturity of vocational attitudes and learning processes in adolescence. Paper presented at the 17th Annual Convention of the International Congress of Applied Psychology, Liege, Belgium, 1971.

Crites, J. O. *Theory and research handbook for the Career Maturity Inventory.* Monterey, Calif.: CTB-McGraw-Hill, 1973; 1978.

Darley, J. B. The structure of the systemic case study in individual diagnosis and counseling. *Journal of Counseling Psychology,* 1940, *4,* 215–220.

Davidson, P. E., & Anderson, H. B. *Occupational mobility in an American community.* Palo Alto: Stanford University Press, 1937.

Ginzberg, E., Ginsburg, S. W., Axelrad, S., & Herma, J. L. *Occupational choice.* New York: Columbia University Press, 1951.

Kilby, R. W. Some vocational counseling methods. *Educational and Psychological Measurement,* 1949, *19,* 173–192.

Miller, D. C., & Form, W. H. *Industrial sociology.* New York: Harper & Row, 1951.

Oliver, L. Verbal reinforcement of career choice realism in relation to career attitude maturity. Unpublished manuscript, Department of Psychology, University of Maryland, 1973.

Pepinsky, H. B., & Pepinsky, P. N. *Counseling theory and practice.* New York: Ronald, 1954.

Robinson, F. P. *Principles and procedures in student counseling.* New York: Harper, 1950.

Super, D. E. *The dynamics of vocational adjustment.* New York: Harper, 1942.

Super, D. E. *Appraising vocational fitness.* New York: Harper, 1949.

Super, D. E. Vocational adjustment: Implementing a self-concept. *Occupations,* 1951, *30,* 88–92.

Super, D. E. Career patterns as a basis for vocational counseling. *Journal of Counseling Psychology,* 1954, *1,* 12–20.

Super, D. E. The dimensions and measurement of vocational maturity. *Teachers College Record,* 1955, *57,* 151–163.

Super, D. E. The preliminary appraisal in vocational counseling. *Personnel and Guidance Journal,* 1957, *36,* 154–161. (a)

Super, D. E. *The psychology of careers.* New York: Harper, 1957. (b)

Super, D. E. The critical ninth grade: Vocational choice or vocational exploration? *Personnel and Guidance Journal,* 1960, *39,* 106–109.

Super, D. E. (Ed.), *Measuring vocational maturity for counseling and evaluation.* Washington, D. C.: National Vocational Guidance Association, 1974.

Super, D. E., & Overstreet, P. L. *The career maturity of ninth grade boys.* New York: Teachers College Bureau of Publications, 1960.

Tyler, L. E. *The work of the counselor.* (2nd ed.). New York: Appleton-Century-Crofts, 1961.

Williams, J. E. Changes in self and other perceptions following brief educational-vocational counseling. *Journal of Counseling Psychology,* 1962, *9,* 18–30.

Williams, J. E., & Hills, D. A. More on brief educational-vocational counseling. *Journal of Counseling Psychology,* 1962, *9,* 366–368.

Witryol, S. L., & Boly, L. F. Positive diagnosis in personality of college students. *Journal of Counseling Psychology,* 1954, *1,* 63–69.

Behavioral Career Counseling

6

All the approaches to career counseling that we have reviewed thus far have been formulated more in terms of content than process. That is, they have been distinguished by certain central organizing concepts: Trait-and-Factor focuses upon individual differences in ability, interest, and personality; Client-Centered emphasizes the self-concept and phenomenal field; Psychodynamic highlights internal motivating variables and coping mechanisms related to them; and Developmental traces the maturation of career behavior across the life span.

In contrast, the Behavioral approach to career counseling deals almost exclusively with the process of learning as it impinges upon career decision making. The critical question from this orientation is: What are the principles of learning that govern the making of realistic career choices? The substantive aspects of decision making are incidental to an understanding of the behavioral laws that determine *how* career choices are made rather than *what* they are. The underlying assumption is that, once these laws have been explicated, problems in career decision making can be assessed and corrected by instituting changes in the process of learning. Thus, the point of intervention in Behavioral career counseling is where deficient or deviant learning has occurred.

MODEL

It is more accurate to refer to the *models* for this approach rather than the *model*. Goodstein (1972) observes that, although they share common antecedents in the experimental psychology of learning, there are two distinct orientations in behavioral counseling. The *indirect* focuses upon the linguistic mediational variables that precede and elicit overt responses, and the *direct* concentrates upon the consequences of responses—whether they are followed by a rewarding or punishing state of affairs. A further differentiation might also be made between two emphases within direct behavioral counseling, which might be labeled behavioral-*theoretic* and behavioral-*pragmatic*. As these designations connote, the former draws upon concepts and principles from learning theory to explain career behaviors and to deduce counseling methods for changing them. The latter proceeds more inductively and empirically to identify those techniques that work in bringing about behavioral changes, the recognized proponents of the two viewpoints being Goodstein (1972) and Krumboltz and Thoresen (1969; 1976), respectively.

Although Goodstein makes an invaluable contribution to the

analysis and diagnosis of indecision versus indecisiveness (see below), he does not offer a general theory of career choice from which his approach to Behavioral career counseling is deduced. Krumboltz (1978) has at least proposed such a theory, although he has not formally articulated its relationship to career counseling. In this theory, he draws upon both associative and instrumental concepts of learning that explain the career decisions an individual makes. He states the theory in a series of propositions and hypotheses that delineate the positive and negative influences upon:

1 The development of educational/vocational preferences
2 The acquisition of career decision-making skills
3 The factors that affect entry into training programs and the world of work

The theory is calibrated to the time dimension, so that certain events, influencers, and options are seen as preceding others, and it is this temporal sequencing that provides an interface with the steps in Behavioral career counseling as Krumboltz and Baker (1973, p. 240) had previously delineated them:

1 Defining the problem and the client's goals
2 Agreeing mutually to achieve counseling goals
3 Generating alternative problem solutions
4 Collecting information about the alternatives
5 Examining the consequences of the alternatives
6 Revaluing goals, alternatives, and consequences
7 Making the decision or tentatively selecting an alternative contingent upon new developments and new opportunities
8 Generalizing the decision-making process to new problems

Together with Goodstein's application of the behavioral-theoretic position, this schema of behavioral-pragmatic career counseling constitutes the model within which behavioral concepts of diagnosis, process, and outcome have been formulated.

Diagnosis

Goodstein (1972) attributes a central role to anxiety in the etiology of behavioral problems in general, and career choice problems in particular. Of the latter, he makes a detailed analysis of the part that anxiety can play, both as an antecedent and a consequent, in career indecision. He distinguishes between what might be called simple *indecision* and pervasive *indecisiveness* (Tyler, 1961). These two types of client choice problems can be conceptualized as shown in Figure 6-1 (Crites, 1969, p. 600), where it can be seen that they develop sequentially from different origins.

The principal etiological factor in simple indecision, according to Goodstein, is lack of information about self and work due to a limitation of experience, much as is assumed in the classical Trait-and-Factor approach. The client cannot make a choice, or possibly makes an unrealistic one, and as a consequent feels anxious about not having mastered the career developmental task of declaring an appropriate vocation, often expressed socially as "What are you going to do when you grow up?" Note that in this process the anxiety is a *consequent,* not an antecedent of the indecision. In contrast, indecisiveness arises from long-standing anxiety associated with decision making that precedes the task of career choice, not infrequently attributed by clients to domineering or overdemanding parents. For this individual, who is often paralyzed in making any kind of choice, anxiety also follows failure to decide upon a career, that is, anxiety is both an antecedent *and* a consequent, thereby compounding the client's feelings of discomfort and inadequacy.

To differentially diagnose indecision and indecisiveness, that is, to distinguish between them, after career counseling is not particularly difficult. If a client who comes in with "no choice" is still undecided after career counseling, during which relevant information on self and occupations was given, then she or he is most likely indecisive. In other words, the indecision is not simply a function of lack of information; otherwise, she or he would have made a decision. But being able to make a diagnosis post hoc is of little or no use in career counseling. How can this be done before the process begins or, at least, during the first few interviews? There is little research on indecision versus indecisiveness, but what there is in combination with clinical experience suggests this diagnostic procedure. First, administer a reliable and valid measure of anxiety, such as the Spielberger, et al. (1970), which yield scores for both trait and state anxiety. Note which is higher, the indecisive client typically having a higher trait anxiety score. Second, administer the Attitude Scale and Competence Test of the Career Maturity Inventory (Crites, 1978) to assess availability of experience and amount of information about the career choice process. Finally, interpret this configuration of scores to make a diagnosis. Clients with simple *indecision* will usually have low to average trait anxiety scores, but average to above-average state scores; their CMI scores will be about

(Indecision)

Limitation of experience → Inadequate or non-adaptive behavior → Failure → Anxiety (Consequent)

(Insufficient opportunity to acquire or learn adaptive or adequate responses) → (No vocational choice; unrealistic vocational choice) → (Unable to solve choice problem) → (Conflict between inability to solve choice problem and social pressure to do so)

(Indecisiveness)

Availability of experience → Anxiety (Antecedent) → No use of learning opportunities → Inadequate or non-adaptive behavior

(Sufficient opportunity to acquire or learn adaptive or adequate responses)

(Making a choice is anxiety-arousing, because it may mean defying parents, becoming independent, etc., all of which "cue" anxiety)

(May have appropriate information for making a choice but anxiety prevents him from utilizing it, or anxiety may interfere with acquisition of information, even though opportunity to learn it is available)

Inadequate or non-adaptive behavior (No vocational choice of unrealistic choice)

Failure (Unable to solve choice problem)

Anxiety (Consequent) (Conflict between inability to solve choice problem and social pressure to do so)

Figure 6-1 Indecision versus indecisiveness in career choice. *(Crites, 1969, p. 600)*

147

average, with the Competence Test low on Self-Appraisal and Occupational Information. In contrast, clients with pervasive *indecisiveness* will have high trait anxiety scores with average state scores; their CMI-Attitude scores will be average to low, but their Competence Test will be average to high. Of course, some clients who suffer from both antecedent anxiety associated with decision making *and* limitation of experience will have high trait and state anxiety scores and low CMI scores. They would placed be in the maladjusted category discussed in Chapter 2.

Krumboltz and Thoresen (1969) eschew this diagnostic approach in their pragmatically oriented version of Behavioral career counseling. They seldom mention either anxiety or diagnosis, preferring the rubrics *behavioral analysis* or *problem identification,* and they closely relate these to the specification of goals for counseling. That is, the client's difficulties are complementary to the goals (outcomes) that client and counselor strive to achieve through their interaction with each other. Thus, if the client's presenting problem is that she or he has "no career choice," then the goal of career counseling is to make a career choice. Krumboltz and Thoresen (1969, pp. 9–18) enumerate seven general categories of problems (difficulties in formulating goals) that may beset clients in counseling:

1 The problem is someone else's behavior.
2 The problem is expressed as a feeling.
3 The problem is the absence of a goal.
4 The problem is that the desired behavior is undesirable.
5 The problem is that the client does not know his behavior is inappropriate.
6 The problem is a choice conflict.
7 The problem is a vested interest in not identifying any problem.

Of these problems, those which bear upon career counseling are indecision (absence of a goal), unrealism (expressed feeling about overly high aspirations), and multipotentiality (choice conflict among equally desirable alternatives). Within each of these problem types, specific behaviors can be delineated as the goals of career counseling (see "Outcomes").

Process

In the behavioral-theoretic view of career counseling, if it is determined diagnostically that a client's decision-making problems are a function of antecedent anxiety, then it is assumed that this anxiety must be eliminated before effective cognitive consideration of career choice can be undertaken. In other words, the elimination of anxiety is a sine qua non for subsequent career decision making. In this case, then, the process of career counseling has two stages, much as Shoben (1949) has proposed for psychotherapy. During the first stage, the counselor attempts to eliminate the anxiety associated with decision making, whether career or otherwise, primarily through counterconditioning it. In the second stage, after the client has been freed of the interfering effects of anxiety, instrumental learning can occur in which the client can acquire those responses needed to choose a career, for example, information seeking.

If the client's problem is one of simple indecision, however, with no evidence of debilitating previous anxiety, then career counseling would begin with stage two, instrumental learning. What this client needs to learn is *how* to make a career choice, *which* options are available to him or her, and *what* the consequences of each are. He or she is exposed to the experiences that have not been available in prior career development. Thus, the process of career counseling, as deduced from behavior theory primarily by Goodstein (1972), varies with the etiology of the client's problem. If the problem involves antecedent anxiety (indecisiveness), there are two stages, one of counterconditioning and the other of instrumental learning. If the problem stems from limited experience (indecision), it involves only instrumental learning.

More specifically, the counterconditioning process can be schematized as shown in Figure 6-2. The unconditioned stimulus (UCS) is the client's talk about making decisions, whether in the past or present. This talk elicits the unconditioned response (UCR), which is the anxiety the client experiences when talking about making decisions. In other words, through the learning process anxiety has become associated with decision making. To counteract this bond, the conditioned stimulus (CS) of the relationship with the counselor is paired (contiguous in time) with the talk of the client about decision making. If the relationship is nonthreatening, that is, it fulfills the conditions of acceptance or nonretaliatory permissiveness and unconditional positive regard or warm concern (see Chapters 3 and 4), then it should stimulate in the client feelings of comfort, safety, confidence, and hopefulness, which are the conditioned response (CR). As the CR becomes stronger, it eventually replaces the UCR in the client's response hierarchy. Now the client can talk about decision making without the competing response of anxiety, which has been counterconditioned through the relationship

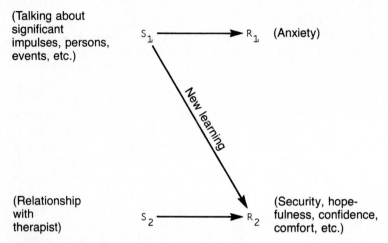

(Talking about significant impulses, persons, events, etc.)

$S_1 \longrightarrow R_1$ (Anxiety)

New learning

(Relationship with therapist)

$S_2 \longrightarrow R_2$ (Security, hopefulness, confidence, comfort, etc.)

Figure 6-2 Counterconditioning anxiety associated with career decision making. *(Shaffer & Shoben, 1956, p. 534)*

with the counselor. Note that it is critical to establish the security of the relationship with the client *before* dealing with material that is anxiety-arousing. Otherwise, the client will become so anxious she or he will most likely break contact. Conversely, if the relationship is established without talking about anxiety-arousing topics, there is the likelihood of fostering a dependence in the client that is prolonged and nonproductive.

Juxtaposed to this model is that of Krumboltz, Thoresen, and others, the most recent exposition of which has been summarized by Krumboltz and Baker (1973, p. 240 passim), who have enumerated eight steps taken by the counselor and client in the course of career counseling previously mentioned. This series of mutual actions on the part of the counselor and client generally follows informed opinion on how career decisions can best be made (Gelatt, 1962; Yabroff, 1969), but it is not necessarily invariant: "The sequence may vary, but the priorities remain" (Krumboltz & Baker, 1973, p. 240). Conspicuous by its absence in this process is any mention of anxiety or its reduction. Rather, the focus is upon "the external environment of each client and the interaction of the person with his environment" (Krumboltz & Baker, 1973, p. 262). Behavioral-pragmatic career counseling, therefore, appears to be closely aligned with the view expressed by Eysenck (1960) and others that:

anxiety elimination should not be the counselor's primary concern, but rather that therapy should be directed at the elimination of nonadjustive behavior patterns and/or providing conditions for learning more adjustive responses (Goldstein, 1972, p. 274).

Outcomes

The two hypothesized outcomes of behavioral-theoretic career counseling are (1) elimination or reduction of both antecedent and consequent anxiety and/or (2) acquisition of decision-making skills. Whether both outcomes are expected depends upon the extent to which anxiety preceded the emergence of the client's problem, as mentioned earlier (Figure 6-1). An experimental paradigm for evaluating the effectiveness of this variety of behavioral counseling is outlined in Figure 6-3 (Crites, 1969, p. 602). Included in it are measures of anxiety (Manifest Anxiety Scale) and career maturity (Career Maturity Inventory), not only as criterion variables but also (on pretest) as possible diagnostic indicators of indecision versus indecisiveness. The design also allows for the operational differentiation of indecision and indecisiveness. That is, those clients with "no choice" on pretest who still are undecided on posttest, after having been exposed to an informational intervention, are operationally defined as *indecisive*. In contrast, those who make a choice after being given information are defined as having had *indecision*. For these clients the informational experience was sufficient to resolve their choice problem, but for the indecisive clients it was not. They need counterconditioning of their anxiety associated with career decision making. If this process is effective, then they should have the same levels of manifest anxiety and career maturity as those with indecision on posttest.

The goals of behavioral-pragmatic career counseling are akin to the general one of skill acquisition but are more idiosyncratic. Krumboltz (1966a, pp. 154–155) states that any set of goals for counseling should satisfy three criteria:

  1 *The goals of counseling should be capable of being stated differently for each individual client . . .*
  2 *The goals of counseling for each client should be compatible with though not necessarily identical to the values of the counselor . . .*
  3 *The degree to which the goals of counseling are attained by each client should be observable . . .* (italics in original).

Given these constraints, he then identifies three counseling goals which

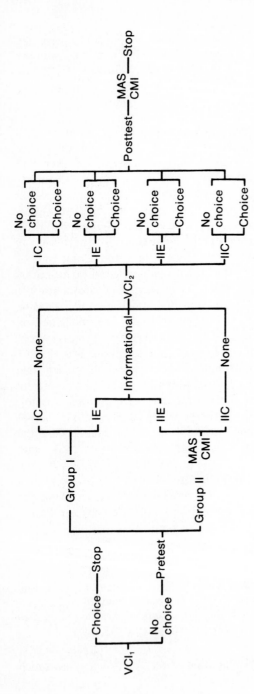

Figure 6-3 Experimental design for relationship of manifest anxiety and career maturity to indecision and indecisiveness. *(Crites, 1969, p. 602)*

are consistent with them: (1) altering maladaptive behavior, (2) learning the decision-making process, and (3) preventing problems. Ultimately, however, Krumboltz (1966a, p. 155) contends that any "type of behavior change desired by a client and agreed to by his counselor," regardless of the above criteria, is an acceptable goal (outcome) of counseling, whether it deals with career or some other aspect of functioning. Stated in this way, the problem of evaluating the effectiveness of career counseling is greatly simplified. Rather than attempting to evaluate the gains of all clients on some common criterion, hits and misses for each client's goals, however different they may be, can be totalled to determine an overall success percentage for all clients.

To assess the efficacy of the behavior-pragmatic approach to career counseling, the learning paradigm is that depicted in Figure 6-4. This is the familiar operant model for acquisition or elimination of responses as a function of their consequences. In S_1 cues are present in the counselor-client relationship which elicit salient responses, for example, information-gathering behavior. If cues are not present, the counselor may shape (suggest) them so that they are elicited from the client. In R_1 the free-response rate or operant level of the behavior engaged in by the client is established. In other words, this is the baseline for the behavior *before* any intervention by the counselor. Next, in S_2 the counselor invokes positive or negative reinforcement or punishment of the target behavior. Since these terms are sometimes confused, Table 6-1 can be used to define them.

The diagram works as follows: If a positive stimulus is applied, the effect is positive reinforcement, or what is more commonly known as reward, and so forth. Misunderstanding usually surrounds the distinction between punishment and negative reinforcement; they are *not* the same. Punishment occurs either when a positive stimulus is withdrawn or when a negative stimulus is applied, whereas negative reinforcement comes from withdrawing a negative stimulus.

METHODS

The methods of Behavioral career counseling, whether behavioral-theoretic or pragmatic, sometimes strike counselors of other persuasions as "cookbookish" and unduly specific, and they question their expediency in terms of broader goals and values (Patterson, 1964), for example, the "self-actualization" of the client. The behaviorists are quick to reply that they subscribe fully to such ideals as self-actualization, but "as a counseling goal, the abstract and ambiguous terminology makes it

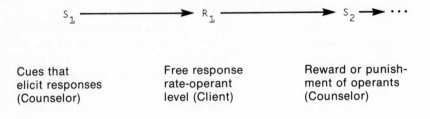

$S_1 \longrightarrow R_1 \longrightarrow S_2 \rightarrow \cdots$

| Cues that elicit responses (Counselor) | Free response rate-operant level (Client) | Reward or punishment of operants (Counselor) |

$\cdots \longrightarrow R_2$

Increased or decreased operant rate (Client)

Figure 6-4   Operant model of client learning in career counseling.

difficult for clients or counselors to know what they are trying to do and when they have succeeded" (Krumboltz & Thoresen, 1969, p. 2). Hence the emphasis upon, and commitment to, whatever counseling technique works. What may seem like blatant pragmatism to some, however, is tempered by the behavioral career counselor's recognition of his or her relationship to the client as a basic dimension of their interaction, along with communication. Goodstein (1972, p. 281) notes that:

> Several writers in this area, especially Wolpe (1958; 1969), point out the need for establishing a good interpersonal relationship as an integral part of the treatment process. Indeed, it has been noted that an essential role for the counselor to play is that of a reinforcing agent, a role that depends upon the developing counseling relationship.

It should be understood, therefore, that the interview techniques, methods of test interpretation, and uses of occupational information described below are sketched in relief against a background of the relationship that develops between counselor and client.

Interview Techniques

For the alleviation of anxiety, particularly that which is etiologically significant in aberrant career decision-making processes, Goodstein

Table 6-1 Definitions of Reinforcement

	Apply	Withdraw
Positive stimulus	positive reinforcement (reward)	punishment
Negative stimulus	punishment	negative reinforcement

(1972) proposed three procedures which are widely used in behavioral-oriented psychotherapy and which are applicable to career counseling:

1 *Adaptation or desensitization* This procedure ". . . involves the presentation of the anxiety-arousing stimulus at very weak strengths so that it will not be strong enough to actually elicit the anxiety response. The strength of the stimulus is then gradually increased, always taking care to keep the strength of the stimulus below that which is required to elicit anxiety. Eventually even the presentation of the stimulus at full strength is no longer an effective cue for eliciting the response" (Goodstein, 1972, p. 265).

In other words, the anxiety cues are kept just below the threshold of anxiety responses, the principle being to adapt the client to the increasing intensity of the noxious stimulus. In career counseling, this would be the proscribed career developmental task of making a career choice. To approach the high level of anxiety that this task may arouse in the client, the counselor may construct with the client's collaboration an "anxiety hierarchy" (Wolpe, 1958), graded from minimal anxiety-producing decisions (for example, what to wear in the morning), through intermediate ones (for example, which courses to take next semester), to maximal ones (for example, college major and career choice). The counselor then asks the client to imagine the situations that would produce the least anxiety and progressively they work through the hierarchy until the client can conceive of making a career choice without feeling anxious. In this process, it is essential for the counselor to be alert to any indications of anxiety in the client (for example, restlessness, flushing, perspiring, and so forth) and keep the cues below threshold. Note also that this procedure is only desensitization; it is *not* paired with a competing response, such as relaxation, which would be counterconditioning.

2 *Inhibitory conditioning or internal inhibition*   This technique "... involves presenting the anxiety-producing cues in sufficient strength to elicit the anxiety response, and these cues are either continuously presented or are presented for periods of time, without any additional primary reinforcement, but with only brief intervals of rest interspersed between their presentation. The continual or very frequent presentation of such stimulation will result in a virtually continuous response; such continual responsiveness will in turn lead to fatigue and other changes in the organism, which will eventually lead to the cessation of the response despite the continued presence of the anxiety-arousing cue" (Goodstein, 1972, p. 267).

This process will be recognized as the familiar one of *experimental extinction,* in which exposure to massed trials of the stimulus is neither rewarded nor punished. The application of inhibitory conditioning to career counseling would be constant talk about decision making, possibly on a daily interview schedule, or weekly interviews with the client keeping a decisional diary between interviews. The critical consideration is the constancy of exposure to the anxiety-arousing cues. If the interval between their presentation is too long, extinction due to other factors (for example, fatigue) will not occur.

3 *Counterconditioning*   This procedure was discussed at some length in the section on "Process" and was outlined in Figure 6-2, but some further comments on its application are apropos. It should be recognized that, as a consequence of higher-order conditioning, anxiety may generalize to the conditioned stimulus, or, in this instance, the counselor-client relationship, which is now compounded with that associated with decision making, may become so intense that she or he may "break contact." All the more reason for the counselor to introduce anxiety-producing decisional topics only when the relationship has been securely established. Another consideration is that counterconditioning occurs only if the client is actually experiencing anxiety about making a career choice *during* the interview. A change in cognitive behavior, or what is often referred to as "insight," is not sufficient to reduce or eliminate anxiety around career decision making. Goodstein (1972, p. 264) notes that these techniques are theoretically distinguishable, but that most "... real-life attempts to eliminate or reduce anxiety would seem to involve some combination of these methods, and it is difficult to find pure procedures." Of the three methods, therefore, the most general, and hence the most potent, of them is counterconditioning, which involves desensitization as well.

In the behavioral-theoretic approach to career counseling, anxiety reduction using the techniques just described precedes instrumental learning or skills acquisition, which necessitate different counseling methods. Again, Goodstein (1972) delineates three procedures that he considers effective in assisting the client with new learning:

1 *Reinforcement* The counselor selectively reinforces those client responses that facilitate the career decision-making process. "The positive reinforcers may range from statements of direct approval such as 'I'm glad you did (or told me) that,' to such indirect and subtle procedures as head nodding or the client-centered 'Mm-Humm.' The negative reinforcers range from a failure to make any response to direct threats to discontinue the therapeutic relationship" (Goodstein, 1972, p. 274). For example, in response to a client remark about finding out more about an occupation, the counselor might say: "That sounds like a good idea to me. Let me know next time what you find out."

2 *Social modeling and vicarious learning* Goodstein (1972, p. 276) points out that ". . . virtually all of the learnings that can be acquired through direct experience can also be acquired vicariously, that is, through observation of other people's behavior and its consequences for them." The counselor as a role model, therefore, becomes a potent factor in the process of career counseling by emulating for the client optimal decision making—information-gathering, goal selection, planning, and problem-solving (Crites, 1978). Modeling can also be more formal, as Krumboltz and Schroeder (1965) have demonstrated, by exposing clients to audio/video tapes of how individuals make realistic career choices.

3 *Discrimination learning* As applied to career decision making, teaching the client to distinguish among the various aspects of the choice problem probably has its greatest import for learning mature career choice attitudes. The counselor can discriminate for the client between attitudes that mediate realistic career decision making, including the use of career choice competencies, and those that do not. In discussing the client's responses to the CMI-Attitude scale, for example, the counselor can explain why the attitude "A person can do any kind of work she or he wants as long as she or he tries hard" is immature and unrealistic, whereas the attitude "You should choose an occupation, then plan how to enter it" is mature and realistic. Such discrimination learning by the client often breaks down self-defeating global misconceptions of how career choices are made.

Much more specialized interview techniques than those outlined by Goodstein have been gathered together in two books on behavioral counseling methods by Krumboltz and Thoresen (1969; 1976). No attempt will be made here to review and summarize these procedures. It should be noted, however, that they stem from the behavioral-pragmatic orientation and consequently do not assume anxiety reduction before direct intervention upon maladaptive behaviors.

Test Interpretation

Allusions to the use of tests in career counseling, much less extended discussions, by either those of a theoretical or pragmatic behavioral bent are difficult to find. The reason is, of course, that they subscribe to an S-R or operant model, whereas most tests are constructed within an R-R model, with S (items) held constant (standardized) across individuals (Underwood, 1957; Crites, 1961). In other words, test scores measure individual differences in behavior, but they seldom reflect individual-environmental interactions, which are of primary concern to the Behavioral career counselor. Consequently, traditional tests (aptitude, interest, and personality) are typically eschewed and objective indices of behavior in situ are gathered, although some effort is being expended to assess S-R situations with paper-and-pencil instruments (Goldfried & D'Zurilla, 1969). Krumboltz and Baker (1973, p. 255) do allow that: "Objective empirical data can be useful to counselor and client in their study of outcome probabilities" as part of "examining the consequences of alternatives" (see "Process" above), and they present a counselor-client dialogue, in which the counselor reports entrance test scores as expectancy data much as a Client-Centered career counselor would.

As compared with the Trait-and-Factor approach, for example, the use of tests in Behavioral career counseling is considerably more circumscribed, although not as much so as in the Client-Centered orientation. In the Behavioral approach, more emphasis is accorded to interest inventories than other standardized measures, particularly aptitudes, presumably because Krumboltz and Baker (1973, pp. 273–274) assume interests are more subject to the impact of learning:

> From the behavioral [pragmatic] viewpoint, vocational interests and career development in general are the outgrowth of an individual's experiences. Why does an individual select one alternative over another? The behavioral counselor would answer that he experienced greater satisfaction (received more positive reinforcement) with the chosen alternative, or one similar to it, in the past.

At that stage in Behavioral career counseling given to "generating alternative solutions" in career decision making, interest inventories may serve two purposes:

First, the client's mere responding to inventory items may stimulate discussion about various occupational alternatives. Second, scores from the inventory may indicate a pattern of interests in occupations that neither the client nor counselor would have considered.

Test data other than those from interest inventories, used in this exploratory fashion, are typically not generated in the Behavioral approach to career counseling.

Occupational Information

Some of the most creative and imaginative contributions that have been made by Behavioral career counselors are in the area of occupational information. Krumboltz and his associates (Krumboltz & Bergland, 1969; Bergland & Krumboltz, 1969; Hamilton & Krumboltz, 1969; Krumboltz & Sheppard, 1969) have systematically devised a set of problem-solving career kits that simulate selected activities from twenty different occupations, including accountant, electronics technician, police officer, X-ray technologist, and so forth. The specifications for these kits were as follows (Krumboltz & Sheppard, 1969, pp. 293–294).

1 The problem should be realistic and representative of the type of problems faced by members of the occupation.
2 95 percent of the target population (high school students) should have no difficulty in passing the problem.
3 The problem should be considered intrinsically interesting by the majority of the target population.
4 At least 75 percent of the target population should be able to read the material and solve the problem successfully within 50 minutes.
5 The problem should be completely self-contained and self-administered.

Evidence from tryouts and evaluations by experts indicates that the kits largely fulfill these criteria. Results are also available from several studies (Krumboltz, Sheppard, Jones, Johnson, & Baker, 1967; Krumboltz, Baker, & Johnson, 1968) that establish that the kits are useful in stimulating further career exploration and decision making. Career counselors can use them with the expectation that clients will learn at least as much, if not considerably more, about different careers than they will from printed occupational information. Sample materials from the Job Experience Kits (Science Research Associates) are shown in Figure 6-5.

MATERIALS

To illustrate the Behavioral approach to career counseling, a case has been selected from the writer's private practice, which is one considerably different from the modal client engaged in the decision-making process but one that highlights a choice problem that has received increasing (and necessary) attention in recent years. This is the person in midlife who is experiencing a career crisis or who is considering a second career or both. In this case, the client is in crisis *and* choosing a second career. He is Jim Calhoun, a 38-year-old captain in the United States Air Force, with twelve years of active duty, who asked for career counseling because he had been passed over for promotion, was being mustered out of the service, and did not know what he wanted to do.

Diagnosis

This presenting problem was exacerbated by Jim's having to make some decisions that would have long-term ramifications within a week from his first interview. In short, he was faced with the alternatives of (1) retiring from the Air Force with a large lump-sum ($15,000) severance emolument but with no future benefits, (2) staying in the Air Force as an enlisted person (staff sergeant), or (3) applying for a warrant officer's grade in the Army. In discussing these options with him, his decisional style became immediately apparent: He was indecisive with high anxiety, vascillating back and forth among the different courses of action. He could see pros and cons for each, but his anxiety kept him from making a decision. Rather than focusing upon the conditions of the conflict in an effort to eliminate them, he responded to his symptomatic anxiety and attempted to reduce it by drinking excessively. As a result, he felt better momentarily, but as soon as the alcohol wore off his problem reappeared, more acutely than ever. The counselor pointed this out to him, and he agreed to make a short-term contract not to drink until after he decided his service status, with the understanding that he could call or see the counselor at any time during the week. To the best knowledge of the counselor, he kept this agreement and decided to leave the Air Force and enter civilian life.

Once the initial crisis in career choice had been resolved, the longer-term problem of Jim's anxiety around decision making in general

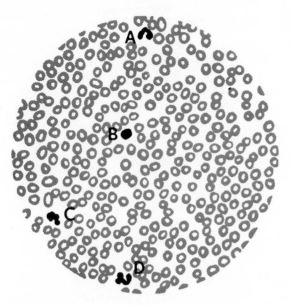

Figure 6-5 Illustrative materials from the Job Experience Kits. *(Science Research Associates, 1970)*

became the focus of his career counseling. Two interviews spent on his decisional history indicated that he had really never had to assume personal responsibility for choices, largely because of a dependence relationship with his mother, in which she made decisions for him, and his years in the Air Force, when it made decisions for him. As a consequence, not only was he experiencing consequent anxiety associated with his present choice situation, but also he experienced antecedent anxiety conditioned to his lack of experience in making choices. In other words, the counselor saw Jim as indecisive rather than simply undecided. To check this diagnosis, as well as to assess his career maturity, the counselor asked him to take both the Spielberger Trait and State Anxiety Questionnaire and the Career Maturity Inventory. On the former, according to expectation, Jim had both high trait and state anxiety, which correspond, respectively, to antecedent and consequent anxiety in Goodstein's (1972) analysis of indecisiveness. He also had relatively low scores on the CMI Attitude Scale and Competence Test, possibly attributable to the protected life he led first with his mother and then the Air Force. Because of his dependence, his career developmental experiences were limited and his career maturity was lower than would be expected for someone at his stage in life.

Process

Given the diagnosis of indecisiveness, the counselor started the career counseling with Jim by attempting to countercondition his antecedent anxiety around decision making. The counselor might have relied upon the developing relationship to pair its cues of hopefulness and security (see Figure 6-2) with discussion of past decision making, but he felt that reducing Jim's anxiety this way might not be systematic enough, particularly since the client used drinking for symptomatic relief of anxiety. In other words, because drinking affords almost instantaneous anxiety reduction, the counselor had to offer a potent alternative, along with Jim's agreement to refrain from drinking. Consequently, the counselor opted for a counterconditioning procedure that paired desensitization with relaxation. With Jim's collaboration, he built a hierarchy of increasingly anxiety-arousing decisional situations, which culminated with the client's present quandary of deciding upon a second (civilian) career. He also instructed Jim in relaxation, which could be used not only during the interview sessions as part of the counterconditioning but also extraclinically when the client had anxiety attacks. The counselor hoped that the use of relaxation at these times would substitute for and reduce the likelihood of Jim's drinking. Utilizing this approach, Jim and the counselor engaged in what appeared to be effective counterconditioning for six interviews.

The second stage of this behavioral-oriented career counseling involved instrumental learning by Jim to acquire those attitudes and competencies that would increase his career maturity and facilitate making a realistic career choice. In the fifth interview, the counselor started a systematic interpretation of the CMI, beginning with the Attitude Scale. He gave Jim a copy of the inventory as well as his Career Maturity profile, with the mature and immature keyed responses to each item printed on it. They then went through the inventory and discussed each of Jim's answers and why a particular response was mature or immature. This technique of "teaching the test" has been found to significantly increase CMI scores as well as resulting in greater realism of career choice (Crites, 1971; 1973). Similarly, the counselor went through the Competence Test with Jim but supplemented discussion with suggested activities. He reinforced whatever information-gathering responses the client made during the interviews and directed him to relevant resources in the community. Jim also worked the exercises in a self-administered decision-making program for adults called *Decisions and Outcomes,* published by the Educational Testing Service. By the end of his career counseling, Jim had not only acquired more mature career decisional attitudes and competencies, but also he used these to make a career choice. He decided to combine his Air Force background in administration and management with his interest in science to train for a career in computer systems.

Outcomes

The outcomes of Jim's career counseling were apparent from the process. First, he resolved his immediate choice crisis by deciding to leave the Air Force rather than stay in a lower grade. Moreover, he was apparently able to make this decision without drinking to excess (his verbal report). Second, the first stage of career counseling, counterconditioning antecedent anxiety associated with decision making, was evidently effective because Jim overcame his indecisiveness by the second stage and made a career choice. If antecedent anxiety had still been a competing response, he could not have decided to enter a specific occupation. Finally, later feedback from him indicated that he was considerably less anxious and more effective in his daily living than he had been; that he had quit drinking entirely; and that he was expanding his recreational activities and his circle of friends. He had applications in for several positions, but it was too soon to hear anything definite. In general, then, he seemed to have benefited not only from his career counseling by reducing choice anxiety and making a career decision, but also by resolving these conflicts and issues, he released energy to expand the perimeter of his life. Again, the intimacy between career development and personal development has been accentuated.

COMMENT

Krumboltz (1966b) has heralded the behavioral approach as no less than a "revolution in counseling," and the temptation to agree unreservedly would be great, were it not that several disquieting issues are yet to be resolved. Foremost among these issues is the role of anxiety in the etiology of problems in career decision making. If a counselor follows the current formulation of behavioral-pragmatic career counseling, he or she would take the client's presenting problem of "no choice," for example, at face value and most likely agree to work toward the goal of "deciding upon a career," using reinforcement, modeling, and simulation in the process. For insufficient prior learning experiences, this would probably be effective career counseling, but for the client with pervasive indecisiveness, the outcome would be problematical.

How many of these clients have career counselors expended their best information-giving and decision-making efforts on, only to have them terminate counseling with the epitaph, "Well, I still don't really know what I want to do." It is not long before the mounting frustration of the counselor prompts him or her to wonder whether there is some competing response tendency that inhibits the client from making a career decision, given the relevant information about self and work. The behavioral-theoretic point of view would posit that it is the anxiety associated with decision making, occasioned by punishing past experiences, that prevents the indecisive client from declaring a career choice. Once this anxiety has been sufficiently reduced, information-seeking and decisional responses can be learned, or made if they were already in the client's behavioral repertoire, and the instrumental phase of career counseling can proceed. A resolution of this issue, both theoretically and pragmatically, appears critical, if a coherent system of Behavioral career counseling is to be formulated.

REFERENCES

Bergland, B. W., & Krumboltz, J. D. An optimal grade level for career exploration. *Vocational Guidance Quarterly,* 1969, *18,* 29–33.

Crites, J. O. A model for the measurement of vocational maturity. *Journal of Counseling Psychology,* 1961, *8,* 255–259.

Crites, J. O. *Vocational psychology.* New York: McGraw-Hill, 1969.

Crites, J. O. *The maturity of vocational attitudes in adolescence.* Washington, D.C.: American Personnel and Guidance Association, Inquiry Series, No. 2, 1971.

Crites, J. O. *Theory and research handbook for the Career Maturity Inventory.* Monterey, Calif.: CTB/McGraw-Hill, 1973; 1978.

Eysenck, J. H. (Ed.), *Behavioral therapy and the neuroses.* New York: Macmillan, 1960.

Gelatt, H. B. Decision-making: A conceptual frame of reference for counseling. *Journal of Counseling Psychology,* 1962, *9,* 240–245.

Goldfried, M. R., & D'Zurilla, T. J. A behavioral analytic model for assessing competence. In C. D. Spielberger (Ed.), *Current topics in clinical and community psychology.* Vol. 1. New York: Academic Press, 1969. Pp. 151–196.

Goodstein, L. D. Behavioral views of counseling. In B. Stefflre & W. H. Grant (Eds), *Theories of counseling.* New York: McGraw-Hill, 1972. Pp. 243–286.

Hamilton, J. A., & Krumboltz, J. D. Simulated work experience: How realistic should it be? *Personnel Guidance Journal,* 1969, *48,* 39–44.

Krumboltz, J. D. Behavioral goals for counseling. *Journal of Counseling Psychology,* 1966, *13,* 153–159. (a)

Krumboltz, J. D. A social learning theory of career selection. In J. M. Whiteley & A. Resnilkoff (Eds), *Career counseling*. Monterey, Calif.: Brooks/Cole, 1979. Pp. 100–127.

Krumboltz, J. D., & Baker, R. D. Behavioral counseling for vocational decision. In H. Borow (Ed.), *Career guidance for a new age*. Boston: Houghton Mifflin, 1973. Pp. 235–283.

Krumboltz, J. D., Baker, R. D., & Johnson, R. G. Vocational problem-solving experiences for stimulating career exploration and interest: Phase II. Final Report, Office of Education Grant 4-7-070111-2890. School of Education, Stanford University, 1968.

Krumboltz, J. D., & Bergland, B. W. Experiencing work almost like it is. *Educational Technology*, 1969, *9*, 47–49.

Krumboltz, J. D., & Sheppard, L. E. Vocational problem-solving experiences. In J. D. Krumboltz & C. E. Thoresen (Eds), *Behavioral counseling: Cases and techniques*. New York: Holt, Rinehart, & Winston, 1969. Pp. 293–306.

Krumboltz, J. D., Sheppard, L. E., Jones, G. B., Johnson, R. G., & Baker, R. D. Vocational problem-solving experiences for stimulating career exploration and interest. Final Report, Office of Education, Stanford University, 1967.

Krumboltz, J. D., & Schroeder, W. W. Promoting career planning through reinforcement. *Personnel and Guidance Journal*, 1965, *43*, 19–26.

Krumboltz, J. D., & Thoresen, C. E. (Eds), *Behavioral counseling: Cases and techniques*. New York: Holt, Rinehart & Winston, 1969; 1976.

Patterson, C. H. Counseling: Self-clarification and the helping relationship. In H. Borow (Ed.), *Man in a world at work*. Boston: Houghton Mifflin, 1964. Pp. 434–459.

Shoben, E. J., Jr. Psychotherapy as a problem in learning theory. *Psychological Bulletin*, 1949, *46*, 366–392.

Spielberger, C. D., Gorsach, R. L., & Lushene, R. E. *The State-Trait Anxiety Inventory*. Palo Alto: Consulting Psychologists Press, 1970.

Tyler, L. E. *The work of the counselor*. (2d ed.). New York: Appleton-Century-Crofts, 1961.

Underwood, B. J. *Psychological research*. New York: Appleton-Century-Crofts, 1957.

Wolpe, J. *Psychotherapy by reciprocal inhibition*. Stanford, Calif.: Stanford University Press, 1958.

Wolpe, J. *The practice of behavior therapy*. New York: Pergammon, 1969.

Yabroff, W. Learning decision making. In J. D. Krumboltz & C. E. Thoresen (Eds), *Behavioral counseling: Cases and techniques*. New York: Holt, Rinehart & Winston, 1969. Pp. 329–343.

Comprehensive Career Counseling:
Models, Methods, and Materials

In the preceding chapters, a review of the major approaches to assisting clients engaged in decision making was made, along with limited critical analysis of each. More specifically, the five approaches to career counseling listed across the horizontal dimension of Figure 7-1 were respectively considered and summarized down the vertical axis, which enumerates the more salient and presumably universal continuua along which they can be described and differentiated. The model of an approach to career counseling explicates its theoretical framework, its conceptual outline, its raison d'être. It encompasses the three principal chronological stages of any career counseling encounter, regardless of temporal span: the beginning, during which a diagnosis of the client's problem is typically made; the middle, when the process of intervention with the client is implemented; and the end, when the outcomes of the experience are enumerated and evaluated by the client and counselor.

In contrast, the methods of career counseling are pragmatic, rather than theoretic, their purpose being to translate the model into operational terms. In career counseling, they include the interview techniques used by the counselor, the test interpretation procedures engaged in by client and counselor, and the acquisition/use of occupational information by the client. Together, the model and methods of career counseling serve to define the unique parameters of a given approach, and they provide a schema for synthesizing the several approaches into a comprehensive one that has maximal applicability.

That none of the major approaches to career counseling was sufficient with respect to its model and methods emerged from the previous review. But each approach has its contribution to make to a comprehensive approach. To extrapolate what these are and to integrate them into a cogent and coherent system of career counseling, a synthesis of the approaches for each aspect of model and method has been attempted. That is, reading across the rows of Figure 7-1, a "provisional try" has been made to synthesize the best theory and practice, buttressed by confirmatory experiential and empirical evidence on diagnosis, process, outcomes, interview techniques, test interpretation, and occupational information. What has resulted is, hopefully, more than an eclectic grafting together of disparate parts. The objective was to articulate a comprehensive approach to career counseling based upon an explicit rationale for the interrelationship of its elements. In the discussion that follows, the latter are delineated first (across the rows of Figure 7-1), and then are interrelated within the context of the client/counselor interaction. Thus, this outline of a comprehensive approach to career counseling is divided into one section on model (or theory), a second on methods (or techniques), and a concluding one on materials (or case studies), which illustrates its principles and procedures with an account and analysis of a recent career counseling case.

MODEL

In formulating a model of Comprehensive career counseling, concepts and principles have been utilized that come not only from the major approaches already reviewed, but also from more general systems of counseling and psychotherapy (Ford & Urban, 1963; Corsini, 1973). Moreover, the model reflects experience gained from many case conference presentations and supervisory sessions that leaven and authenticate its formal characteristics. The concepts of diagnosis, process, and outcomes that it embraces, therefore, have been derived experientially as well as logically, the purpose being to blend the theoretical and pragmatic as meaningfully as possible.

Diagnosis

The central issue in synthesizing this facet of the model for Comprehensive career counseling is whether or not to diagnose. All but the Client-Centered approach would affirm the value of diagnosis in identifying and solving the client's problems, although viewpoints vary on the type of diagnosis which should be made (see below). The Client-Centered position is that diagnosis shifts the locus of responsibility for decision making to the counselor and fosters critical. or evaluative attitudes that interfere with "unconditional positive regard" for the client. Yet Client-Centered career counselors (for example, Patterson, 1964; 1973) actually make two kinds of diagnoses but nevertheless assume that they have not usurped the client's decision-making prerogatives. First, they assume that all clients have the same problem, namely, a lack of congruence between perceptions of self and perceptions of reality (Rogers, 1951). In other words, they diagnose but not differentially. Second, they distinguish among the life areas in which a lack of congruence may arise, thus allowing for career counseling as a treatment modality peculiarly suited to vocational problems (Patterson, 1964). This inconsistency in Client-Centered views of diagnosis is not only conceptual; it is also empirical. Findings from both the Chicago (Kirtner & Cartwright, 1958) and the Wisconsin (Rogers, Gendlin, Kiesler, & Truax, 1967) studies have revealed that Client-Centered counseling is not uniformly effective with all types of psychological disorders. It works better with some clients—more intelligent, less

		Trait-and-Factor	Client-Centered
M o d e l s	**Diagnosis**	Different courses of treatment stem from a determination of what is wrong with the client	Rogers and Patterson consider diagnosis as disruptive of the client/counselor relationship; instead, they determine whether or not the client has a "vocational problem"
	Process	Involves largely the counselor in gathering and interpreting data on the client; client assists only in the actual determination of treatment or counseling to effect desired adjustment, and in follow-up	Patterson sees the process as encompassing Rogers' highest stage of personal adjustment in psychotherapy; the adjustment level of a client following psychotherapy approximates that of a vocational client before counseling when he is finding out who he is and what his needs are
	Outcomes	Immediate goal is to resolve the presenting problem of client; longer-term objective is to help him/her better understand and manage his/her own assets and liabilities, so s/he can solve future problems	Goal is to facilitate the clarification and implementation of the self-concept in a compatible occupational role at whatever point the client is; relates to psychotherapy's overall outcome of an individual's reorganized self that can accept and convert into reality a picture of himself and role in the work world

Figure 7-1   Summary of major approaches to career counseling.

Psychodynamic	Developmental	Behavioral
Bordin stipulates that diagnosis must form the basis for the choice of treatment; wants more psychologically based constructs (choice anxiety, dependence, self conflict) to be used in diagnosis	Super coins "appraisal" rather than diagnosis; delineates three types that focus on the client's potentialities and problems: (a) Problem Appraisal (b) Person Appraisal (c) Prognostic Appraisal; client is active in the appraisal process	Goodstein, in his behavioral-theoretic approach, attributes a central role to anxiety in the diagnosis of behavioral and career-choice problems; Krumboltz and Thoresen focus fully on behavioral analysis or problem identification in the specification of goals for counseling; in this behavioral-pragmatic approach, they do not focus on anxiety or diagnosis
Bordin defines three stages of process: (a) exploration and contract setting stage (b) critical decision stage in which client decides what facets of personal adjustment other than just vocational s/he would pursue (c) "working for change" stage in which increased understanding of self is aimed at in counseling	The immediate objective is to facilitate the client's career development; Super states that the broader goal is to bring about improvements in the individual's general personal adjustment (represents a synthesis of trait-and-factor and client-centered orientations)	According to Goodstein, process varies with the etiology of the client's problem—antecedent anxiety necessitates counter-conditioning and instrumental learning, while consequent anxiety necessitates only the latter; Krumboltz and Thoresen, on the other hand, aim at the elimination of nonadjustive behavior patterns
Results are twofold: (a) assist the client in career decision-making and (b) in broader terms, to effect some positive change in the client's personality	The process of career development progresses from orientation and readiness for career choice to decision-making and reality testing; the counselor initiates counseling at that point in the process that the client has reached	Goodstein's theoretic outcomes are (a) elimination of antecedent and consequent anxiety and (b) acquisition of decision-making skills, Krumboltz and Thoresen's pragmatic goals involve skill acquisition—altering maladaptive behavior, learning decision-making process, and preventing problems

(Continued on following page)

	Trait-and-Factor	Client-Centered
Interview technique	Involves a pragmatic technological method of establishing rapport, cultivating self-understanding, advising a program of action, carrying out a plan, and referring the client to other personnel for more assistance	Counselor will make responses during the interview geared to helping the client experience and implement the self-concept in an occupational role
Test Interpretation	Involves the counselor who makes authoritative interpretations of the test results, and draws conclusions and recommendations from them for the client's deliberation	Counselor proposes that tests be used primarily for the client's edification and wants; use only as needed and requested by client; termed by Super as "precision testing"
Use of occupational info	Counselor provides this information to either confirm a choice already made or resolve indecision between two equally attractive options; may help a client readjust an inappropriate choice; also used to involve the client actively in the decision-making process	Introduced when there is a recognized need for it on the part of the client; counselor must recognize that such information has personal meanings to the client which must be understood and explored within the context of needs and values, and objective reality

The left side of the table is labeled vertically: **Methods**

Figure 7-1 *(Continued)*

Psychodynamic	Developmental	Behavioral
Bordin enumerates three interpretive counselor response categories that can be used: (a) clarification - to focus the client's thinking and verbalizations (b) comparison and (c) the interpretation of "wish-defence" systems; *represents a synthesis of psychoanalytic practices, trait-and-factor, client-centered approaches	Super's "cyclical" approach is to respond directly to content statements by the client and nondirectly to expressions of feeling	Goodstein proposes techniques of psychotherapy for the alleviation of anxiety; he joins with Krumboltz and Thoresen in their pragmatic stance that the counselor should reinforce desired client responses, encourage social modeling, and teach discrimination learning in the acquisiton of decision-making skills
Bordin defines three major uses: (a) that the client be an active participant in selecting the tests (as in the client-centered approach) (b) that the tests provide diagnostic information for counselor to give client and stimulate self-exploration and (c) that the counselor verbally present the test interpretation—introduce as needed rather than presenting it all at once as in trait-and-factor	The most appropriate information is the description of career patterns in different occupational pursuits; Super observes that there are approximately six types of descriptive data on career patterns that are needed for this approach	Test use, in either a theoretical or pragmatic stance, is almost negligible since they measure individual differences in behavior rather than reflect individual-environment interaction—a primary concern to a behavioral counselor; objective indices of behavior are therefore gathered
Information that is based upon a "need analysis" of job duties and tasks is needed; resembles the trait-and-factor approach of matching men with jobs, but differs in that variables are personality needs and gratifying work conditions, rather than static characteristics of the individual and occupation	The purpose is to maximize the value of tests in decision-making by administering them in a discriminating way, and by involving the client in each phase of the process; represents "precision" testing rather than "saturation" testing as in the trait-and-factor approach	Behavioral counselors have developed "career kits" that are more useful in stimulating further career exploration and decision-making than simply printed information

disturbed ones—than it does with others. Thus, diagnosis appears necessary for Client-Centered as well as other approaches to career counseling.

Given this precept as an integral part of the model for comprehensive career counseling, several questions immediately arise: What is meant by "diagnosis"? How are diagnoses made, and can they be made reliably? What is the relationship of diagnosis to process in career counseling? From the Trait-and-Factor approaches comes the well-known concept of diagnosis as the *differential* classification of clients according to the distinguishing characteristics of their career problems. For example, individuals who cannot state which occupation they intend to enter upon completion of their training (Crites, 1969) are designated as having "no choice" or being "undecided" (Williamson, 1939). Several systems for the differential diagnosis of vocational problems have been developed, but they have foundered primarily because of the unreliability of counselors in using them. Interjudge agreement seldom exceeds 25–30 percent (Crites, 1969, Chapter 7). Moreover, the categories in these systems are neither mutually exclusive nor exhaustive. Thus, some clients can be classified into more than one problem category and others cannot be classified into any category. To rectify these shortcomings, Crites (1969, pp. 292–303) has proposed a system which eliminates subjective judgments and hence is perfectly reliable and which consists of exclusive and exhaustive categories, at least for the diagnostic criteria used. In brief, it defines differential career problems by identifying the discrepancies that exist between career choice, on the one hand, and aptitudes and interests, on the other hand. To illustrate, if a client chooses an occupation that requires greater aptitude than she or he has, then the client is diagnosed as "unrealistic." Without further elaboration, let it suffice to say that the system can be used reliably and validly by counselors for the differential diagnosis of client career problems.

Differential diagnosis addresses the question: What is the client's career decisional problem? *Dynamic diagnosis* asks the question: Why does the client have the problem? The answer has been formulated largely within the psychodynamic approach to career counseling. Bordin (1946) early criticized differential diagnostic systems (for example, Williamson, 1939) because they failed to identify the causes of psychological problems. As noted in the review of this approach (Crites, 1974a), he then proposed diagnostic constructs, such as choice anxiety and dependence, that focused upon the etiology of the client's problem rather than simply its symptomatology. More recently, Bordin and

Kopplin (1973) have formulated another set of problem categories, based upon an analysis of "motivational conflicts," but both sets have been plagued with low interjudge agreement that has limited their usefulness. As with differential diagnosis, what is needed are explicit operational criteria for the definition of etiological factors in career problems that clearly distinguish their dynamics. One such analysis has been made by Crites (1969; 1974a) to explicate the role of anxiety in indecision as contrasted with indecisiveness. Given only the differential diagnosis of "no choice" (Williamson, 1939), it is difficult, if not impossible, for a career counselor to know whether the client's problem is one of simple indecision or pervasive indecisiveness, unless a dynamic diagnosis of how anxiety has affected antecedent decisional experiences is made. Recent research (Schrader, 1970) as well as current studies, following an experimental paradigm suggested by Crites (1969, pp. 599–604), have indicated that indecision and indecisiveness can be dynamically differentiated early in career counseling by administering standardized measures of manifest anxiety and career maturity. There is emerging evidence, based upon reliable test scores rather than unreliable judgments, that indecisive clients are more anxious and less mature than those with simple indecision.

To make differential and dynamic diagnoses is necessary but not sufficient to identify a client's problem(s). These types of diagnosis attend primarily to the content of career choice; they do not directly deal with the process of career choice. The distinction between the content and process of career choice has not been generally recognized (Crites, 1974b), although it is implicit in both the developmental and behavioral approaches to career counseling. Career choice content pertains to which occupation the client intends to enter. In contrast, career choice process refers to how the decision was made. Knowing only that a client has "no choice" (differential diagnosis) and that she or he is "indecisive" (dynamic diagnosis) in most decision-making situations does not identify whatever problems arise in the client's approach to career choice. To determine deviations or disjunctions in how career choices are made necessitates a *decisional diagnosis*. A conceptual framework and assessment methodology for this kind of diagnosis can be extrapolated from an integration of Behavioral and Developmental career counseling. From the former comes a schema for optimal career decision making (Gelatt, 1962; Gelatt, Varenhorst, & Carey, 1972; Krumboltz & Baker, 1973) that delineates the sequence a client might follow to arrive at a realistic career choice and from the latter is derived a model of career maturity (Crites, 1974c) which casts this process into a developmental context. A client's career maturity at any given point in time can be assessed and diagnosed. For example, a client's scores on the Career Maturity Inventory, which was constructed to measure maturity in optimal career decision making (Crites, 1973), may indicate below average goal selection for the client's stage of career development. The decisional diagnosis might be that the client's problem lies in the process of relating self to work, not in gathering information, and consequently career counseling would focus upon this facet of decision making rather than others.

Synthesis   When a client requests career counseling, a twofold conceptual and pragmatic issue is posed. What is the client's problem and why does she or he experience it? If it is granted that diagnosis is necessary to address this issue, and to ultimately choose an appropriate course of treatment, irrespective of the interventive orientation, then a comprehensive approach to career counseling would involve this synthesis of what is known about diagnosis. First, a differential diagnosis of the client's career problem would be made, using a system such as that proposed by Crites (1969), in which the principal categories are indecision and unrealism. Second, once the nosological classification of the client's problem has been made, a dynamic diagnosis is undertaken to identify the antecedents and contingencies that have generated the problem. Here, although research findings are suggestive (Schrader, 1969), the basic procedure is inferential, using constructs such as those formulated by Bordin (1946; Bordin & Kopplin, 1973). The most reliable and valid reasoning starts on the data-language level (demographic and psychometric information, interview impressions), moves to the theory-language level with the formulation of hypotheses, and returns to the data-language level for hypothesis testing (Goldman, 1964; McArthur, 1954). Thus, the dynamics of the client's career problem are extrapolated from an ongoing interaction between the empirical and the conceptual, the purpose being to understand the so-called causes of the client's felt difficulty. Third, against this background of the what and the why of the client's problem, a decisional diagnosis of disjunctions in the process of career choice is attempted. How career-mature in choice attitudes and competencies, as assessed by an instrument like the Career Maturity Inventory, is the client and how are these attitudes and competencies related to the choice content problem? Taken together, the differential, dynamic, and decisional diagnoses of the client's career problem allow the counselor to draw better than chance conclusions about what the problem is, why it has occurred, and how it is being dealt with. They also have import for deciding upon which career counseling processes may be most appropriate for assisting the client to resolve the problem.

Process

The basic unit of process in career counseling is the interview interaction between client and counselor (compare Kiesler, 1973). Career counseling may consist of only one interview, but typically the overall process is comprised of a series of interviews. Whether one interview or many, however, the process corresponds to an opening interview, in which the counselor collects data on the client, a second interview during which tests are interpreted, and a third interview when occupational information is presented. The Client-Centered approach varies from this schema somewhat, depending upon the inclinations of the counselor, but the broad outlines are the same: opening self-exploration of difficulties in career decision making, intermediate internalizing or "owning" of these problems, and eventual resolution of them through "the experiencing of real and effective choice" (Patterson, 1964, p. 394). Similarly, psychodynamic career counseling, as largely formulated by Bordin (1968), proceeds through three stages: exploration and contract setting, critical decision, and working for change. In the Developmental approach, much the same phasing is apparent, the process beginning with orientation to and readiness for decision making, progressing through exploration of self and work, and culminating in planning for the future. Behavioral career counseling, whether theoretic or pragmatic, follows much the same three-phased cycle of problem identification, intervention (for example, counterconditioning, modeling), and generalization.

The lead-in to the first stage of the process of career counseling is diagnosis. Both test and nontest data are gathered by the counselor, not only to identify the parameters of the client's problem, but also to get to know the client. What are the antecedents of the client's current decision making? How career-mature are the client's choice attitudes and competencies? Have the client's experiences with career and other choices been positive or negative? The focus is upon a wide-ranging exploration of the client's presenting problem and the background factors that have possibly occasioned it. Using a conceptual framework such as that proposed by Ginzberg, Ginsburg, Axelrad, and Herma (1951), and a measure of career maturity like the CMI, the counselor can locate the place the client has reached on the continuum of career development (Super, 1955) and then collaborate with the client in establishing goals for the career counseling which, if achieved, will further the client's growth along that continuum toward greater career maturity in both choice content and process (see "Outcomes" below). Equally important during this first stage of career counseling, however, are the counselor's perceptions of the relationship which the client is establishing with her or him. Often it becomes readily apparent that a central facet of the client's career choice problem is avoiding personal responsibility for resolving the problem. Rather, in any one of a number of ways, most notably passive dependence, the client attempts to shift the locus of this responsibility to the counselor. The content of the client's problem thus becomes inextricably interwoven with the dynamics of the client's relationship with the counselor, and the task of the opening gambit of career counseling emerges as the complex one of clarifying the client's responsibility in decision making while concomitantly dealing wth its substance.

The middle stage in career counseling process occupies most of the time that the client and counselor spend together. It is a time of problem clarification and specification. The client and counselor collaboratively identify the attitudes and behaviors in the career problem that are interfering with the decision-making process and together they survey the range of possible solutions. The counselor emphasizes collaboration in the relationship to counteract the typical dependence of the undecided client and the defensiveness of the unrealistic client. Moreover, a collaborative client/counselor interaction achieves an optimal balance between the characteristic paternalism of traditional Trait-and-Factor career counseling and the laissez faire orientation of the early Client-Centered approach. These extremes are moderated by the counselor's willingness to accept the client's perception of reality as valid, on the one hand, and to disclose his or her personal experiences as meaningful and facilitative to the client, on the other hand. What evolves is a higher-order relational experience in which client and counselor share responsibility for problem solution. If a collaborative relationship can be fashioned as the career counseling moves through this intermediate phase, it not only increases the involvement of the client in the decisional process, but it also may have salutary effects upon the client's self-esteem. For many clients, it may be the first time in their lives that a "significant other" (usually an adult) has taken an active interest in their problems, and it may be the first time that they realize they *are* competent to cope effectively with their lives. This stage of career counseling is critical, then, to both the explication of the client's career problems and to the client's assumption of responsibility for solutions to the problems.

The process of career counseling culminates in a stage that can best be characterized as problem resolution. If the client has become aware of the nature of his or her problem and has become actively engaged in its solution, then the career counseling turns to a consideration of what the client must do. What behaviors are now necessary? The focus is upon instrumental learning: How can information about self and work be gathered? What negative decisions need to be made in career goal selection in order to narrow the range of options? What are the steps to be followed in reaching the goal (means and cognizance) and how are they ordered along the temporal dimension (planning)? How are unforeseen contingencies dealt with when they interfere with goal attainment? Through modeling and shaping and reinforcement (see "Interview Techniques" below), the counselor sets the learning conditions for the client to acquire those career-mature behaviors that are problem-resolving. But probably more important, the counselor encourages the generalization of these behaviors to the solution of other life problems. If the career counseling is efficacious, the client learns an approach to problem solving and decision making that can be used not only in future career adjustments, but also in personal, marital, and social adjustments. Furthermore, the client gains confidence in his or her competence to solve problems and make decisions independently of others. The client becomes a responsible individual, personally as well as vocationally.

Synthesis That stages occur in the process of career counseling is posited by all approaches at least in broad outline, if not also in detail. The stages are delineated essentially in terms that correspond to generally recognized steps in problem-solving: background of the problem, statement of the problem, and resolution of the problem. Superimposed upon the stages are the complementary dimensions of any client/counselor interaction: communication and relationship. The content of the communication between client and counselor defines the parameters of the problem: its etiology, its symptomatology, and its possible solutions. The dynamics of the relationship set the conditions for the extent to which the client learns to assume personal responsibility for career decision making, both in the present and the future. Together, communication and relationship are universal dimensions of career counseling to which all approaches contribute. The Trait-and-

Factor and Behavioral have emphasized communication concerning the substantive aspects of the problem and the formulation of solutions to it. The Client-Centered has contributed an understanding of the conditions which facilitate such communication, and the Psychodynamic has identified the dynamics of the relationships which can be formed between client and counselor. The Developmental has sketched the background against which client growth can be calibrated in moving toward greater career maturity.

Outcomes

The expected outcomes of career counseling are largely implied by diagnosis of a client's problem, that is, its differential, dynamic, and decisional diagnosis. It is anticipated that the type of career counseling intervention that the client and counselor collaboratively agree upon will lead to resolution of the problem. For example, if the client and counselor decide together that the career problem is one of inadequate information about self and work, then the desired outcome of career counseling is the client's becoming more knowledgeable in these areas. Whatever the client's problem, all of the major approaches to career counseling are oriented to its solution. More succinctly, the outcomes of career counseling are the solutions that are most appropriate to the client's problems. Too often, however, the outcomes are conceptualized as epiphenomena that have no antecedents. They are frequently seen as appearing only after the career counseling has been completed. Actually, as Grummon (1972) observes, outcomes are part of, and emerge from, process; they can be traced, and assessed, across the course of career counseling (compare Kiesler, 1973). In other words, successive cross-sectional assessments of process collectively define a trend line for the outcomes of career counseling. At any one point in time, in comparison with other preceding ones, movement toward the goals that client and counselor established for the career counseling can be determined.

The most generally recognized of these goals—and one that cuts across all of the major approaches to career counseling—is to assist the client in making a career choice. The long-standing societal expectation that everyone be "occupied," preferably in some economically gainful pursuit (particularly males), is an unquestioned assumption of career counseling. Seldom, if ever, is the avowed outcome of career counseling to help a client decide *not* to work, as legitimate as this outcome may be personally. Sometimes career counselors allow for clients to postpone their decisions, but usually they feel a sense of lack of closure if a decision may be developmentally premature. Super (1960) points out that the exploratory stage of career development should be "open-ended" until the individual has had the opportunity to clarify the self-concept and to learn about the occupational roles that are available and suitable. Similarly, Ginzberg et al. (1951) note the pitfalls in career decision making of pseudo-crystallization in choice, stemming from (1) the persistence of childhood interests, (2) powerful fantasies about being admired and successful, and (3) responsiveness to parental pressure (Crites, 1969, p. 171). Strong's (1943; 1955) research on the development of vocational interests indicates that certain interest patterns, specifically Social Service, do not emerge until relatively late in adolescence, whereas others (for example, Physical Sciences) crystal-lize earlier (compare Sinnett, 1956). Thus, for the principal outcome of career counseling to be the making of a career decision is theoretically and empirically contraindicated. Not making a career decision may be equally desirable for the client's degree or rate of career development (Crites, 1961).

A second outcome of career counseling, which only recently has been articulated by the Developmental and Behavioral approaches, is the acquisition of decisional skills. In contrast to Trait-and-Factor and, to a lesser extent, Client-Centered and Psychodynamic career counsel-ing, the Developmental and Behavioral orientations have emphasized choice process, not choice content. Both have addressed the question: How can the client best make a realistic career choice? In answering this question they have gone beyond choice content, although this too is seen as an outcome (Thompson, 1954), and have focused upon choice process. Super (1963) has enumerated the career developmental tasks with which the client must contend in making a choice, and Krumboltz and Baker (1973) have outlined the necessary steps in arriving at a decision. Drawing upon these schemata, as well as general decision theory (Edwards, 1954; 1961), Crites (1973) has constructed the CMI Competence Test as a measure of the stages in optimal career decision making: information gathering (self and work), goal selection, planning, and problem-solving. Presumably a client not only passes through these stages, as needed in career counseling, but also explicitly learns them as a modus operandi for decision making in the future. Thus, the client acquires a way of coping with career problems that is not time- or content-bound. She or he has an approach to the decision-making situations of life, whether career or otherwise, that transcends career counseling and changes in the world of work. The problem-specific constraints imposed by career counseling oriented only to choice content are obviated by career counseling which provides a client with a process paradigm for decision making which is "contentless."

Still another outcome of career counseling, and one which has been obscured by its nonvocational nature, is the enhanced general adjustment status of the client. Accruing evidence (Williams, 1962; Williams & Hills, 1962) indicates that career counseling results in the client being better adjusted in areas of life functioning other than just the vocational. There are probably several reasons why this is true. The psychodynamic point of view, drawing upon Freud's (1962) conclusion that the hallmarks of maturity are *arbeiten und lieben* (compare Shoben, 1956), would contend that the person who can work effectively as well as love fully is better adjusted. Moreover, most of our working hours are spent in either preparing for or engaging in work; it is not surprising, therefore, that the better adjusted worker is also the better adjusted individual generally. A corollary is that, if a client learns to cope with her or his career problem, it is likely that she or he will be better able to cope with other problems. Furthermore, learning to cope with one's career problems generates an overall feeling of greater self-esteem that is reflected in a heightened adjustment level. Unfortunately, this intimate relationship between career and general adjustment is not widely recognized by either career counselors or personal counselors. Rarely do the former explore with a client the implications and applications of what was learned in career counseling to other areas of adjustment, and equally infrequently do the latter discuss with a client what impact personality changes have for career development.

Synthesis   In Comprehensive career counseling, a basic premise is that all aspects of life functioning and development are interrelated (Super, 1955). If a specific decision concerning career is made, or if career decisional attitudes and competencies are learned, then the impact of these outcomes of career counseling upon philosophy of life, interpersonal relationships, self-concept, etc., should be examined. All of the major approaches to career counseling would concur in the humanistic value that their common goal (outcome) is to further the development or growth of clients towards being more fully functioning individuals, whether intellectually, personally, socially, or vocationally. In comprehensive career counseling, the focus is upon the vocational outcome but embraces the others. Super (1957, p. 300) summarizes it this way:

By relieving tensions, clarifying feelings, giving insight, helping attain success, and developing a feeling of competence in one important area of adjustment, the vocational, it is possible to release the individual's ability to cope more adequately with other aspects of living, thus bringing about improvement in [his or her] general adjustment.

METHODS

For many years, dating back to Parsons and the early work of the Minnesota vocational psychologists, the methods of career counseling—interview techniques, test interpretation, and occupational information—could be characterized as largely didactic and directive. They came out of an educational tradition that highlighted the expertise of the counselor as the transmitter of information to the client. The Rogerian revolution in the early 1940s, however, brought a dramatic change in the techniques used by career counselors, who either adopted a nondirective style (Bixler & Bixler, 1946; Seeman, 1948) or alternated between it and a directive style (Kilby, 1949; Super, 1957). In recent years, both styles have been modified and combined with behavioral methods to the extent that a synthesis can now be extrapolated that reflects the best of the several approaches to career counseling.

Interview Techniques

The techniques available to the career counselor encompass all of those reviewed previously that have been proposed by the major approaches to career counseling (Crites, 1974a), as well as others that have been developed in personal counseling and psychotherapy (Kiesler, 1973). The problem in formulating a system of Comprehensive career counseling is not one of the availability of interview techniques, but rather of how and when to best use them. The Developmental and Behavioral approaches have been most explicit in addressing this problem, but several issues remain unresolved. One of these is: Which interview techniques are most appropriate for different client career problems? Neither a conceptual nor an empirical linkage has been made between these variables, despite Bordin's (1946, p. 170) observation that:

> the most vital characteristic of a set of diagnostic classifications is that they form the basis for the choice of treatment. This means that there should be some understandable and predictable relationship between the characteristics which define the construct and the effects of treatment processes.

A second issue is: How do differential interview techniques relate to the identifiable stages in the process of career counseling? Presumably, the career counselor would make different responses early in the process, during problem exploration, rather than later on when engaged with the client in problem solution, but this phasing of interview techniques in career counseling has not been articulated. A third issue is: what relationship exists between interview techniques and the expected outcomes of career counseling? More specifically, are there classes of counselor responses that are more conducive to a particular outcome, for example, making a specific career decision, than to others (compare Robinson, 1950)?

To illustrate how diagnosis and interview techniques can be related, consider the client whose differential diagnosis is "undecided" (no career choice), whose dynamic diagnosis is "indecisive," and whose decisional diagnosis is "immature goal selection," as measured by the CMI. Clinical experience with this type of client indicates that he or she almost invariably places the responsibility for career choice upon the counselor. If the counselor responds by saying something like "I can't make your decision for you, you have to do that for yourself," a response that is not atypical of most of us, then we have communicated what amounts to a "paradoxical injunction" (Watzlawick, Beavin, & Jackson, 1967). We have said on an "object language" level that we are absolving ourselves of any responsibility for the client's problem, but on a metacommunication level we have given the client the injunction that she or he has to make the career choice. This is much the same response the passive dependent career client elicits from most people in the extraclinical situation. Consequently, they react to the counselor as they do to others—they become even more indecisive! If the career counselor "prescribes the symptom," however, by saying to the client: "Don't make any decision," the effect is usually for the client to react to this extreme injunction by making a commitment to the career choice process and gradually assuming personal responsibility for it. In other words, the client is faced with the choice whether to make a choice. If she or he chooses not to make a choice, then career counseling can be terminated with this goal accomplished; if she or he chooses to make a choice, then career counseling can proceed but with the client now actively involved in the decision making.

The interview techniques that are most appropriate to the several stages of the career counseling process range along a continuum from more to less general in form and content. And they correspond to the foci of the stages. In the first stage, the career counselor's responses are more general, in order to facilitate exploration of the background of the problem as presented by the client during the early interviews. Of the response repertoire available to the counselor, the most frequently used responses are those of (1) restatement and (2) reflection of both content and feeling (Dipboye, 1954; Robinson, 1950). These kinds of responses serve to open up discussion of the etiology and nature of the client's problem. In the second stage, the counselor narrows the scope of the problem and moves toward an explicit statement of it through what Colby (1951) calls "interpositions" and "juxtapositions." The former are open-ended questions, such as: "What do you mean, you never made a *right* decision?", and the latter are comparisons or contrasts, for example: "On the one hand, you have difficulty making decisions, and, on the other, you tell me that your father always told you what to do. Do you see any relationship between these two?" Problem clarification progresses through the counselor's posing of questions like these and the client's responding to them. In the third and last stage of career counseling, problem resolution is furthered by the counselor's becoming more active and directive. Client responses are openly shaped and reinforced, and the counselor interacts in a way that models a mature relationship between two adults who are collaborating in solving a common problem.

As was mentioned previously, the outcomes of career counseling are intimately related to the process, and both are a function of the interview techniques used by the counselor. How often do career counselors initiate interviews with a client with no more explicit rationale for the responses they are going to make than the "good intention" of helping the client to solve a choice problem? Each counselor response should ideally be fashioned to achieve an explicitly agreed-upon goal (as part of the collaborative relationship between client and counselor), rather than a random responding to whatever the current content of the interview happens to be. The dictum for the counselor is: "Know why you said what you said." Equally important is the timing of counselor responses. If she or he allows the first stage of the career counseling process (problem exploration) to last too long, then the most likely outcome is increased dependence of the client upon the counselor, as manifested in redundant and circuitous recounting of the problem. If she or he moves too quickly to the second or third stages of career counseling, then the client may feel threatened or rejected and "break contact." Pacing responses to coincide with the stages in the career counseling process achieves not only immediate goals, but also longer-range outcomes. Still another interview technique, which facilitates personal as well as career development, is *yoking*. The counselor draws implications from the client's talk about career for life in general. Thus, the counselor might point out how dependent the client is upon her or him to make a career choice and then comment: "I wonder whether you rely upon others in the same way to make other decisions in life." Here the focus is upon dependence in career decision making, but the extrapolation is to decision making in general, particularly in terms of interpersonal relationships.

Synthesis   The principal modus operandi of career counseling are the interview techniques by which diagnosis, process, and outcomes are realized. Each of these facets of the model of Comprehensive career counseling are implemented by how the counselor responds to the client. During the beginning of the process, the most relevant interview techniques are those advocated by the Client-Centered and Developmental approaches. Problem exploration appears to be best facilitated by nondirective counselor responses. The middle stage of career counseling is characterized by a predominance of interpretive counselor responses, designed to clarify the predisposing and precipitating factors in the client's problem. These interview techniques come largely from Psychodynamic career counseling. During the terminal stage of career counseling the methods of review and reinforcement from the Trait-and-Factor and Behavioral approaches seem to be most apropos. They are peculiarly suited to problem resolution, which involves instrumental learning and goal-directed behavior. Comprehensive career counseling, therefore, incorporates and applies interview techniques from the other major approaches that implement the diagnostic, process, and outcome model along the communication and relationship dimensions of the client/counselor interaction.

Test Interpretation

From its inception, the heart of Trait-and-Factor career counseling was test interpretation. The raison d'etre of this approach was that tests can predict future career adjustment (success and satisfaction) and that these predictions provide the client with a rational basis for career choice. When Client-Centered career counseling emerged, however, the pendulum swung away from test interpretation to a focus upon the emotional side of decision making, and it has not appreciably swung back. Both Psychodynamic and Behavioral career counseling largely eschew tests, or they use them in unique ways (Crites, 1974a). Developmental career counseling has been hung on the dilemma that measures of its central concepts, namely, career maturity, have not been generally available. Moreover, increasing evidence has accumulated that the initial promise of tests has not been realized; their predictive validity has left much to be desired (Bloom, 1964; Ghiselli, 1966; Holland & Lutz, 1967). The upshot of this disenchantment with tests has been for career counselors to overact by not using them even when appropriate. That a role for tests in Comprehensive career counseling exists, however, can be contended not only conceptually, but also experientially (Crites, 1974a). Experimentation and experience with tests in career counseling suggests new modes and methods for their integration with diagnosis, process, and outcomes that revitalize their potential for assisting clients with problems in career decision making.

For differential diagnosis, both general aptitude tests and vocational interest inventory scores, as well as nontest data on career choice, are needed to identify a client's problem within the system described previously (Crites, 1969). These data also provide the basis for dynamic diagnosis, but they must be supplemented with interview interactions. Process notes on the latter from one contact to another are synthesized with the psychometric data to formulate and test the counselor's understanding of the "hypothetical client." Obviously, the client is intimately involved in this process and collaborates with the counselor in accumulating greater self-knowledge. It should be emphasized that testing is part of the ongoing career counseling; it is not a separate activity that takes place disjunctively from the client/counselor interaction. This is particularly true in decisional diagnosis, where the client and counselor systematically analyze whatever problems may be identified in how choices are made. To illustrate, suppose the differential diagnosis for a client, arrived at mutually with the counselor, is unrealism in decision making due to choice at a level higher than measured aptitude, and the dynamic diagnosis is that of an individual who has been impulsive in decision making. The decisional diagnosis may center, then, upon which phase of the choice process the client is circumventing or subverting. For example, the CMI Competence Test may reveal low scores on self-appraisal and occupational information, thus indicating that the client may be impulsively bypassing the information-gathering stage of decision making and prematurely engaging in goal selection (Crites, 1973). Test interpretation in relation to all aspects of diagnosis becomes an integral part of career counseling, not an adjunctive disparate activity.

The relationship of test interpretation to the process of career counseling is that of microcosm to macrocosm. Not only are there the beginning, middle, and terminal stages of test interpretation, but woven through them is the interplay between communication and relationship. From these universal dimensions of client/counselor interactions, in conjunction with the diagnosis, are derived the most appropriate techniques for interpreting tests. For example, if a client has "no choice" (either indecision or indecisiveness), tests are probably best interpreted by not directly presenting the results to the client. Rather, as questions arise during the career counseling process that the client and counselor collaboratively agree might be answered with tests, they are taken with the understanding that the counselor will "feed-back" the information from them to the client as the two of them talk about the choice problem. Thus, in response to a client's expressed indecision about whether she or he might be satisfied with a career in engineering, the counselor might say, depending upon what the test results were, "The interest inventory you took indicates that your interests are very much like those of engineers. The chances are pretty good, about 3½ to 1, that if you went into that occupation you would stay in it and feel relatively satisfied." By interpreting tests in this way, communication is maximized, because the test interpretation is stated within the client's conceptual and linguistic frame of reference, *not* psychometric jargon, and relationship is furthered, because responsibility for interpreting the tests is shared by the client and counselor, not assumed almost wholly by the latter as expert. In contrast to the traditional approach to test interpretation, in which profiles are presented and scores are explained didactically, this new technique has become known as "interpreting the tests without the tests" (Crites, in press).

Its value lies not only in the immediate outcomes of facilitating the ongoing process of career counseling, but also in the longer-term goals of retention and understanding. There is reliable research evidence that test results interpreted in the traditional way are either distorted or forgotten by clients (for example, Froehlich & Moser, 1954). Counseling experience and preliminary experimental findings (Rubinstein, 1978) suggest that "interpreting the tests without the tests" increases both accuracy and duration of test information and enhances self-understanding. What apparently happens in this approach, although all the dynamics are far from being explicated, is that the test results are translated by the counselor into the vernacular of the client who, in turn, thinks and talks about them in terms of the decision-making process. The test scores thus become imbedded in the contextual meaning of such considerations as "What kind of person am I?" "What career roles are most compatible with the person I am?" "What are the problems I have in becoming that person in a career?" Both person and problem appraisal (Super & Crites, 1962) are furthered and, as a consequence, general self-knowledge. Hence, test interpretation assumes a critical valence in achieving the desired outcomes of career counseling. It provides the client with relevant information for making a specific career choice; it models decisional skills and how they can be used in problem solving; and it contributes to better adjustment through greater self-understanding and resultant self-confidence in coping effectively.

Synthesis Although the procedure of "interpreting the tests without the tests" contrasts dramatically with the Trait-and-Factor approach, it is nevertheless built upon a common premise—that test information has empirically established usefulness for person and problem appraisal, if not also prognostic appraisal, in Comprehensive career counseling. Even contemporary Client-Centered precepts allow for the value of information about self and reality other than that coming solely from within the phenomenal field (Grummon, 1972; Hart & Tomlinson, 1970). Consistent with this point of view is the technique of "interpreting the tests without the tests," which deliberately casts objective test information into the client's perception of the world. Presumably, this new method of test interpretation would also be compatible with Behavioral career counseling, in which there is a central focus upon the decision-making process. More specifically, introducing and discussing tests results as part of the client's and counselor's "examining the consequences of alternatives" (Krumboltz & Baker, 1973) appears to fit the behavioral model of how career choices are made, although this approach is not test-oriented (Crites, 1974a). Communicating test scores in client/counselor interchanges on the content and process of career choice comes closest to the techniques that are advocated in Developmental and Psychodynamic career counseling. Both of these orientations emphasize the dynamics of decision making, which are clarified and learned by the client when test results are imparted interactively.

Occupational Information

Of the various methods of career counseling, the use of occupational information has been the most inarticulate. Voluminous amounts of occupational information have been published over the years with dubious impact. Some critics (for example, Barry & Wolf, 1962) have questioned whether it has *any* salience for career decision making, whereas others (for example, Hoppock, 1963) have highlighted its centrality in both career choice and counseling. Most counselors seem to pay lip service to it, regarding the presentation of occupational information to the client as necessary but uninspiring. As a result, they either do a poor job of the presentation or neglect it altogether. In one unpublished study (Crites, 1965), for example, it was found that most counselors of a university career counseling service simply referred their clients to the "occupational file" in the center for information about the world of work. A tally of those clients who actually used the file indicated that only about 5 percent availed themselves of it! More novel approaches to the dissemination of occupational information (for example, Magoon, 1964) may be more effective, but the problem remains that this aspect of decision making does not appear to be integrated with career counseling. There are some new methods, however, that have promise for meaningfully relating occupational information to diagnosis, process, and outcomes in Comprehensive career counseling.

If the combined differential, dynamic, and decisional diagnosis suggests that a client's problem is simple indecision, then the use of occupational information by the counselor to increase knowledge of the world of work is appropriate. Clients with this problem typically have had inadequate or insufficient opportunities to learn about occupations, either directly or indirectly, and they can benefit from information about job duties and tasks, employment opportunities, lines of advancement, and future trends. In contrast, the client diagnosed as indecisive usually has acquired the necessary occupational information for career choice but is unable to use it in decision making due to antecedent anxiety (Crites, 1969; 1974a). Occupational information only exacerbates the anxiety by emphasizing the presenting problem; the client's decisional processes are paralyzed by anxiety, not lack of information. Once the anxiety has been reduced, then the indecisive client can utilize the previously obtained occupational information and engage in career choice. If the diagnosis is unrealism, then direct presentation of occupational information is indicated. The unrealistic client characteristically colors the world of work to look *as if* it is consistent with his or her career choice when it is not. To establish such distortions, and to rectify them, confrontive reality testing against objective occupational information is often the best counseling method.

Three principal processes are available for imparting occupational information to the client. First, the counselor can directly present it to the client in the interview. This procedure has the advantage of integrating the use of occupational information with the overall context of career counseling, but it has the twofold disadvantage of casting the counselor into the role of an "expert," rather than a "collaborator," who must then keep abreast of the voluminous information about occupations that is constantly changing in today's rapidly developing economy. Second, the client can be shaped and reinforced by the counselor to gather information on his or her own outside the interview situation. This approach has merit in fostering client independence in making a career choice, as well as acquiring a relevant competency, but it needs to be incorporated into the ongoing course of the career counseling. Otherwise, the information may not be meaningfully used by the client in decision making. Third, a computerized occupational information system (Super, 1970) may be utilized as an adjunct to career counseling, in which the client becomes familiar with the world of work by asking the computer questions about possible careers. Again, the potential drawback is that this experience becomes an end in itself, without relation to client/counselor interactions on career choice. The obvious synthesis of these methods, of course, is to use them concomitantly, with the counselor orienting the client to information, including computerized systems, and reinforcing the client in their exploration. The client then discusses the import of the occupational information for career goal selection with the counselor as part of the career counseling process.

The immediate outcome of this general method of using occupational information in career counseling is increased knowledge of the world of work, particularly that segment that most closely corresponds to the career choices the client is considering. Until recently, there has been no standardized measure of occupational information to assess the extent to which this outcome has been achieved. The Occupational Information Test of the Career Maturity Inventory was published for this purpose (Crites, 1973). Preliminary findings from research in progress indicate that scores on this subtest increase significantly after exposure to an occupational information intervention (the Job Experience Kits). The remote outcomes of acquiring occupational information include realistic career choice and greater career maturity. The former can be appraised by the agreement of choice with aptitudes and interests, and the latter with the CMI or comparable instruments (Super, 1974).

Increased incidence of information-seeking behavior, for example, might be reflected on both the CMI occupational information subtest and the Attitude Scale, which can be scored for involvement as well as independence in career choice. Together, the immediate and remote outcomes of occupational information in career counseling should also contribute, through generalization, to the client's effectiveness in functioning in other areas of life adjustment. Thus, having learned how to collect and use information about occupations in making career decisions, she or he might follow the same process in gathering information for a consumer or business decision.

Synthesis   It is difficult to synthesize the positions of the major approaches to career counseling on occupational information, not only because of divergences among them, but also because of the discrepancy between precept and practice. Occupational information is the most neglected aspect of career counseling, yet it is as important as self-knowledge in career decision making, according to the Trait-and-Factor approach. Similarly, Behavioral and Psychodynamic career counseling accord a role to occupational information in deciding about a career, although their emphases differ (Crites, 1974a). In the Developmental orientation, one of the major dimensions of career maturity is occupational information (Super & Overstreet, 1960). Only in the Client-Centered approach has objective information been eschewed, but even Patterson (1964) allows for it and Grummon (1972) states that it is necessary. Thus, it can be concluded that a Comprehensive approach to career counseling would encompass the use of occupational information in assisting a client to make a career choice. The problem is how to integrate this activity, which is largely one of accumulating facts and figures, with the career counseling process. One solution is to reinforce the client for gathering occupational information outside the contact hour and to use the latter for counseling rather than dissemination. Both the counselor and the client can fulfill the collaborative roles they have assumed for themselves in their relationship, and career counseling can proceed as an interactive process.

MATERIALS

Materials of Comprehensive career counseling means the subject matter of client-counselor interactions, including talk and tests, from the initial interview to the last. Sometimes called case materials or case studies, they constitute the warp and woof of career counseling; they give it operational definition. Thus, to provide experiential meaning for the comprehensive approach to career counseling that has been outlined here, the materials of the process must be presented. Ideally, cases that exemplify all of the parameters of Comprehensive career counseling would be described, but space obviously does not permit such a survey. A case has been selected, however, that illustrates many of these facets. This was a seven-interview sequence with Karen, a 17-year-old high-school senior, who was self-referred for career counseling during the 1974-75 academic year. She was seen by the author on a weekly basis, with one break over the Christmas vacation period. The materials from the case—interview excerpts, test results, biographical and demographic data, and so forth—have been organized according to the model for Comprehensive career counseling: diagnosis, process, and outcomes. The method of interview, test interpretation, and use of occupational information are discussed in relation to the model, the former being the means for implementing the latter.

Diagnosis

I saw Karen for a relatively short (less than the standard 50-minute appointment) screening interview to make arrangements for her career counseling and to gain some initial impression of why she wanted to see me. Her presenting problem was one of uncertainty about her career choice. She said that she had been considering teaching and social work and possibly music, but had been having difficulty deciding among them. I responded with largely open-ended questions, such as "How do you mean you are uncertain?" and "Why has it been difficult for you to decide what you want to do?", in order to further problem exploration. Her answers to these and similar questions suggested that her problem might be less one of uncertainty than indecision. For example, she said, "I keep going back and forth between teaching and social work. My mother is a third-grade teacher, and I like what she does, but if I were a social worker I could help people." The reaction she elicited in me was like others I had had when I could not decide between what appeared to be equally desirable alternatives. I shared this by saying: "I have had much the same feeling of uncertainty you are expressing, or what I call indecision, when I have been trying to make a choice about something. Perhaps it is indecision rather than uncertainty that is troubling you." I explained what I considered to be the difference between the two states or conditions, uncertainty being defined as the dissonance that follows a choice rather than the anxiety that precedes a decision (Crites, 1969; Hilton, 1962; James, 1963). She agreed that she was experiencing indecision, and we settled upon this as her differential diagnosis.

Whether the indecision was simple or not, however, had to be determined by making a dynamic diagnosis, which continued through approximately three interviews. I had to identify the antecedent conditions in which she had decisional experiences, starting with the family and school. Since she was a high-school senior, I asked her what she planned to do after she graduated, and she said she was going to college. Which college or university had she decided upon? Her preference had been a small Southern college, where she felt she could develop closer personal relationships with other students than she had had in high school. But her father questioned her choice, not only because the tuition would be higher, she would be farther from home, and other objective reasons, but also because he implied that she really did not know what she wanted for herself. He devalued her need for "closer personal relationships" and encouraged (coerced?) her to attend the state university where she could continue the "reputation of achievement" she had established in high school. She acquiesced and followed her father's wishes. I asked her: "Has this happened with other decisions you have made?" and she answered affirmatively. I continued with questions about how she felt when she was faced with a decision, and she reported what amounted to an accentuated state of anxiety. She said: "I really feel up tight. I'm afraid of what he will say." From her description of past experiences with decision making, particularly vis-à-vis her father, I developed the dynamic diagnosis of indecisiveness. Subsequent interviewing and testing tended to confirm that she had considerable difficulty in making not only career decisions but other decisions as well.

The pervasiveness of Karen's indecisiveness extended to her self-concept and self-esteem. In one of the early interviews in the overall sequence, I asked her to describe herself, and she said that she couldn't. She added: "I don't know who I am." Since knowing oneself is a central part of mature career decision making, I suggested that it would be useful to assess her self-knowledge objectively, as well as some of the other career choice competencies and attitudes that are related to the decisional process. I described the Career Maturity Inventory, which was designed to measure these variables, and Karen thought that taking it would be worthwhile. Her scores are shown in Figure 7-2 on the Career Maturity Profile (1973 edition), the percentile ranks being from the norms for twelfth graders. She was above average on all of the parts of the Competence test, except Self-Appraisal. On this subtest she had a raw score of 10 out of a possible total score of 20 and a percentile rank of 15, which placed her considerably below average. In other words, both her degree and rate of maturity (raw score and percentile rank, respectively) (Crites, 1961) revealed that she was career-immature

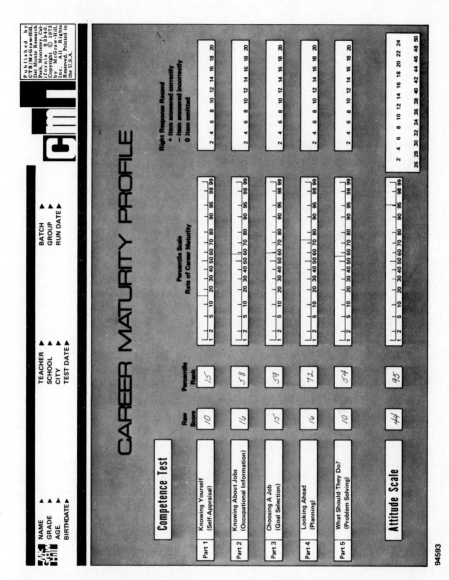

Figure 7-2 Karen's Career Maturity Profile. *(From Career Maturity Inventory devised by John O. Crites. Reprinted by permission of the publisher, CTB/McGraw-Hill, Del Monte Research Park, Monterey, CA 93940. Copyright © 1978 by McGraw-Hill, Inc. All rights reserved. Printed in U.S.A.)*

in making self-appraisals. Also, although her Attitude Scale score was high, the items that she endorsed in the career-immature direction corroborated her doubts and uncertainties about herself, as well as indecisiveness concerning career choice. The decisional diagnosis, therefore, was career immaturity in self-appraisal.

Process

The first stage in the process of career counseling with Karen, which included the screening and initial interviews, was primarily oriented to problem exploration. It focused upon diagnosis of her problem. It also opened the complex process of establishing effective communication with Karen and of developing a working relationship with her. I found that she interacted readily but rather glibly. The client/counselor "talk ratio," which is a good index of the extent to which each is assuming responsibility for the interaction, was about 50/50. What bothered me was not the quantity of Karen's communication but its quality. Her analysis of her career decisional problem was, at least initially, rather glossy and superficial. To break through this facade, I asked open-ended questions designed to expose aspects of her problem that I felt she had not previously considered or been aware of. When she commented that she "didn't know" what kind of person she was, I asked, "Why not?" and added, "Who is going to know who you are if not you?" She responded that she usually looked to her parents, particularly her father, for an answer to this question. To clarify the nature of our relationship, I came back with: "Do you expect me to tell you what kind of person you are?" Karen: "I guess I did before, but I don't think you're going to." Me: "That's right, but I'll try to help you find out." Her: "O.K. I'd like to do that." Problem explored and explicated, communication opened up, relationship begun, initial contract entered: these goals of the first stage of the career counseling process were achieved.

The second stage in my career counseling witb Karen became more intensive. We tried to clarify her problem further and identify the factors that had contributed to it. Most of these involved her family. Her father is a hard-driving, achievement-oriented man who expected the same attitudes of Karen. In contrast, her mother is a family-centered elementary school teacher who encouraged Karen to consider social service careers. Her indecisiveness thus mirrored the divergent values of her parents and her mixed allegiances to them. I came to see much of her conflict concerning career choice as emanating from anxiety associated with these divided loyalties: If she made a decision, then she was rejecting one or the other parent. Compounded with this dilemma was what emerged as an unwillingness to compromise—since, as evolved later—to do so would have meant making a career choice, thereby running the risk of alienating one of her parents. When I pointed this out to Karen, using the declarative responses more typical of the second stage of career counseling, she cried and said: "But how can I free myself from them? What can I do to be my own person?" At this point in the career counseling process, I renegotiated our "contract" to include a consideration of Karen's relationships with her parents, in general, and how they impinged upon her career decision making, in particular. We agreed (collaborative relationship) that we would look at how she might resolve her problems with her parents and thereby resolve her career choice problem.

In the third stage of Karen's career counseling, which consisted of the fifth, sixth, and seventh interviews, we talked about various options she had available to her to do what she wanted to do rather than what her parents wanted her to do. She balked at times in considering some of these alternatives, tearing at the prospect of behaving counter to her parents' expectations, but she gradually came to the understanding that her life was her own, if she would assume responsibility for it, which she did. The issue of which college she would attend had been settled, primarily because of financial considerations, but we discussed at some length how she might extricate herself from what appeared to be an impossible family situation. The mother tried to have the family together at dinner time, but the father subverted this, either by having to work late or by playing the stereo at maximum volume when he was at home for dinner, so that dinnertable interaction was impossible. Moreover, her time at home never seemed to be her own; someone was always intruding upon her privacy. The resolution that we arrived at was for her to create time for herself. She felt it was impossible for her to shed any of her home responsibilities, but she was receptive to my suggestion that she go to bed earlier in order to have some "quiet time" to herself in the morning hours before others were up. She did this as well as exploring possible careers for herself (reading "I Can Do Anything," Mitchell, 1978). In discussing these careers, I introduced the results from the tests she had taken—Differential Aptitude Tests, Holland Vocational Preference Inventory, and Career Maturity Inventory—and tried to draw implications from them for her career choice. The third stage of Karen's career counseling ended with a review of the career options that were possibly open to her in light of current occupational information, and a resolution of her career choice problem to the extent that she was no longer indecisive, for reasons that had previously been inexplicable to her. She planned to use the summer not only for further career exploration, but also to live away from home. Thus, she arrived at a resolution of her choice problem that alleviated the conditions of conflict and posed opportunities for their effective elimination.

Outcomes

Implicit in the process of my career counseling with Karen are the outcomes. First, although she did not arrive at a specific career choice, she learned why she was having difficulty in making a decision. She realized that she was usually unwilling to compromise her lofty ambitions and standards and consequently was frequently indecisive in all areas of her life functioning, not only the vocational. By the end of her career counseling, she was able to compromise more appropriately and to make such decisions as to live away from home during the summer. Second, she started to know herself better and to be able to communicate her self-concept to me. She clarified many of her feelings about her parents, and she moved toward a greater understanding of how she related to peers. She became aware that she often put them off by acting toward them much as her father acted toward her— directive, demanding, and critical. As a result, she felt used by others who sought her advice and help, but who kept her on the fringe of their social groups. Karen resolved to tone down her active-directive characteristics and to moderate her expectations of others. All these changes contributed to an increased facility for self-appraisal and thus enhanced this aspect of her career maturity. Finally, Karen seemed to be better adjusted upon the completion of her career counseling. Not only did she feel more competent to cope with her career decisions, but she also expressed greater confidence in running her own life. Both her career and her personal adjustment appeared improved from her experience in Comprehensive career counseling.

CONCLUSION

The Comprehensive approach to career counseling described in this chapter and extrapolated from the previous review of major approaches to career counseling is necessarily incomplete. It is a first approximation to a system of career counseling that ideally would be applicable and useful with all possible combinations of clients and counselors in both individual and group interactions. To test and extend its applicability is the next task. Laboratory studies on what are called career counseling *modules,* such as "interpreting the tests," are currently being conducted to determine whether several of these units might be identified that could then be used in optimal combinations for different client/ counselor parameters. If they can, then research to replicate the laboratory findings in the field will be undertaken, the goal being to make career counseling as comprehensive as possible. In the meantime, clinical work continues as the comprehensive approach is tried out with more and different client/counselor dyads (and groups). Males and females, blacks and other minorities, disabled and handicapped, sick and well: all should be able to benefit from Comprehensive career counseling.

REFERENCES

Barry, R., & Wolf, B. *Epitaph for vocational guidance.* New York: Bureau of Publications, Teachers College, Columbia University, 1962.

Bixler, R. H., & Bixler, V. H. Test interpretation in vocational counseling. *Educational and Psychological Measurement,* 1946, *6,* 145–156.

Bloom, B. S. *Stability and change in human characteristics.* New York: Wiley, 1964.

Bordin, E. S. Diagnosis in counseling and psychotherapy. *Educational and Psychological Measurement,* 1946, *6,* 169–184.

Bordin, E. S. *Psychological counseling.* (2d ed.). New York: Appleton-Century-Crofts, 1968.

Bordin, E. S., & Kopplin, D. A. Motivational conflict and vocational development. *Journal of Counseling Psychology,* 1973, *20,* 154–161.

Colby, K. M. *A primer for psychotherapists.* New York: Ronald, 1951.

Corsini, R. *Current psychotherapies.* Itasca, Ill.: Peacock, 1973.

Crites, J. O. A model for the measurement of vocational maturity. *Journal of Counseling Psychology,* 1961, *8,* 255–259.

Crites, J. O. Measurement of vocational maturity in adolescence: I. Attitude Test of the Vocational Development Inventory. *Psychological Monographs,* 1965, *79* (2, Whole No. 595).

Crites, J. O. *Vocational psychology.* New York: McGraw-Hill, 1969.

Crites, J. O. *Theory and research handbook for the Career Maturity Inventory.* Monterey, Calif.: CTB/McGraw-Hill, 1973; 1978.

Crites, J. O. Career counseling: A review of the major approaches. *The Counseling Psychologist,* 1974, *4,* (3), 3–23. (a)

Crites, J. O. A reappraisal of vocational appraisal. *Vocational Guidance Quarterly,* 1974, *23,* 272–279. (b)

Crites, J. O. Career development processes: A model of vocational maturity. In E. L. Herr (Ed.), *Vocational guidance and human development.* Boston: Houghton Mifflin, 1974. Pp. 296–320.

Crites, J. O. Integrative test interpretation. In C. Shinkman & D. Montross (Eds), *Career development in higher education and business: Theory and practice.* In press.

Diphoye, W. J. Analysis of counselor style by discussion units. *Journal of Counseling Psychology,* 1954, *1,* 21026.

Edwards, W. The theory of decision-making. *Psychological Bulletin,* 1954, *51,* 380–417.

Edwards, W. Behavioral decision theory. *Annual Review of Psychology,* 1961, *12,* 473–499.

Ford, D. H., & Urban, H. B. *Systems of psychotherapy.* New York: Wiley, 1963.

Freud, S. *Civilization and its discontents.* New York: Norton, 1962.

Froelich, C. P., & Moser, W. E. Do counselees remember test scores? *Journal of Counseling Psychology,* 1967, *14,* 131–136.

Gelatt, H. B. Decision-making: A conceptual frame of reference for counseling. *Journal of Counseling Psychology,* 1962, *9,* 240–245.

Gelatt, H. B., Varenhorst, B., & Carey, R. *Deciding.* New York: College Entrance Examination Board, 1972.

Ghiselli, E. E. *The validity of occupational aptitude tests.* New York: Wiley, 1966.

Ginzberg, E., Ginsburg, S. W., Axelrad, S., & Herma, J. L. *Occupational choice.* New York: Columbia University Press, 1951.

Goldman, L. The process of vocational assessment. In H. Borow (Ed.), *Man in a world at work.* Boston: Houghton-Mifflin, 1964. Pp. 389–410.

Grummon, D. L. Client-centered theory. In B. Stefflre & W. H. Grant (Eds), *Theories of counseling* (2d ed.). New York: McGraw-Hill, 1972. Pp. 73–135.

Hart, J. T., & Tomlinson, T. M. (Eds), *New directions in client-centered therapy.* Boston: Houghton Mifflin, 1970.

Hilton, T. L. Career decision-making. *Journal of Counseling Psychology,* 1962, *9,* 291–298.

Holland, J. L., & Lutz, S. W. Predicting a student's vocational choice. *ACT Research Reports,* 1967, No. 18.

Hoppock, R. *Occupational information* (2d ed.) New York: McGraw-Hill, 1963.

James, F., III. Comment on Hilton's model of career decision-making. *Journal of Counseling Psychology,* 1963, *10,* 303–304.

Kiesler, D. J. *The process of psychotherapy.* Chicago: Aldine, 1973.

Kilby, R. W. Some vocational counseling methods. *Educational and Psychological Measurement,* 1949, *9,* 173–192.

Kirtner, W. L., & Cartwright, D. S. Success and failure in client-centered therapy as a function of initial in-therapy behavior. *Journal of Counseling Psychology,* 1958, *22,* 329–333.

Krumboltz, J. D., & Baker, R. D. Behavioral counseling for vocational decisions. In H. Borow (Ed.), *Career guidance for a new age.* Boston: Houghton-Mifflin, 1973. Pp. 235–283.

Magoon, T. Innovations in counseling. *Journal of Counseling Psychology,* 1964, *11,* 342–347.

McArthur, C. Analyzing the clinical process. *Journal of Counseling Psychology,* 1954, *1,* 203–208.

Mitchell, J. S. *I can be anything: Careers and colleges for young women* (Rev. ed.). Princeton, N.J.: The College Board, 1978.

Patterson, C. H. Counseling: Self-clarification and the helping relationship. In H. Borow (Ed.), *Man in a world at work.* Boston: Houghton Mifflin, 1964. Pp. 434–459.

Patterson, C. H. *Theories of counseling and psychotherapy.* (2d ed.). New York: Harper & Row, 1973.

Robinson, F. P. *Principles and procedures in student counseling.* New York: Harper, 1950.

Rogers, C. R. *On becoming a person.* Boston: Houghton Mifflin, 1951.

Rogers, C. R., Gendlin, E. T., Kiesler, D. J., & Truax, C. G. *The therapeutic relationship and its impact.* Madison: University of Wisconsin Press, 1967.

Rubinstein, M. R. Integrative interpretation of vocational interest inventory results. *Journal of Counseling Psychology,* 1978, *25,* 306–309.

Schrader, C. H. *Vocational choice problems: Indecision vs. indecisiveness.* Unpublished doctoral dissertation, University of Iowa, 1970.

Seeman, J. A. A study of client self-selection of tests in vocational counseling. *Educational and Psychological Measurement,* 1948, *8,* 327–346.

Shoben, E. J., Jr. Work, love and maturity. *Personnel and Guidance Journal,* 1956, *34,* 326–332.

Sinnett, E. R. Some determinants of agreement between measured and expressed interests. *Educational and Psychological Measurement,* 1956, *16,* 110–118.

Strong, E. K., Jr. *Vocational interests of men and women.* Palo Alto: Stanford University Press, 1943.

Strong, E. K., Jr. *Vocational interest 18 years after college.* Minneapolis: University of Minnesota Press, 1955.

Super, D. E. The dimensions and measurement of vocational maturity. *Teachers College Record,* 1955, *57,* 151–163.

Super, D. E. *The psychology of careers.* New York: Harper, 1957.

Super, D. E. The critical ninth grade: Vocational choice or vocational exploration. *Personnel and Guidance Journal,* 1960, *39,* 106–109.

Super, D. E. The definition and measurement of early career behavior: A first formulation. *Personnel and Guidance Journal,* 1963, *41,* 775–780.

Super, D. E. (Ed.), *Computer-assisted counseling.* New York: Teachers College Press, 1970.

Super, D. E. (Ed.), *Measuring vocational maturity for counseling and evaluation.* Washington, D.C.: National Vocational Guidance Association, 1974.

Super, D. E., & Crites, J. O. *Appraising vocational fitness.* (Rev. ed.). New York: Harper & Row, 1962.

Super, D. E., & Overstreet, P. L. *The vocational maturity of ninth grade boys.* New York: Teachers College Bureau of Publications, 1960.

Thompson, A. S. A rationale for vocational guidance. *Personnel and Guidance Journal,* 1954, *32,* 533–535.

Watzlawick, P., Beavin, J. H., & Jackson, D. D. *Pragmatics of human communication.* New York: Norton, 1967.

Williams, J. E. Changes in self and other perceptions following brief educational-vocational counseling. *Journal of Counseling Psychology,* 1962, *9,* 18–30.

Williams, J. E., & Hills, D. A. More on brief educational-vocational counseling. *Journal of Counseling Psychology,* 1962, *9,* 366–368.

Williamson, E. G. *How to counsel students.* New York: McGraw-Hill, 1939.

Comprehensive Career Counseling: Special Applications

The raison d'être for Comprehensive career counseling, as a synthesis of the models and methods of other approaches, is to make it as generally applicable as possible to the problems clients encounter in their career decision making. There are certain special applications, however, which although the career counselor may make them as needed, warrant further explication and discussion. The case of Karen, presented in the last chapter, for example, illustrates how Comprehensive career counseling can be used with a young woman in exploring and choosing from among the spectrum of career options available. But there are broader issues in the career counseling of women that cut across the career development continuum and need to be addressed. Similarly, with minority and racial group members and with the handicapped and disabled, there are special applications of Comprehensive career counseling that may not be apparent without further discussion. Although allusions were made throughout the book to how Comprehensive career counseling and the other major approaches interface with group and programmatic approaches, particularly the latter which have become popular in recent years, some comments on their special applications should be made. Therefore, this chapter, to indicate the further applicability of Comprehensive career counseling, covers the following topics: (1) "Comprehensive Career Counseling with Women, Racial and Ethnic Minorities, and Disabled"; (2) "Comprehensive Career Counseling in Groups": and (3) "Comprehensive Career Counseling and Programmatic Approaches."

COMPREHENSIVE CAREER COUNSELING WITH WOMEN, RACIAL AND ETHNIC MINORITIES, AND THE DISABLED

Although much has been written about the career counseling of these groups, especially during the past ten years, most of it has been commentary rather than systematic theory construction, and research has been disparate rather than programmatic and focused. Thus, most of what is known about the career counseling of these special groups is more speculative and experiential than demonstrated and integrated. What expertise has accumulated, however, can be organized according to the "models, methods, and materials" taxonomy, with some emendations, and general guidelines for the adaptation of Comprehensive career counseling to the special problems can be outlined.

Women

The *model* for Comprehensive career counseling of women varies more in its substantive aspects than its formal ones. That is, because there are significant variations in the process of career development for women (Super, 1957; Osipow, 1975; Fitzgerald & Crites, 1980), and because the socialization of career roles for women and men differs markedly, *diagnosis, process,* and *outcomes* in Comprehensive career counseling with women pose unique issues in conceptualization and intervention. Idiosyncratic to the present, although not necessarily the future, existential condition of women in making a career choice is the possible conflict between mothering and working. Another problem is the consideration of a broader range of career options, as in the case of Karen, than has been traditionally sex-stereotyped for women (Germaine, 1974), particularly since women are demonstrably more mature in their career choice attitudes yet make less realistic decisions (Rathburn, 1973). Compounded with these problems is what Horner (1968) has called "fear of success," especially for creative and high ability women who feel that their outstanding potential will bring them into direct conflict and competition with prospective life partners (Mathews, 1974; Torrance, 1965). Not nearly as clear as the diagnosis of such problems is whether the process of Comprehensive career counseling is appropriate for their resolution. Within the general phasing of the process through problem exploration, clarification, and resolution there should be interwoven a confrontation of the issues occasioned by sex stereotyping, the outcomes being those chosen with full awareness by the female client. Although the counselor's values may differ from those of the client, the goal of Comprehensive career counseling is for the client to know and choose those options that she feels are best for her (Fitzgerald & Crites, 1980).

The *methods* of Comprehensive career counseling for achieving these outcomes are generally the same as those interview techniques, test interpretation procedures, and uses of occupational information for other clients, but there are certain notable differences for women. Fitzgerald and Crites (1980, p. 56) suggest some of the following techniques for assisting women, for example, at the critical point of occupational entry:

> . . . practice in writing a resumé, role-playing job interviews, making appointments with prospective employers at the career planning and

placement office, and variants of assertiveness training applicable to job hunting.

They also recommend "participation in a group experience with others (women) who are seeking employment," such as the "Me, For a Change" program designed by Leonard, Tanney, Hill, and Clancy (1978, p. 507) to " . . . help women examine their achievement needs in the vocational and career areas." Such programs can incorporate test interpretation procedures in a group context, or tests can be utilized in individual interview sessions. In either situation, it is imperative that the Comprehensive career counselor be aware of the sexist bias that can affect tests and their interpretation (Diamond, 1975). In using the Strong-Campbell Interest Inventory (SCII), for example, there is increasing evidence that, although efforts were made to eliminate sexist bias from this instrument, score interpretation *may* actually *reinforce* sex stereotyping in career choice (Johnson, 1977; Crites, 1978a). Similarly, Birk, Cooper, and Tanney (1973) have found that some of the most widely available occupational information (for example, the *Occupational Outlook Handbook*) is fraught with sexist bias, depicting women in the lower level, assistant or helper, less powerful careers. There is no question, therefore, that Comprehensive career counseling with women must be adapted to take into consideration and counteract these biases.

Instead of presenting case studies as *materials* illustrative of Comprehensive career counseling with women, some comments on what unique resources are available for assisting women in the decisional process may be more useful. Schiffer (1978) has suggested a check list of counseling related to career interest inventories, and Zytowski (1978) has suggested methods for evaluating such inventories so that counselors can modify their techniques depending on the particular instrument they are using. Stebbins, Ames, and Rhodes (1975) have developed materials that illustrate ways of ensuring "sex-fair counseling" (Fitzgerald & Crites, 1980, p. 51). Tests free of sexist bias, particularly in the domain of interest measurement, which is often the most salient for a woman's choice, are difficult to find. The American College Testing program's UNIACT II interest inventory, with "sex-balanced" items, is one possibility, but the psychometric work on it is only beginning (Rayman, 1976). Cautious interpretation of the SCII can sometimes be useful in the career counseling of women, but there is the danger, due to the construction of the instrument (Crites, 1978a), that stereotypic interests will be perpetuated. This is particularly true on occupational scales for the opposite sex in traditional careers (Johnson, 1977). It is recommended that, until the revision of the SCII currently in progress has been completed, it be interpreted only on the "like-sex" scales. In other words, for women this means discussion only of the female occupational scales of the SCII. Another resource that is frequently helpful in suggesting a broader range of career options for women, and that counteracts the biases in more standard sources of occupational information, is Mitchell's (1978) revised and expanded edition of *I Can Be Anything: Careers and Colleges for Young Women.* For other materials on the career counseling of women, see the Counseling Psychologist series on this and related topics, as well as Hansen and Rapoza's (1978) edited volume on the career development of women.

Racial and Ethnic Minorities

Adapting the *model* of Comprehensive career counseling to minorities is difficult for two reasons: First, it was largely evolved from career counseling with individuals from favored educational and economic circumstances and from majority racial and ethnic backgrounds; and, second, because of the diversity of minority group members, how can general recommendations about diagnosis, process, and outcomes be made? As Vontress (1973) has astutely observed, there are several "psychosocial barriers" to the translation of the major approaches to career counseling reviewed in this book into effective interventions with minority clients. Among these barriers are: differences in making self-disclosures, self-hatred, machismo, personalism, modes of listening, and modesty. Without defining each of these with variations from one minority group to another, their import is that the dual dimensions of Comprehensive career counseling—communication and relationship—are significantly affected by whatever ethnic and racial differences exist between counselor and client. For example, Vontress (1973, p. 5) points out:

> In order to communicate effectively with minority group clients, the counselor must be able to understand the verbal and non-verbal language of his counselees, for each aspect is dependent on the other. If a counselor listens only to the speaker's words, the counselor may get as much

distortion as if he "listened" only to body language. To understand the meaning of gestures, postures and inflections, it is important to know a people, their institutions, values and lifestyle.

Similarly, establishing *trust* in the relationship is often a sine qua non for understanding the minority client's problem and creating facilitative counseling conditions. Creating such trust comes largely from the counselor's willingness to cross ethnic and racial barriers and to learn the folkways, mores, and customs of those who are culturally different.

Which *methods* of Comprehensive career counseling are effective in assisting minority clients has long been an imponderable question, principally because there has been no resolution of why minorities *appear* to be less favored. There is increasing sentiment and conviction, however, if not clinical and empirical evidence, that counseling and programmatic interventions do make a difference in the career development of ethnic and racial groups (Crites, 1978b). Gordon (1974, p. 471) argues that:

> If the problem of social disadvantage is truly a reflection more of the environment in which poverty/minority populations exist rather than the result of predetermined and inherent characteristics, then the principal function of the counselor or guidance specialist should be that of environmental encounters calculated to best complement individual human potential and needs.

He goes on to conclude that:

> . . . counseling efforts directed at encouraging active behavioral change and effective environment intervention on behalf of the counselee, seem to be the most promising techniques for dealing with the socially disadvantaged if the individual counseling approach is to be utilized (Gordon, 1974, p. 468).
>
> . . . If the traditional instruments of assessment are employed, they will produce a static measurement of the (client's) current status, whereas the use of a qualitative analysis would be more descriptive of his functioning and would provide clues to his potential (Gordon, 1974, p. 469).

A more comprehensive approach would be to use standardized measures, within their limitations (Samuda, 1975) and supplement the test results with relevant clinical and demographic data (Crites, 1977).

What can be suggested as *materials* for career counseling of minority clients are more conceptual and experiential than they are substantive. With the possible exception of Samuda's (1975) excellent book mentioned previously, available resources for assisting the "culturally different" with problems in career decision making are limited. A systematic approach to their formulation and conceptualization, however, has been proposed in the "flow chart" outlined by Sue (1977, p. 423) in Figure 8-1. In this comprehensive schema for the counseling of minorities, he considers all possible combinations of appropriate process and goals from before the time the client enters the counseling process until he or she leaves. He describes the flow as follows:

> At the preentry level, culturally different clients inherit a whole constellation of cultural and class values, language factors, and life experiences. Further, the counselor is also a product of his or her culture, class, language, and experiences. This will influence the counseling activity as well as the particular school of counseling that is chosen by the counselor. Upon entering the *process of counseling,* counselors choose a general approach, style, or strategy in working with clients . . . Closely linked to the actual process of counseling are certain implicit or explicit goals; insight, self-actualization, behavior change, or more specific goals: studying better, dealing with aggression, or interviewing for jobs (Sue, 1977, p. 423).

Obviously, the best (and most comprehensive) approach to career counseling is the one which combines "appropriate process and appropriate goals." As Sue (1977, p. 423) points out: ". . . *equal treatment in counseling* (with the culturally different) *may be discriminatory treatment"* (italics in original).

Disabled

To refer to Comprehensive career counseling with the disabled may be less preferred by some than to use the term *handicapped,* but, as Hershenson (1974, p. 479) has noted, these terms have "suffered from confusion and inexactitude of definition." More operationally, he states that:

> For the vocational counselor, however, probably three concepts should

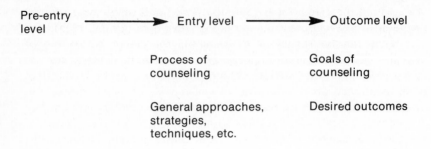

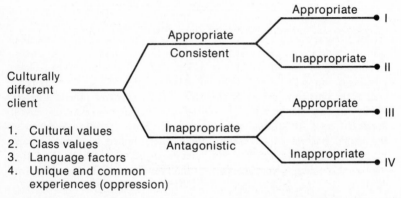

Figure 8-1 Four conditions in counseling the culturally different. *(Sue, 1977, p. 423)*

> suffice to describe the handicapped clients with whom he will work:
> "chronic condition" may refer to the long-term impact of the disease
> process on the individual's physical and/or mental integrity (for example,
> an amputated foot); "functional limitation" may refer to the consequent
> reduction in capacity to carry out activities of living; and "adjustment"
> may refer to the individual's mode of coping physically and emotionally
> with his "chronic condition" and its resultant "functional limitation."

Given these concepts, perhaps a choice between terms is unnecessary,
but for convenience in this discussion *disabled* has been selected because
it is generally considered the generic term, and it has less perjorative
surplus meaning.

In articulating a *model* of Comprehensive career counseling with
disabled clients, it is important to note, as both Hershenson (1974) and

Osipow (1976) have, that the career development of the disabled is not necessarily the same as that for the nondisabled. Osipow (1976) goes further to enumerate the negative assumptions that are often made about the career development of the disabled (see Table 8-1). To counteract such assumptions, Hershenson (1974, p. 487) has suggested:

> . . . a model for vocational behavior which, while developed with reference to the general population, appears to have particular applicability to the handicapped. This model utilizes five constructs: the individual's background (physical and psychosocial), his work personality (his constellation of psychological traits and attitudes which mediate adaptation to work), his competences, his work choice, and his work adjustment (the satisfaction with his working behavior by himself and others). Thus, at any given time, his background partly determines his work personality, work competences, and work choice. These three also influence each other, and the output of this system is his work adjustment.

This interactive system is depicted in Figure 8-2, where it can be seen that the several elements or components are mutually influential and that their "looping back" effects take place over time. In other words, Hershenson's model is a developmental one with certain antecedents, intervening variables, and consequents.

The *methods* of Comprehensive career counseling with disabled clients include those previously discussed, but with certain emendations and additions. Hershenson (1974, p. 490) comments that:

> Traditionally, vocational guidance contains at least three elements: evaluation, occupational information, and counseling. Sometimes the fourth element of job placement is added, and more rarely the fifth element of adjustment to the job on which the client has been placed. Vocational guidance with the handicapped has utilized all of these and added certain special services which are unique to this group, such as sheltered workshops and work adjustment programs.

More specifically, Sinick (1979) highlights the necessity of adopting usual career counseling procedures to facilitate the decision-making process for disabled clients. He suggests that "individual testing is preferable to group testing, as handicapped persons may have low test-taking sophistication and high test anxiety" and that nontest methods of assessment be used with disabled clients because of "the unfamiliarity of persons deprived of life's experiences—for example,

Table 8-1   Career Development under Ideal Conditions versus Disability Conditions

Assumptions about career development in the ideal	Assumptions about career development in the disabled
1 Career development is systematic.	1 Career development is unsystematic, influenced by chance (i.e., the disabled better take what they can get).
2 Career development is psychologically influenced.	2 Career development is not psychological since the disabled don't have much subjective, psychological life.
3 Career development is culturally based.	3 Career development is not important for the disabled.
4 The total person is involved in career development.	4 The disability itself overrides the individual's other characteristics in determining career behavior.
5 People are multipotential regarding careers.	5 The career options of the disabled are very limited.
6 Career behavior is developmental.	6 The career development of the disabled (and the general development as well) is all arrested or retarded.
7 Career development is stressful at choice points.	7 The career development of the disabled is stressful at all points.

Source: Osipow, 1976, p. 56

with the content of interest inventory items" (Sinick, 1979, p. 253). Once assessment of the disabled client's vocational capabilities has been made, the counseling process

> . . . must focus largely on the question of *adjustment* to chronic condition and/or functional limitation, particularly as related to work. Toward this aim, all the elements usually present in vocational counseling must be brought into consideration (personality, abilities, interests, available options, goals, etc.) as influenced by the issue of adjustment to handicap (Hershenson, 1974, p. 492).

The underlying principle of Comprehensive career counseling methods with disabled clients is reflected in the *materials* that can be used in this process, i.e., an individualized approach that takes into consideration the limitations imposed upon the disabled person by whatever defects or deficiencies she or he has. One resource is the series of *Interviewing Guides for Specific Disabilities* (U.S. Department of Labor) and another is the edited volume of assessment methods by Boulton (1976). Particularly useful for "first-hand experiences" with the world of work are job visits. Sinick (1979, p. 254) has suggested the following "Outline for Visits to Work Sites":

I   The business or industry
    A Name and address of firm
    B Name and address of firm
    C Major operations performed
II Physical features of the environment
    A Transportation to and from firm
    B Mobility on premises
       1 Location of parking lot, access to buildings
       2 Location of cafeteria, washrooms, fire exits
       3 Space for movement, condition of floors
    C Lighting, heat, humidity, ventilation
    D Sanitation, orderliness
    E Noise, vibration
    F Health and accident hazards
    G Other physical features
III Psychosocial features of the environment
    A Characteristics of employees
       1 Predominant age range
       2 Male vs. female

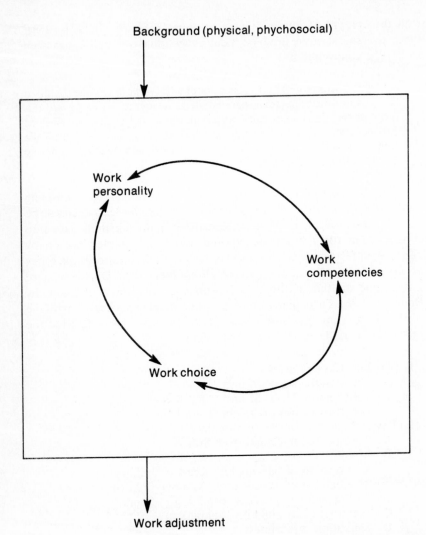

Figure 8-2   A model of career development for the disabled. *(Hershenson, 1974, p. 488)*

        3 Minority group members
        4 Physically disabled
   B Interpersonal relations
        1 Isolated task vs. joint operation
        2 Opportunity for conversation
        3 Close vs. occasional supervision
   C Other psychosocial features
IV Physical demands of work performed
   A Sitting vs. standing
   B Limbs required
   C Visual acuity
   D Color vision
   E Other sensory requirements
   F Finger dexterity
   G Weight lifted
   H Other physical demands
V Psychological demands of work performed
   A Range of intelligence
   B Memory or other mental demands
   C Precision and other pressures
   D Repetitiveness vs. variety
   E Adaptability
   F Other psychological demands
VI Psychological rewards of work performed
   A Autonomy, freedom of behavior
   B Responsibility vs. lack of responsibility
   C Exercise of initiative, judgment, creativity
   D Direct or indirect service to others
   E Other psychological rewards

COMPREHENSIVE CAREER COUNSELING IN GROUPS

Although much has been written about career counseling in groups (e.g., Bennett, 1963; Reardon & Burck, 1975), it has *not* been widely adopted as a preferred modus operandi for assisting clients with their decisional problems. It is certainly an economical mode of service in intervention, but it is difficult to adapt to the individual career concerns of clients. Perhaps for this reason, it is not even discussed in classical treaties on group counseling (for example, Ohlson, 1977). In other words, group career counseling is recognized as a desirable approach to facilitating career development, but it has not been conceptualized and implemented in a way that has encouraged its use. With a change of emphasis or frame, however, it is possible to formulate a model of Comprehensive *group* career counseling that has both conceptual soundness and practical utility.

Model

The principle upon which this approach to group career counseling is based is the distinction made in Chapter 5 between career choice *content* and career choice *process* (Crites, 1978b). Briefly summarized, the former refers to the client's declared occupation. In response to the question "Which occupation do you intend to enter after you have finished your education or training?", the client responds with an occupational title (for example, computer programmer or medical technologist), unless she or he has made no decision. In contrast, career choice process involves the steps the individual takes in arriving at career choice content. Traditionally, the focus of group career counseling has been upon content, usually as revealed by scores on an interest inventory, such as the SCII. The difficulty with this approach is that, first, each group member's profile is different, and, second, as a consequence, the group process typically devolves into a dialogue between the counselor and each client separately. It is tantamount to doing individual career counseling in a group context, which violates a common model for group interaction. This is the "wheel" concept in which interaction takes place not only from the center (counselor) to individual clients but also among the latter around the group perimeter.

Methods

By concentrating upon career choice process, rather than content, interaction among group members, as well as the counselor, can be facilitated by assessment *methods* that measure the critical attitudes and competencies in career decision making. These are the following, which were also discussed in Chapters 5 and 7.

Career Choice Attitudes:

1 Involvement in career decision making
2 Independence in career decision making
3 Orientation to career decision making
4 Compromise in career decision making
5 Decisiveness in career decision making

Career Choice Competencies:

1 Self-Appraisal
2 Occupational information
3 Goal selection
4 Planning
5 Problem solving

Discussion of these attitudes and competencies is general, although each group member has her or his own configuration of scores indicating areas of maturity and immaturity. By outlining the process of career decision making each group member learns the ideal way to make a career choice and at the same time identify personal strengths and weaknesses. These can be discussed by the group and ways of becoming more career mature suggested. Thus, all group members are involved, along with the counselor, in what becomes the career choice process per se.

Materials

To make the discussion specific, scores on the CMI can be interpreted to elucidate the career choice process variables (attitudes and competencies) and other tests and inventories which measure career choice content can be taken when appropriate. Having gained some group cohesiveness through discussion of the decision-making process, career choice content problems can now be introduced without the interpretation becoming a dialogue between the counselor and a particular client. Of course, the career choice content measures can be interpreted individually, rather than in the group, if sufficient counseling resources are available. Hoyt (1955) has reported that concurrent individual and group career counseling is more effective than either alone. This may be particularly true when the group deals with career choice process issues and the individual interview with career choice content problems.

COMPREHENSIVE CAREER COUNSELING AND PROGRAMMATIC APPROACHES

In recent years, particularly since Marland (1974) introduced the concept of "career education," there has been a widespread interest in developing what might be termed *programmatic approaches* to Comprehensive career counseling. These encompass paper-and-pencil booklets,

such as Holland's (1973) *Self-Directed Search* (SDS); package "modules" on decision making, such as the DECIDING program by Gelatt,
Varenhorst, and Carey (1972); and a variety of computer-assisted
approaches (Super, 1970), such as Harris' (1972) Computerized Vocational Information System (CVIS). A useful compilation of the various
types of programs that are available, mostly for use in secondary school
guidance programs, has been made and annotated by Campbell,
Rodebaugh, and Shaltry (1978). The list of these programmatic
approaches is so extensive no attempt will be made here to systematically review or critique them. Suffice it to say that most of them have *not*
been empirically evaluated, using experimental/control group designs,
to determine their effectiveness. Of those which have been field tested,
however, it is encouraging to note that most produce some kind of
change in career development as a result of the intervention. In a review
of over 200 studies with the CMI, it was found that approximately 75
percent of the programs used, ranging in sophistication from "home-
made" units on career education in social studies courses to highly
developed published materials, yield significant changes or gains in
career choice attitudes and competencies (Crites, 1971; 1978b). There is
evidence, therefore, that programmatic interventions can impact the
process of career development, but most of these findings have been for
secondary school programs. In the sections that follow, the model,
methods, and materials for a comprehensive program of career counseling and development at the college and university level are described.

Model

The model for a programmatic approach to Comprehensive career
counseling has been extrapolated from contemporary career development theory and research and from experience over twenty years in a
university counseling service. The model is graphically represented in
Figure 8-3, where the horizontal dimensions are the successive *stages* in
career development through the college years, and the vertical axis
represents the narrowing range or increasing *specificity* in career choice.
In typical career development through the higher educational experience, it would be expected that the freshman year would be devoted
largely to exploration—to surveying and identifying those career
options that are appropriate or feasible for the individual. During the
sophomore year, the process of crystallization takes place, in which
greater certainty and specificity in career options is achieved. Negative
decisions are made, and the range of possibilities is narrowed. Specification occurs in the junior year, when the career developmental task of

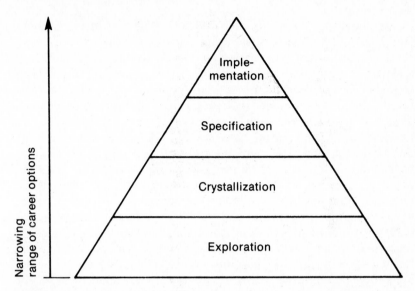

Figure 8-3 Model for a comprehensive career development program in higher education.

"declaring a major" is encountered. It is at this time that commitment to a career decision is made, and the college student begins to concentrate academically in a particular subject-matter area. The last stage is that of implementation, when the individual acts upon the series of prior career decisions and begins the search for employment, culminating with "taking a job." This is the *modal* pattern of career development through a four-year college or university, from which there may be at least two deviations. For students in two-year colleges, the career decisional process may be accelerated, much like it is for terminal high school graduates. And, for some students, whether in two- or four-year colleges, their career development may not keep pace with the time frame of their higher education, and they become increasingly career immature. It is not unusual, for example, for some college seniors having little or no idea of their career capabilities or the position requirements to apply for job interviews.

Methods

A variety of interventive methods can be used to implement a programmatic approach to Comprehensive career counseling in the college or university. A typical plan is to begin with needs assessment during the freshman orientation program. Both measures of career choice content and process (see below) can be administered, but with the focus upon the latter to identify areas of career immaturity in making decisions. For example, the CMI was given to 3,000 incoming freshmen during orientation to appraise possible immaturities in their career choice attitudes and competencies. Interventions were then designed for both individual and group participation to facilitate career development where needed. Thus, students who scored below average on the Occupational Information subtest of the CMI (Adult Edition) were referred to groups which met periodically to visit work sites and gather information about the range of career options open to them. Other activities were organized to correspond to each of the dimensions of career maturity measured by the CMI. To evaluate the effectiveness of the program and to provide a "checkpoint" for career development in succeeding years, the CMI was readministered at the end of the freshman year, and, on the basis of each student's scores, recommendations were made for further experiences to enhance their career maturity. Similarly, for the crystallization, specification, and implementation stages, programs for individuals and groups were formulated, with administration through the counseling center or career planning and placement office, to facilitate the career development of students throughout their college years.

Materials

The materials used in this comprehensive approach to career counseling during the period of higher education, including those especially adapated for two-year colleges, are too extensive to reproduce here, but many of them can be made available from the author upon request. Outlines of prototypic programs can be found, however, in the following sources:

Brandt, J. B. Model for the delivery of career development programs by the college counseling center. *Journal of Counseling Psychology,* 1977, *24,* 494–502.

Harris, N. C., & Grede, J. F. *Career education in colleges.* San Francisco: Jossey-Bass, 1977.

Reardon, R. C., & Burck, H. D. (Eds), *Facilitating career development: Strategies for counselors.* Springfield, Ill.: Charles C. Thomas, 1975.

In addition, consideration should be given to the administration of appraisal instruments, such as the Career Maturity Inventory (Adult Edition) and the Strong-Campbell Interest Inventory, as measures of the central variables in career choice process and career choice content, respectively.

SUMMARY

This chapter on special applications of Comprehensive career counseling has necessarily been open-ended, much like the approach itself. For career counseling to be comprehensive, it must incorporate those components of models and methods reviewed in this book that make it generally applicable to all clients but that also, in unique combinations and syntheses, make it idiosyncratically appropriate to each client. The challenge for the imaginative career counselor is to combine creatively the elements of Comprehensive career counseling to facilitate the client's career development while concurrently improving her or his general quality of life.

REFERENCES

Bennett, M. E. *Guidance and counseling in groups.* (2d ed.) New York, McGraw-Hill, 1963.

Birk, J. M., Cooper, J., & Tanney, M. F. *Racial and sex role stereotyping in career illustrations.* Paper presented at the meeting of the American Psychological Association, Montreal, Quebec, Canada, August 1973.

Boulton, B. L. (Ed.), *Handbook of measurement and evaluation in rehabilitation.* Baltimore: University Park Press, 1976.

Campbell, R. E., Rodebaugh, H. D., & Shaltry, P. E. *Building comprehensive career guidance programs for secondary schools: A handbook of programs, practices, and models.* Columbus, Ohio: The National Center for Research in Vocational Education, 1978.

Crites, J. O. *The maturity of vocational attitudes in adolescence.* Washington, D.C.: American Personnel and Guidance Association, Inquiry Series, No. 2, 1971.

Crites, J. O. *Test reviews for the Division of Veterans Benefits.* Washington, D.C.: Veterans Administration, 1977.

Crites, J. O. Review of the Strong-Campbell Interest Inventory. In O. K. Buros (Ed.), *The eighth mental measurements yearbook.* Highland Park, N.J.: Gryphon Press, 1978. Pp. 1621–1624. (a)

Crites, J. O. *Theory and research handbook for the Career Maturity Inventory.* Monterey, Calif.: CTB/McGraw-Hill, 1978. (b)

Diamond, E. (Ed.), *Issues of sex bias and sex fairness in career interest measurement.* Washington, D.C.: National Institute of Education, 1975.

Fitzgerald, L. F., & Crites, J. O. Toward a career psychology of women: What do we know? What do we need to know? *Journal of Counseling Psychology,* 1980, *27,* 44–62.

Gelatt, H. B., Varenhorst, B., & Carey, R. *Deciding.* New York: College Entrance Examination Board, 1972.

Germaine, L. *Longitudinal trends in the career choices of adolescent females.* Unpublished manuscript, University of Maryland, 1974.

Gordon, E. W. Vocational guidance: Disadvantaged and minority populations. In E. L. Herr (Ed.), *Vocational guidance and human development.* Boston: Houghton Mifflin, 1974. Pp. 452–477.

Hansen, L. S., & Rapoza, R. S. (Eds), *Career development and counseling of women.* Springfield, Ill.: Charles Thomas, 1978.

Harris, J. *Analysis of the effects of a computer-based vocational information system on selected aspects of vocational planning.* Unpublished doctoral dissertation, Northern Illinois University, 1972.

Hershenson, D. B. Vocational guidance and the handicapped. In E. L. Herr (Ed.), *Vocational guidance and human development.* Boston: Houghton Mifflin, 1973. Pp. 478–501.

Holland, J. L. *The Self-Directed Search.* Palo Alto, Calif.: Consulting Psychologists Press, 1973.

Horner, M. S. *Sex differences in achievement motivation and performance in competitive and non-competitive situations.* Unpublished doctoral dissertation, University of Michigan, 1968.

Hoyt, D. P. An evaluation of group and individual programs in vocational guidance. *Journal of Applied Psychology,* 1955, *39,* 26–31.

Johnson, R. W. Relationships between female and male interest scales for the same occupation. *Journal of Vocational Behavior,* 1977, *11,* 239–252.

Leonard, M. M., Tanney, M. F., Hill, C. E., & Clancy, L. B. Me, for a change. *Personnel and Guidance Journal,* 1978, *56,* 507–509.

Marland, S. P., Jr. *Career education.* New York: McGraw-Hill, 1974.

Mathews, E. E. The vocational guidance of girls and women in the United States. In E. L. Herr (Ed.), *Vocational guidance and human development.* Boston: Houghton Mifflin, 1974. Pp. 419–451.

Mitchell, J. S. *I can be anything: Careers and colleges for young women* (Rev. ed.) Princeton, N.J.: College Entrance Examination Board, 1978.

Ohlson, M. M. *Group counseling* (2d ed.). New York: Holt, Rinehart & Winston, 1977.

Osipow, S. H. (Ed.), *Emerging woman: Career analysis and outlooks.* Columbus, Ohio: Charles E. Merrill, 1975.

Osipow, S. H. Vocational development problems of disabled. In H. Rusalem & D. Malikan (Eds), *Contemporary vocational rehabilitation.* New York: New York University Press, 1976.

Rathburn, C. *Developmental trends in the career choice attitudes of male and female adolescents.* Unpublished manuscript, University of Maryland, 1973.

Rayman, J. R. Sex and the single interest inventory: The empirical validation of sex-balanced interest inventory items. *Journal of Counseling Psychology,* 1976, *23,* 239–246.

Reardon, R. C., & Burck, H. D. (Eds), *Facilitating career development: Strategies for counselors.* Springfield, Ill.: Thomas, 1975.

Samuda, R. J. *Psychological testing of American minorities: Issues and consequences.* New York: Harper & Row, 1975.

Shiffler, I. J. Legal issues regarding sex bias in the selection and use of career interest inventories. In C. K. Tittle & D. G. Zytowski (Eds), *Sex-fair interest measurement: Research and implications.* Washington, D.C.: National Institute of Education, 1978.

Stebbins, L., Ames, N., & Rhodes, I. *Sex-fairness in career guidance: A learning kit.* Cambridge, Mass.: Abt. Associates, 1974.

Sue, D. W. Counseling the culturally different: A conceptual analysis. *Personnel and Guidance Journal.* 1977, *55,* 422–425.

Super, D. E. *The psychology of careers.* New York: Harper, 1957.

Super, D. E. (Ed.), *Computer-assisted counseling.* New York: Teachers College Press, 1970.

Torrance, E. P. Helping the creatively gifted girl achieve her potentiality. *Journal of the National Association of Women Deans and Counselors,* 1965, *29,* 28–33.

Vontress, C. E. Counseling the racial and ethnic minorities. *Focus on guidance,* 1973, *5,* 1–10.

Zytowski, D. G. Implications for counselors of research on sex fairness in interest measurement. In C. K. Tittle & D. G. Zytowski (Eds), *Sex-fair interest measurement: Research and implications.* Washington, D.C.: National Institute of Education, 1978.

Bibliography

The references listed below constitute as complete a bibliography on career counseling as could be compiled through June 1980. They are mostly published sources, since these are the core literature on career counseling, but some unpublished, potentially useful citations have been included. Only those works referenced at the end of each chapter have been cited in the text. The others are provided here for general use in theory, research, and practice.

Aiken, J., & Johnston, J. A. Promoting career information seeking behaviors in college students. *Journal of Vocational Behavior,* 1973, *3,* 81–87.

Anderson, R. G. Reported and demonstrated values of vocational counseling. *Journal of Applied Psychology,* 1959, *33,* 460–473.

Apostal, R. A. Two methods of evaluating vocational counseling. *Journal of Counseling Psychology,* 1960, *7,* 171–175.

Arnold, W. M. Vocational guidance and vocational education: The common goal. *Vocational Guidance Quarterly,* 1967, *16,* 2–6.

Ash, P. Pre-retirement counseling. *Gerontologist,* 1966, *6,* 97–99.

Aubrey, R. F. Historical development of guidance and counseling and implications for the future. *Personnel and Guidance Journal,* 1977, *55,* 288–295.

Baer, M. F., & Roeber, E. C. *Occupational information: Its nature and use.* Chicago: Science Research Associates, 1951.

Barahal, G. D., Brammer, L. M., & Shostram, E. L. A client-centered approach to vocational counseling. *Journal of Consulting Psychology,* 1950, *14,* 256–260.

Barrett, G. V., & Otis, J. L. The semantic differential as a measure of changes in meaning in educational and vocational counseling. *Psychological Reports,* 1967, *20,* 335–338.

Barry, R., & Wolf, B. *Epitaph for vocational guidance.* New York: Bureau of Publications, Teachers College, Columbia University, 1962.

Beardsley, S. W. The ideal vocational counselor. *Occupations,* 1948, *26,* 528–531.

Bennett, M. E. *Guidance and counseling in groups* (2nd ed.). New York: McGraw-Hill, 1963.

Berdie, R. F. Counseling: An educational technique. *Educational and Psychological Measurement,* 1949, *9,* 89–94.

Berg, I. A. Test score interpretation and client confusion. *Personnel and Guidance Journal,* 1956, *34,* 576–578.

Berger, E. M. Willingness to accept limitations and college achievement. *Journal of Counseling Psychology,* 1961, *8,* 140–146.

Bergland, B. Group social models and structured interaction in teaching. *Vocational Guidance Quarterly,* 24, *1,* 28–35.

Bergland, B. W., & Krumboltz, J. D. An optimal grade level for career exploration. *Vocational Guidance Quarterly,* 1969, *18,* 29–33.

Biggers, J. L. The use of information in vocational decision making. *Vocational Guidance Quarterly,* 1971, *19,* 171–176.

Birk, J. M., Cooper, J., & Tanney, M. F. *Racial and sex role stereotyping in career illustrations.* Paper presented at the meeting of the American Psychological Association, Montreal, Canada, August 1973.

Bixler, R. H., & Bixler, V. Clinical counseling in vocational guidance, *Journal of Clinical Psychology,* 1945, *1,* 186–192.

————. Test interpretation in vocational counseling. *Educational and Psychological Measurement,* 1946, *6,* 145–155.

Bonar, J. R., & Mahler, L. R. A center for "undecided" college students. *Personnel and Guidance Journal,* 1976, *54,* 481–484.

Bordin, E. S. Diagnosis in counseling and psychotherapy. *Educational and Psychological Measurement,* 1946, *6,* 169–184.

————. Four uses for psychological tests in counseling. *Educational and Psychological Measurement,* 1951, *11,* 779–781.

————. *Psychological counseling.* New York: Appleton-Century-Crofts, 1955.

————. *Psychological counseling* (2d ed.). New York: Appleton-Century-Crofts, 1968.

Bordin, E. S., & Bixler, R. H. Test selection: A process of counseling. *Educational and Psychological Measurement*, 1946, *6*, 361–373.

Bordin, E. S., & Kopplin, D. A. Motivational conflict and vocational development. *Journal of Counseling Psychology*, 1973, *20*, 154–161.

Bordin, E. S., Nachmann, B., & Segal, S. J. An articulated framework for vocational development. *Journal of Counseling Psychology*, 1963, *10*, 107–116.

Borman, C. Effects of a reinforcement style of counseling on information-seeking behavior. *Journal of Vocational Behavior*, 1972, *2*, 255–259.

Borow, H. (Ed.), *Man in a world at work*. Boston: Houghton Mifflin, 1964.

Boulton, B. (Ed.), *Handbook of measurement and evaluation in rehabilitation*. Baltimore: University Park Press, 1976.

Bown, O. H. The client-centered approach to educational and vocational guidance. *The Personal Counselor*, 1947, *2*, 1–5.

Brayfield, A. H. Putting occupational information across. In A. H. Brayfield (Ed.), *Readings in modern methods of counseling*. New York: Appleton-Century-Crofts, 1950. Pp. 212–220.

————. "Dissemination" of occupational information. *Occupations*, 1951, *29*, 411–413.

————. Research on vocational guidance: Status and prospect. In H. Borow (Ed.), *Man in a world at work*. Boston: Houghton Mifflin, 1964. Pp. 310–323.

Brender, M. Toward a psychodynamic system of occupational counseling. *Journal of Counseling Psychology*, 1960, *7*, 96–102.

Burnett, C. W., & Basham, J. Evaluative criteria for the VA Vocational Counseling Service. *Journal of Counseling Psychology*, 1958, *5*, 178–183.

Byrne, R. H. Proposed revision of the Bordin-Pepinsky diagnostic constructs. *Journal of Counseling Psychology*, 1958, *5*, 184–187.

Callis, R. et al. *A casebook of counseling*. New York: Appleton-Century-Crofts, 1955.

Campbell, R. E., Rodebaugh, H. D., & Shaltry, P. E. *Building comprehensive career guidance programs for secondary schools: A handbook of programs, practices, and models*. Columbus, Ohio: The National Center for Research in Vocational Education, 1978.

Carlson, H. B., & Vandever, M. G. The effectiveness of directive and nondirective counseling in vocational problems as measured by the T.A.T. Test. *Educational and Psychological Measurement*, 1951, *11*, 212–223.

Catron, D. W. Educational-vocational group counseling: The effects on perception of self and others. *Journal of Counseling Psychology*, 1966, *13*, 202–208.

Cautela, J. R. The factor of psychological need in occupational choice. *Personnel and Guidance Journal*, 1959, *38*, 46–48.

Cherry, N. Clients' experience of vocational guidance. *Journal of Vocational Behavior*, 1974, *4*, 67–76.

Christensen, T. E. Functions of occupational information in counseling. *Occupations*, 1949, *28*, 11–14.

Clark, F. E., & Murtland, C. Occupational information in counseling: Present practices and historical development. *Occupations*, 1946, *24*, 451–475.

Combs, A. W. Nondirective techniques and vocational counseling. *Occupations*, 1947, *25*, 261–267.

Cover, B. N. Nondirective interviewing techniques in vocational counseling. *Journal of Consulting Psychology*, 1947, *11*, 70–73

Crites, J. O. Ego-strength in relation to vocational interest development. *Journal of Counseling Psychology*, 1960, *7*, 137–143.

————. A model for the measurement of vocational maturity. *Journal of Counseling Psychology*, 1961, *8*, 255–259.

————. Parental identification in relation to vocational interest development. *Journal of Educational Psychology*, 1962, *53*, 262–270.

————. Proposals for a new criterion measure and research design. In H. Borow (Ed.), *Man in a world at work*. Boston: Houghton Mifflin, 1964. Pp. 324–340.

————. Measurement of vocational maturity in adolescence: I. Attitude Test of the Vocational Development Inventory. *Psychological Monographs*, 1965, *79* (2, Whole No. 595).

————. *Vocational Psychology*. New York: McGraw-Hill, 1969.

————. *The maturity of vocational attitudes in adolescence*. Washington, D.C.: American Personnel and Guidance Association, Inquiry Series, No. 2, 1971.

————. *Theory and research handbook for the Career Maturity Inventory*. Monterey, Calif.: CTB/McGraw-Hill, 1973, 1978.

————. Career counseling: A review of major approaches. *The Counseling Psychologist*, 1974, *4*(3), 3–23. (a)

————. A reappraisal of vocational appraisal. *Vocational Guidance Quarterly*, 1974, *23*, 272–279. (b)

————. Career development processes: A model of vocational maturity. In E. L. Herr (Ed.), *Vocational guidance and human development*. Boston: Houghton Mifflin, 1974. Pp. 296–320. (c)

Darley, J. G. The structure of the systematic case study in individual diagnosis and counseling. *Journal of Counseling Psychology*, 1940, *4*, 215–220.

————. Conduct of the interview. In A. H. Brayfield (Ed.), *Readings in modern methods of counseling*. New York: Appleton-Century-Crofts, 1950. Pp. 265–272.

Diamond, E. (Ed.), *Issues of sex bias and sex fairness in career interest measurement.* Washington, D.C.: National Institute of Education, 1975.

Dole, A. A. The vocational sentence completion blank in counseling. *Journal of Counseling Psychology,* 1958, *5,* 200–205.

Doleys, E. J. Are there "kinds" of counselors? *Counseling News and Views,* 1961, *13,* 5–9.

Dolliver, R. H., & Nelson, R. E. Assumptions regarding vocational counseling. *Vocational Guidance Quarterly,* 1975, *24,* 12–19.

Dressel, P. L., & Matheson, R. W. The effect of client participation in test interpretation. *Educational and Psychological Measurement,* 1950, *10,* 693–706.

Dulsky, S. G. Vocational counseling. I. By use of tests. *Personnel Journal,* 1941, *20,* 16–22.

Dysinger, W. S. Two vocational diagnoses compared. *Personnel and Guidance Journal,* 1944, *22,* 304–308.

Egner, J. R., & Jackson, D. J. Effectiveness of a counseling intervention program for teaching career decision-making skills. *Journal of Counseling Psychology,* 25, *1,* 45–51.

Failor, C. C., & Mahler, C. A. Examining counselors' selection of tests. *Occupations,* 1959, *28,* 164–167.

Faries, M. A therapeutic approach to test interpretation. *Personnel and Guidance Journal,* 1957, *35,* 523–526.

Fitzgerald, L. F., & Crites, J. O. Toward a career psychology of women: What do we know? What do we need to know? *Journal of Counseling Psychology,* 1980, *27,* 44–62.

Flake, M. H., Roach, A. J., Jr., & Stenning, W. F. Effects of short-term counseling on career maturity of tenth-grade students. *Journal of Vocational Behavior,* 1975, *6,* 73–80.

Folds, J. R., & Gazda, G. M. A comparison of the effectiveness and efficiency of three methods of test interpretation. *Journal of Counseling Psychology,* 1966, *13,* 318–324.

Foreman, M. E., & James, L. E. Vocational relevance as a factor in counseling. *Journal of Counseling Psychology,* 1973, *20,* 99–100.

Forgy, E. W., & Black, J. D. A follow-up after three years of clients counseled by two methods. *Journal of Counseling Psychology,* 1954, *1,* 1–8.

Forster, J. R. Comparing feedback methods after testing. *Journal of Counseling Psychology,* 1969, *16,* 222–226.

Froehlich, C. P. Bedrock for vocational guidance. *Journal of Counseling Psychology,* 1955, *2,* 170–175.

Froehlich, C. P., & Moser, W. E. Do counselees remember test scores? *Journal of Counseling Psychology,* 1967, *14,* 131–136.

Galinsky, M. D. Personality development and vocational choice of clinical psychologists and physicists. *Journal of Counseling Psychology*, 1962, *9*, 299–305.

Gaudet, F. J., & Kulick, W. Who comes to a vocational guidance center? *Personnel and Guidance Journal*, 1954, *33*, 211–215.

Gaymer, R. Career counseling—teaching the art of career planning. *Vocational Guidance Quarterly*, 1972, *21*, 18–24.

Gelatt, H. B. Decision making: A conceptual frame of reference for counseling. *Journal of Counseling Psychology*, 1962, *9*, 240–245.

Gelatt, H. B., Varenhorst, B., & Carey, R. *Deciding*. New York: College Entrance Examination Board, 1972.

Germaine, L. *Longitudinal trends in the career choice of adolescent females*. Unpublished manuscript, University of Maryland, 1974.

Ghiselli, E. E. *The validity of occupational aptitude tests*. New York: Wiley, 1966.

Gibbs, D. Student failure and social maladjustment. *Personnel and Guidance Journal*, 1965, *43*, 580–585.

Ginzberg, E., Ginsburg, S. W., Axelrad, S., & Herma, J. L. *Occupational choice*. New York: Columbia University Press, 1951.

Ginzberg, E. *Career guidance*. New York: McGraw-Hill, 1971.

Goldberg, S., & Penney, J. A note on counseling underachieving college students. *Journal of Counseling Psychology*, 1962, *9*, 133–138.

Goldman, L. The process of vocational assessment. In H. Borow (Ed.), *Man in a world at work*. Boston: Houghton-Mifflin, 1964. Pp. 389–410.

———. Testing and counseling: The marriage that failed. *Measurement and Evaluation in Guidance*, 1972, *4*, 213–220.

Gonyea, G. G. Appropriateness of vocational choice as a criterion of counseling outcome. *Journal of Counseling Psychology*, 1962, *9*, 213–220.

———. Appropriateness of vocational choice of counseled and uncounseled college students. *Journal of Counseling Psychology*, 1963, *10*, 269–275.

Goodstein, L. D., Crites J. O., Heilbrun, A. B., Jr., & Rempel, P. P. The use of the California Psychological Inventory in a university counseling service. *Journal of Counseling Psychology*, 1961, *8*, 147–153.

Goodstein, L. I., & Crites, J. O. Brief counseling with poor college risks. *Journal of Counseling Psychology*, 1961, *8*, 318–321.

Gordon, E. W. Vocational guidance: Disadvantaged and minority populations. In E. L. Herr (Ed.), *Vocational guidance and human development*. Boston: Houghton Mifflin, 1974. Pp. 452–477.

Gottfredson, G. D. Evaluating vocational interventions. *Journal of Vocational Behavior*, 1978, *13*, 252–254.

Graff, R. W., Danish, S., & Austin, B. Reactions to three kinds of vocational-educational counseling. *Journal of Counseling Psychology*, 1972, *19*, 224–228.

Grumer, M. Aims and scope of vocational counseling. *Journal of Social Casework*, 1949, *30*, 330–335.

Grummon, D. L. Client-centered theory. In B. Stefflre & W. H. Grant (Eds), *Theories of counseling* (2d ed.). New York: McGraw-Hill, 1972. Pp. 73–135.

Gustad, J. W. Test information and learning in the counseling process. *Educational and Psychological Measurement*, 1951, *11*, 788–795.

——. The evaluation interview in vocational counseling. *Personnel and Guidance Journal*, 1957, *36*, 242–251.

Gustad, J. W., & Tuma, A. H. The effects of different methods of test introduction and interpretation on client learning in counseling. *Journal of Counseling Psychology*, 1957, *4*, 313–317.

Gysbers, N. C. Beyond career development—life career development. *Personnel and Guidance Journal*, 1975, *53*, 647–652.

Hahn, M. E., & Kendall, W. E. Some comments in defense of non-nondirective counseling. *Journal of Consulting Psychology*, 1947, *11*, 74–81.

Hale, P. P. Defining vocational counseling and vocational guidance. *Personnel and Guidance Journal*, 1952, *34*, 171–172.

Hamilton, J. A., & Krumboltz, J. D. Simulated work experience: How realistic should it be? *Personnel and Guidance Journal*, 1969, *48*, 39–44.

Hamilton, J. W., & Jones, G. B. Individualizing educational and vocational guidance: Designing a prototype program. *Vocational Guidance Quarterly*, 1971, *19*, 292–298.

Hanna, J. V. The test-obsessed client. *Occupations*, 1950, *28*, 244–246.

Hansen, L. S., & Raposa, R. S. (Eds), *Career development and counseling of women*. Springfield, Ill.: Charles Thomas, 1978.

Hanson, J., & Sander, D. Differential effects of individual and group counseling on realism of vocational choice. *Journal of Counseling Psychology*, 1973, *20*, 541–544.

Harmon, L. R. Test patterns in the vocational clinic. *Educational and Psychological Measurement*, 1947, *7*, 207–220.

Harris, J. *Analysis of the effects of a computer-based vocational information system on selected aspects of vocational planning*. Ph.D. dissertation, Northern Illinois University, 1972.

Healy, C. C. Toward a replicable method of group career counseling. *Vocational Guidance Quarterly*, 1973, *21*, 214–221.

Healy, C. C., Bailey, M. L., & Anderson, E. C. The relation of esteem and vocational counseling to range of incorporation scores. *Journal of Vocational Behavior*, 1973, *3*, 69–75.

Herr, E. L. (Ed.), *Vocational guidance and human development*. Boston: Houghton Mifflin, 1974.

Hershenson, D. B. Techniques for assisting life-stage vocational development. *Personnel and Guidance Journal*, 1969, *8*, 776–780.

————. Vocational guidance and the handicapped. In E. L. Herr (Ed.), *Vocational guidance and human development.* Boston: Houghton Mifflin, 1974. Pp. 478–501.

Hewer, V. H. Group counseling, individual counseling, and a college class in vocations. *Personnel and Guidance Journal,* 1959, *37,* 660–665.

————. What do theories of vocational choices mean to a counselor? *Journal of Counseling Psychology,* 1963, *10,* 118–125.

————. Evaluation of a criterion: Realism of vocational choice. *Journal of Counseling Psychology,* 1966, *13,* 289–294.

Hill, A. H. & Grieneeks, L. Criteria in the evaluation of educational and vocational counseling in college. *Journal of Counseling Psychology,* 1966, *13,* 198–202.

Hills, D. A., & Williams, J. E. Effects of test information upon self-evaluation in brief educational-vocational counseling. *Journal of Counseling Psychology,* 1965, *12,* 275–282.

Hilton, T. L. Career decision making. *Journal of Counseling Psychology,* 1962, *9,* 291–298.

Ho, M. K. Cross-cultural career counseling. *Vocational Guidance Quarterly,* 1973, *21,* 186–190.

Holcomb, W. P., & Anderson, W. P. Vocational guidance research: A five-year overview. *Journal of Vocational Behavior,* 1977, *10,* 341–346.

Holland, J. L. A theory-ridden, computerless, impersonal vocational guidance system. *Journal of Vocational Behavior,* 1971, *1,* 167–176.

————. *The Self-Directed Search.* Palo Alto: Consulting Psychologists Press, 1973.

————. Vocational guidance for everyone. *Educational Researcher,* 1975, *3,* 9–15.

Holmes, J. E. The presentation of test information to college freshmen. *Journal of Counseling Psychology,* 1964, *11,* 54–58.

Hoppock, R. What is the "real" problem? *American Psychologist,* 1953, *8,* 124.

Horst, P. Educational and vocational counseling from the actuarial point of view. *Personnel and Guidance Journal,* 1956, *35,* 164–170.

Hoyt, D. P. An evaluation of group and individual programs in vocational guidance. *Journal of Applied Psychology,* 1955, *39.* 26–31.

Hunt, E. P., & Smith, P. Vocational guidance research: Ten years work by the Birmingham Education Committee. *Occupational Psychology,* 1938, *12,* 302–307.

Impellitteri, J. T., The development of a computer-assisted occupational guidance program. *Journal of Industrial Teacher Education,* Summer 1969, 17–27.

Ivey, A. E. The academic performances of students counseled at a university counseling service. *Journal of Counseling Psychology, 1962, 9,* 347–352.

Jacques, M. (Ed.), Counseling the severely disabled. *Rehabilitation Counseling Bulletin,* 1975, *8,* 1–96.

James, F., III. Comment on Hilton's model of career decision making. *Journal of Counseling Psychology,* 1963, *10,* 303–304.

Johnson, D. G. Effect of vocational counseling on self-knowledge. *Educational and Psychological Measurement,* 1953, *13,* 330–338.

Johnson, R. W. Relationships between female and male interest scales for the same occupation. *Journal of Vocational Behavior,* 1977, *11,* 239–252.

Johnson, W. F., Korn, T. A., & Dunn, D. J. Comparing three methods of presenting occupational information. *Vocational Guidance Quarterly,* 1975, *24,* 62–65.

Kaess, W., & Long, L. An investigation of the effectiveness of vocational guidance. *Educational and Psychological Measurement,* 1954, *14,* 423–433.

Kamm, R. B., & Wrenn, C. G. Client acceptance of self-information in counseling. *Educational and Psychological Measurement,* 1950, *10,* 32–42.

Katz, M. R. A model of guidance for career decision making. *Vocational Guidance Quarterly,* 1966, *15,* 2–10.

Kilby, R. W. Some vocational counseling methods. *Educational and Psychological Measurement,* 1949, *19,* 173–192.

Kirk, B., & Michels, M. E. Counselee reading of occupational materials. *Occupations,* 1950, *28,* 446–450.

Kirk, B. A. How counseling affects vocational goals. *Educational and Psychological Measurement,* 1952, *12,* 692–698.

Kirk, B. Individualizing of test interpretation. *Occupations,* 1952, *30,* 500–505.

Kitson, H. D., & Crane, M. Measuring results of vocational guidance: A summary of attempts, 1932–37. *Occupations,* 1938, *16,* 837–842.

Krivatsy, S. E., & Magoon, T. M. Differential effects of three vocational counseling treatments. *Journal of Counseling Psychology,* 1976, *23,* 112–118.

Krumboltz, J. D. Behavioral goals for counseling. *Journal of Counseling Psychology,* 1966, *13,* 153–159. (a)

Krumboltz, J. D. (Ed.), *Revolution in counseling: Implications of behavioral science.* Boston: Houghton Mifflin, 1966. (b)

Krumboltz, J. D., & Baker, R. D. Behavioral counseling for vocational decision. In H. Borow (Ed.), *Career guidance for a new age.* Boston: Houghton Mifflin, 1973. Pp. 235–283.

Krumboltz, J. D., Baker, R. D., & Johnson, R. G. Vocational problem-solving experiences for stimulatting career exploration and interest: Phase II. Final Report, Office of Education Grant 4-7-070111-2890. School of Education, Stanford University, 1968.

Krumboltz, J. D., & Bergland, B. W. Experiencing work almost like it is. *Educational Technology,* 1969, *9,* 47–49.

Krumboltz, J. D., Mitchell, A. A., & Jones, G. B. A social learning theory of career selection. In J. M. Whiteley & Resnikoff (Eds), *Career counseling*. Monterey, Calif.: Brooks/Cole, 1978. Pp. 100–127.

Krumboltz, J. D., & Sheppard, L. E. Vocational problem-solving experiences. In J. D. Krumboltz & C. E. Thoresen (Eds), *Behavioral counseling: Cases and techniques*. New York: Holt, Rinehart, & Winston, 1969. Pp. 293–306.

Krumboltz, J. D., Sheppard, L. E., Jones, G. B., Johnson, R. G., & Baker, R. D. Vocational problem-solving experiences for stimulating career exploration and interest. Final Report, Office of Education, Stanford University, 1967.

Krumboltz, J. D., & Schroeder, W. W. Promoting career planning through reinforcement. *Personnel and Guidance Journal*, 1965, *43*, 19–26.

Krumboltz, J. D., & Thoresen, C. E. The effect of behavioral counseling in group and individual settings on information-seeking behavior. *Journal of Counseling Psychology*, 1964, *11*, 324–333.

Kuehn, J. Group counseling with undecided college students. *Vocational Guidance Quarterly*, 1974, *22*, 232–234.

Kuna, D. J. The greening of vocational counseling. *Vocational Guidance Quarterly*, 1973, *21*, 276–280.

Lane, D. A comparison of two techniques of interpreting test results to clients in vocational counseling. *Dissertation Abstracts*, 1952, *12*, 591–592.

Langland, L. Projective techniques and counseling psychology. *Journal of Counseling Psychology*, 1960, *7*, 102–107.

Leonard, M. M., Tanney, M. F., Hill, C. E., & Clancy, L. B. Me, for a change. *Personnel and Guidance Journal*, 1978, *56*, 507–509.

Lister, J., & Ohlsen, M. The improvement of self understanding through test interpretation. *Personnel and Guidance Journal*, 1965, *43*, 804–811.

Lofquist, L. H., & Dawis, R. V. *Adjustment to work*. New York: Appleton-Century-Crofts, 1969.

Magoon, T. Innovations in counseling. *Journal of Counseling Psychology*, 1964, *11*, 342–347.

Maola, J., & Kane, G. Comparison of computer-based vs. counselor-based occupational information systems with disadvantaged vocational students. *Journal of Counseling Psychology*, 1976, *23*, 163–165.

Marland, S. P., Jr. *Career education*. New York: McGraw-Hill, 1974.

Mathews, E. F. The vocational guidance of girls and women in the United States. In E. L. Herr (Ed.), *Vocational guidance and human development*. Boston: Houghton Mifflin, 1974. Pp. 419–451.

Matulef, N. J., Warman, R. E., & Brock, T. C. Effects of brief vocational counseling on temporal orientation. *Journal of Counseling Psychology*, 1964, *11*, 352–356.

Melhus, G. E. Computer assisted versus traditional vocational counseling with high- and low-readiness clients. *Journal of Vocational Behavior*, 1973, *3*, 137–144.

Mencke, R. A., & Cochran, D. J. Impact of a counseling outreach workshop on vocational development. *Journal of Counseling Psychology*, 1974, *21*, 185–190.

Mendonca, J. D., & Siess, T. F. Counseling for indecisiveness, problem-solving and anxiety-management training. *Journal of Counseling Psychology*, 1976, *23*, 339–347.

Meyerson, L., & Michael, J. A behavioral approach to counseling and guidance. *Harvard Educational Review*, 1962, *32*, 382–402.

Minge, M. R., & Bowman, T. F. Personality differences among nonclients and vocational educational and personal counseling clients. *Journal of Counseling Psychology*, 1967, *14*, 137–139.

Minor, F. J., Myers, R. A., & Super, D. E. An experimental computer-based educational and career exploration system. *Personnel and Guidance Journal*, 1969, *46*, 565–569.

Mitchell, J. S. *I can be anything: Careers and colleges for young women.* (Rev. ed.) Princeton, N.J.: The College Board, 1978.

Myers, R. A. Research on educational and vocational counseling. In A. E. Bergin and S. L. Garfield (Eds), *Handbook of psychotherapy and behavior change: An empirical analysis.* New York: Wiley, 1971.

McGowan, A. S. Vocational maturity and anxiety among vocationally undecided and indecisive students: The effectiveness of Holland's self-directed search. *Journal of Vocational Behavior*, 1977, *10*, 196–203.

Nachmann, B. Childhood experience and vocational choice in law, dentistry, and social work. *Journal of Counseling Psychology*, 1960, *7*, 243–250.

National Vocational Guidance Association. Principles and practices of vocational guidance. *Occupations*, 1937, *15*, 772–778.

Newman, R. R. When will the educational needs of women be met? Some questions for the counselor. *Journal of Counseling Psychology*, 1963, *10*, 378–383.

Oliver, L. W. Outcome measurement in career counseling research. *Journal of Counseling Psychology*, 1979, *26*, 217–226.

Oliver, L. Verbal reinforcement of career choice realism in relation to career attitude maturity. Unpublished manuscript, Department of Psychology, University of Maryland, 1973.

Osipow, S. H. (Ed.), *Emerging woman: Career analysis and outlooks.* Columbus, Ohio: Charles E. Merrill, 1975.

Parker, C. A. The predictive use of the MMPI in a college counseling center. *Journal of Counseling Psychology*, 1961, *8*, 154–158.

Parker, C., Bunch, S., & Hagberg, R. Group vocational guidance with college students. *Vocational Guidance Quarterly*, 1974, *23*, 168–172.

Parsons, F. *Choosing a vocation*. Boston: Houghton Mifflin, 1909.

Paterson, D. G., & Darley, J. G. *Men, women, and jobs*. Minneapolis: University of Minnesota Press, 1936.

Patterson, C. H. Counseling: Self-clarification and the helping relationship. In H. Borow (Ed.), *Man in a world of work*. Boston: Houghton Mifflin, 1964. Pp. 434–459.

———. Counseling: Vocational or therapeutic? *Vocational Guidance Quarterly*, 1966, *15*, 61–65.

Pepinsky, H. B. The selection and use of diagnostic categories in clinical counseling. *Applied Psychology Monographs*, 1948, No. 15.

Pietrofesa, J. J., & Scholossberg, N. K. Counselor bias and the female occupational role. Detroit: Wayne State University, 1970 (ERIC Document CG 006056).

Pilato, G. T., & Myers, R. A. The effects of computer-mediated vocational guidance procedures on the appropriateness of vocational preferences. *Journal of Vocational Behavior*, 1975, *6*, 61–72.

Pool, D. A. The relation of personality needs to vocational counseling outcome. *Journal of Counseling Psychology*, 1965, *12*, 23–28.

Prediger, D. J., Roth, J. D., & Noeth, R. J. Nationwide study of career development: Summary of results. *ACT Research Report*, No. 61. Iowa City: American College Testing Program, 1973.

Pucel, D. J., Vocational maturity and vocational training. *Journal of Industrial Teacher Education*, 1972, *9*, 30–38.

Rathburn, C. *Developmental trends in the career choice attitudes of male and female adolescents*. Unpublished manuscript, University of Maryland, 1973.

Rayman, J. R. Sex and the single interest inventory: The empirical validation of sex-balanced interest inventory items. *Journal of Counseling Psychology*, 1976, *23*, 239–346.

Reardon, R. C., & Burck, H. D. (Eds), *Facilitating career development: Strategies for counselors*. Springfield, Ill.: Thomas, 1975.

Recktenwald, L. M. Attitudes toward occupations before and after vocational information. *Occupations*, 1946, *24*, 220–223.

Reja, H. Vocational vs. emotional. *Personnel and Guidance Journal*, 1952, *34*, 99–100.

Richardson, L. H. Counseling and ambitious mediocre students. *Journal of Counseling Psychology*, 1960, *7*, 265–268.

Robertson, M. H. A comparison of counselor and student reports of counseling interviews. *Journal of Counseling Psychology*, 1958, *5*, 276–280.

Robinson, F. P. *Principles and procedures in student counseling*. New York: Harper, 1950.

Rogers, C. R. Psychometric tests and client-centered counseling. *Educational and Psychological Measurement*, 1946, *6*, 139–144.

Rogers, L. B. A comparison of two kinds of test interpretation interview. *Journal of Counseling Psychology*, 1954, *1*, 224–231.

Rothney, J. W. M. Interpreting test scores to counselees. *Occupations*, 1952, *30*, 320–322.

Rubinstein, M. R. Integrative interpretation of vocational interest inventory results. *Journal of Counseling Psychology*, 1978, *25*, 306–309.

Rudikoff, L. C., & Kirk, B. A. Test interpretation in counseling. *Journal of Counseling Psychology*, 1959, *6*, 223–228.

Rusalem, H. New insights on the role of occupational information in counseling. *Journal of Counseling Psychology*, 1954, *1*, 84–88.

Ryan, T. A., & Krumboltz, J. D. Effect of planned reinforcement counseling on client decision-making behavior. *Journal of Counseling Psychology*, 1964, *11*, 315–323.

Samaan, M. K., & Parker, C. A. Effects of behavioral (reinforcement) and advice-giving counseling on information-seeking behavior. *Journal of Counseling Psychology*, 1973, *20*, 193–201.

Samler, J. Toward a theoretical base for vocational counseling. *Personnel and Guidance Journal*, 1953, *32*, 34–35.

———. Occupational exploration in counseling: A proposed reorientation. In H. Borow (Ed.), *Man in a world at work*. Houghton Mifflin, 1964. Pp. 411–433.

———. A new psychological speciality: Vocational counseling. *Vocational Guidance Quarterly*, 1966, *15*, 82–89.

———. Vocational Counseling: A pattern and a project. *Vocational Guidance Quarterly*, 1968, *17*, 2–11.

Samuda, R. J. *Psychological testing of American minorities: Issues and consequences*. New York: Harper & Row, 1975.

Schenk, G. E., Johnson, J. A., & Jacobsen, K. The influence of a career group experience on the vocational maturity of college students. *Journal of Vocational Behavior*, 1979, *14*, 284–296.

Schmidt, L. D. Issues in counseling older people. *Educational Gerontology: An International Quarterly*, 1976, *1*, 187–192.

Schneider, L., & Gelso, C. "Vocational" vs. "personal" emphases in counseling psychology training programs. *The Counseling Psychologist*, 1972, *3*, (3) 90–92.

Schrader, C. H. *Vocational choice problems: Indecision vs. indecisiveness*. Ph.D. dissertation, University of Iowa, 1970.

Science Research Associates. *Job Experience Kits*. Chicago: Science Research Associates, 1970.

Seeman, J. A study of client self-selection of tests in vocational counseling. *Educational and Psychological Measurement*, 1948, *8*, 327–346.

————. An investigation of client reactions to vocational counseling. *Journal of Consulting Psychology,* 1949, *13,* 95–104.

————. Psychotechnology and psychotherapy in vocational counseling. *The Personal Counselor,* 1948, *3,* 57–61.

————. A study of client self-selection of tests in vocational counseling. *Educational and Psychological Measurement,* 1949, *8,* 327–346.

Segal, S. J. A psychoanalytic analysis of personality factors in vocational choice. *Journal of Counseling Psychology,* 1961, *8,* 202–210.

Shellow, S. M. The increasing use of clinical psychology in vocational counseling. *Occupations,* 1950, *29,* 302–305.

Shiffler, I. J. Legal issues regarding sex bias in the selection and use of career interest inventories. In C. K. Tittle & D. G. Zytowski (Eds), *Sex-fair interest measurement: Research and implications.* Washington, D. C.: National Institute of Education, 1978.

Shoben, E. J., Jr. Work, love, and maturity. *Personnel and Guidance Journal,* 1956, *34,* 326–332.

Sinnett, E. R. Some determinants of agreement between measured and expressed interests. *Educational and Psychological Measurement,* 1956, *16,* 110–118.

Skovholt, T. M., & Hoenninger, R. W. Guided fantasy in career counseling. *Personnel and Guidance Journal,* 1974, *52,* 693–969.

Sloan, T. J., & Pierce-Jones, J. The Bordin-Pepinsky diagnostic categories: Counselor agreement and MMPI comparisons. *Journal of Counseling Psychology,* 1958, *5,* 189–195.

Smith, R. D., & Evans, J. Comparison of experimental group guidance and individual counseling as facilitators of vocational development. *Journal of Counseling Psychology,* 1973, *20,* 202–208.

Snodgrass, G., & Healy, C. Development of a replicable career decision-making counseling procedure. *Journal of Counseling Psychology,* 1979, *26,* 210–216.

Sprague, D. G., & Strong, D. J. Vocational choice group counseling. *Journal of College Student Personnel,* 1970, *15,* 35–45.

Sprinthall, N. A. Test interpretation: Some problems and a proposal. *Vocational Guidance Quarterly,* 1967, *15,* 248–256.

Stebbins, L., Ames, N., & Rhodes, I. *Sex-fairness in career guidance: A learning kit.* Cambridge, Mass.: Abt Associates, 1975.

Stein, C. I., Bradley, A. D., & Buegel, B. L. A test of basic assumptions underlying vocational counseling utilizing a differential criterion method. *Journal of Counseling Psychology,* 1970, *17,* 93–97.

Stephenson, R. R. Dimensions of educational-vocational test interpretation technique. *American Psychologist,* 1962, *17,* 337–338. (Abstract)

Stone, C. L. The personality factor in vocational guidance. *Journal of Abnormal and Social Psychology,* 1933, *28,* 274–275.

Storey, E. K., Jr. *Vocational interests 18 years after college.* Minneapolis: University of Minnesota Press, 1955.

Stotsky, B. A. Vocational counseling in a neuropsychiatric setting. *Journal of Counseling Psychology,* 1955, *2,* 103–107.

Strang, R. Use in counseling of information about vocations. *School Review,* November 1945, p. 526.

Strong, E. K., Jr. *Vocational interests of men and women.* Palo Alto: Stanford University Press, 1943.

———. *Vocational interest 18 years after college.* Minneapolis: University of Minnesota Press, 1955.

Sue, D. W. Counseling the culturally different: A conceptual analysis. *Personnel and Guidance Journal,* 1977, *55,* 422–425.

Super, D. E. The preliminary appraisal in vocational counseling. *Personnel and Guidance Journal,* 1941, *19,* 323–328.

———. *The dynamics of vocational adjustment.* New York: Harper, 1942. (a)

———. The cross-sectional and developmental methods of vocational diagnosis. *Harvard Educational Review,* 1942, *12,* 283–293. (b)

———. *Appraising vocational fitness.* New York: Harper, 1949.

———. Testing and using test results. *Occupations,* 1950, *29,* 95–97.

———. Vocational adjustment: Implementing a self-concept. *Occupations,* 1951, *30,* 88–92.

———. Career patterns as a basis for vocational counseling. *Journal of Counseling Psychology,* 1954, *1,* 12–20.

———. Personality integration through vocational counseling. *Journal of Counseling Psychology,* 1955, *2,* 217–226. (a)

———. The dimensions and measurement of vocational maturity. *Teachers College Record,* 1955, *57,* 151–163. (b)

———. The preliminary appraisal in vocational counseling. *Personnel and Guidance Journal,* 1956, *36,* 154–161.

———. *The psychology of careers.* New York: Harper, 1957.

———. The critical ninth grade: Vocational choice or vocational exploration? *Personnel and Guidance Journal,* 1960, *39,* 106–109.

———. The definition and measurement of early career behavior: A first formulation. *Personnel and Guidance Journal,* 1963, *41,* 775–780.

———. (Ed.), *Computer-assisted counseling.* New York: Teachers College Press, 1970.

———. (Ed.), *Measuring vocational maturity for counseling and evaluation.* Washington, D.C.: National Vocational Guidance Association, 1974.

Super, D. E., & Bachrach, P. B. *Scientific careers and vocational development theory.* New York: Teachers College Bureau of Publications, 1957.

Super, D. E., & Crites, J. O. *Appraising vocational fitness* (2d ed.) New York: Harper & Row, 1962.

Super, D. E., & Overstreet, P. L. *The career maturity of ninth-grade boys.* New York: Teachers College Bureau of Publications, 1960.

Super, D. E., Starishevsky, R., Matlin, N., & Jordaan, J. P. *Career development: Self-concept theory.* Princeton, N.J.: College Entrance Examination Board, 1963.

Thomas, A. H., & Stewart, N. R. Counselor response to female clients with deviate and conforming career goals. *Journal of Counseling Psychology,* 1971, *18,* 352–357.

Thompson, A. S. A rationale for vocational guidance. *Personnel and Guidance Journal,* 1954, *32,* 533–535.

Thompson, A. S. Personality dynamics and vocational counseling. *Personnel and Guidance Journal,* 1960, *38,* 350–357.

Thoresen, C. E., & Mehrens, W. A. Decision theory and vocational counseling: Important concepts and questions. *Personnel and Guidance Journal,* 1967, *46,* 165–172.

Tilgher, A. Work through the ages. In S. Nosow & W. H. Form (Eds), *Man, work, and society.* New York: Basic Books, 1962. Pp. 11–24.

Tipton, R. M. Relative effectiveness of two methods of interpreting ability test scores. *Journal of Counseling Psychology,* 1969, *16,* 75–80.

Tomita, K. Counseling middle-aged and older workers. *Industrial Gerontology,* 1975, *2,* 45–52.

Tseng, M. S., & Rhodes, C. I. Correlates of the perception of occupational prestige. *Journal of Counseling Psychology,* 20, 6, 522–527.

Tuma, A., & Gustad, J. W. The effects of client and counselor personality characteristics on client learning in counseling. *Journal of Counseling Psychology,* 1957, *4,* 136–141.

Tyler, L. E. The initial interview. *Personnel and Guidance Journal,* 1956, *34,* 466–473.

———. Research on instruments used by counselors in vocational guidance. *Journal of Counseling Psychology,* 1962, *9,* 99–105.

———. *The work of the counselor* (3rd. ed.) New York: Appleton-Century-Crofts, 1969.

Veldman, D. J., & Menaker, S. L. Computer applications in assessment and counseling. *Journal of School Psychology,* 1968, 6, *3,* 167–176.

Vetter, L. Career counseling for women. *Counseling Psychologist,* 1973, *4,* 46–54.

Vontress, C. E. Counseling the racial and ethnic minorities. *Focus on guidance,* 1973, *5,* 1–10.

Wachowiak, D. Personality correlates of vocational counseling. *Journal of Counseling Psychology,* 1973, *20,* 567–568.

Wade, A., & Shertzer, B. Anxiety reduction through vocational counseling. *Vocational Guidance Quarterly,* 1970, *19,* 46–49.

Walker, J. Four methods of interpreting test scores compared. *Personnel and Guidance Journal,* 1965, *44,* 402–405.

Westbrook, F. D. A comparison of three methods of group vocational counseling. *Journal of Counseling Psychology,* 1972, *21,* 502–507.

Williams, J. E., & Hills, D. A. More on brief educational-vocational counseling. *Journal of Counseling Psychology,* 1962, *9,* 366–368.

Williams, J. E. Changes in self and other preceptions following brief educational-vocational counseling. *Journal of Counseling Psychology,* 1962, *9,* 18–30.

Williamson, E. G. *How to counsel students.* New York: McGraw-Hill, 1939. (a)

———. The clinical method of guidance. *Review of Educational Research,* 1939, *9,* 214–217. (b)

———. An historical perspective of the vocational guidance movement. *Personnel and Guidance Journal,* 1964, *42,* 854–859.

———. Vocational counseling: Trait-factor theory. In B. Stefflre (Ed.), *Theories of counseling.* New York: McGraw-Hill, 1965. Pp. 193–214.

———. Counseling and the Minnesota point of view. *Education and Psychological Measurement,* 1968, *7,* 147–157.

———. Trait-and-factor theory and individual differences. In B. Stefflre & Grant (Eds), *Theories of counseling.* (2d ed.) New York: McGraw-Hill, 1972. Pp. 136–176.

Williamson, E. G., & Bordin, E. S. Evaluating counseling by means of a control group experiment. *School & Society,* 1940, *52,* 434–440.

———. The evaluation of vocational and educational counseling: A critique of the methodology of experiments. *Educational and Psychological Measurement,* 1941, *1,* 5–24.

Williamson, E. G. (Ed.), *Vocational counseling: A reappraisal in honor of Donald G. Paterson.* Minneapolis: University of Minnesota Press, 1961.

Woeliner, R. C. Interpretation of test results in counseling. *School Review,* 1951, *59,* 515–517.

Woodcock, P. R., & Herman, A. Fostering career awareness in tenth-grade girls. *School Counselor,* 1978, *25,* 252–263.

Woody, R. H. Vocational counseling with behavioral techniques. *Vocational Guidance Quarterly,* 1968, *17,* 97–103.

Wright, E. W. A comparison of individual and multiple counseling for test interpretation interviews. *Journal of Counseling Psychology,* 1963, *10,* 126–134.

Yabroff, W. Learning decision making. In J. D. Krumboltz & C. E. Thoresen (Eds), *Behavioral counseling: Cases and techniques.* New York: Holt, Rinehart & Winston, 1969. Pp. 329–343.

Zytowski, D. G. Some notes on the history of vocational counseling. *Vocational Guidance Quarterly,* 1967, *16,* 53–55.

———. Toward a theory of career development for women. *Personnel and Guidance Journal,* 1969, *47,* 660–664.

———. Implications for counselors of research on sex-fairness in interest measurement. In C. K. Tittle & D. G. Zytowski (Eds), *Sex-fair interest measurement: Research and implications.* Washington, D.C.: National Institute of Education, 1978.

Index

Name Index

Subject Index